Talking with a map

A Cognitive Analytic Approach to Everyday Conversational Awareness

Steve Potter

Talking with a map

A cognitive analytic approach to better conversations

Published by:

Pavilion Publishing and Media Ltd
Blue Sky Offices
25 Cecil Pashley Way
Shoreham by Sea
West Sussex
BN43 5FF

Tel: 01273 434 943
Email: info@pavpub.com
Web: www.pavpub.com

Published 2022

A catalogue record for this book is available from the British Library.

ISBN: 978-1-914010-86-6

Pavilion Publishing and Media is a leading publisher of books, training materials and digital content in mental health, social care and allied fields. Pavilion and its imprints offer must-have knowledge and innovative learning solutions underpinned by sound research and professional values.

Author: Steve Potter
Production editor: Ruth Chalmers, Pavilion Publishing and Media Ltd
Cover design: Phil Morash, Pavilion Publishing and Media Ltd
Page layout and typesetting: Emma Dawe, Pavilion Publishing and Media Ltd
Printing: CMP Digital Print Solutions

Woodland CARBON
www.woodlandcarbon.co.uk
18CMPUKL
Printed on Carbon Captured paper

Praise for this book

"*Talking with a Map* is a timely reminder of the importance of dialogue and the simplicity and complexity of talking. Beautifully written, it weaves a narrative taking the reader from childhood to adulthood, from our ancestors to current times. It is filled with stories and moments: sweet 'blueberry moments' which speak to your heart, but the author doesn't shy away from difficult topics which need speaking about. We need to remember how to talk now more than ever with the challenges modern society faces. This book starts a dialogue about how to do this. It is one to read over and over until tatty and well-loved."

Dr Jenny Marshall, Consultant Clinical Psychologist, CAT Supervisor and joint trust wide lead for CAT, Tees, Esk and Wear Valleys NHS Foundation Trust

"Conversations around the world could be made easier with the knowledge from this book. Steve Potter shows how mapping enhances our ability to have conversations that are more co-creative and meaningful. *Talking with a Map* builds on his first book, which focused on the use of mapping in therapy, to explore its more versatile application in everyday life by individuals, teams and broader systems. As well as showing us how mapping can be used as an aid to better conversations, it comprehensively describes the underlying mechanisms by which mapping creates conversational and relational awareness – and awareness that ultimately supports us to have a deeper, more integrated connection with ourselves, others, the world around us and beyond."

Dr Siobain Bonfield (DClinPsych), Psychology Discipline Senior, Peninsula Health, Melbourne

"This rich and finely textured analysis of being conversational and relational opens the doors and windows to therapeutic rooms and 'mapscapes' that many experienced psychologists, counsellors and psychotherapists will be unaware even existed, though will instantly recognise as core to their own experience. This is part of the same conversation that Steve began with *Therapy with a Map* and as such will be considered a key text in the world of Cognitive Analytic Therapy. For those who are CAT-curious or interested in conversational awareness in therapy, this book is a gift and a joy."

Sandy McAfee, Clinical Psychologist, Scotland

"This is a beautifully written, deeply curious, wise and compassionate book which teaches us how to develop relational awareness and conversational intelligence through 'mapping' our conversations. Steve Potter puts words on what we already know – how we talk is as important as what we talk about. In teaching us how to 'talk with a map', this book provides us with a tool that can liberate the limiting discourse so prevalent in social and political commentary. It offers a means of having the kind of conversations that we are so desperately in need of, in order to co-create solutions to the challenges of our world as it is today. It is a must read for anyone interested in interpersonal dynamics, or simply interested in living a life with better relationships. Who isn't?!"

Dr Claire Regan, Senior Clinical Psychologist, HSE Carlow/Kilkenny, Ireland

Foreword

Steve Potter gives us an insightful read in *Talking with a Map*. The text is woven with many exciting ideas born of his careful research into conversation and communication over many years.

The book takes us on a creative journey around the actual practical skill of conversation, and the importance it holds in all human life. Mapping together with pen and paper, in small stages, offers a spacious and practical support in making better, clearer and more compassionate conversations.

He writes: 'talking is what makes us human. Being conversational is our superpower.'

He likens the potential of conversation with the musical experience of knowingly being in tune, and in harmony, whatever our differences.

While the map is not the country, making a shared map of how things are between individuals or in groups can hold the bigger picture while each person comes into their own individual understanding. The map is both referee and witness.

Steve draws on his long experience of working with individuals and groups therapeutically, and teaching and supervising psychotherapy in the tradition of Cognitive Analytic Therapy. CAT theory describes well how we all grow within a web of relationship with others, and with all the animate world. Steve's work extends the written and communication skills of the active therapy of CAT and develops it further.

The book offers clear guidelines for the reader to follow, with detailed examples and clearly designed grids to help bring clarity to the words that need to be shared. The grids serve as a guide in the background to the process of mapping. Steve calls on his great skill and experience as a psychotherapist and study and work with Cognitive Analytic Therapy to flesh out initial words shared so that much more is uncovered. As things are questioned and time for pondering allowed, new expressions may unfold that fit the felt experience. Steve calls this process hovering and shimmering. It's inspiring because it allows us to find a flexible way with words which can so often limit our conversation and exchanges. In reading we join Steve in mapping the steps of relating, talking, in silence or spoken.

Steve makes us pause, look and listen, experiment with different words.

How we talk is as important as going into what we are talking about.

Talking with a Map offers a way of rediscovering and healing our ability to talk with one another one-to-one, in groups, at home, work, through art or leisure sport or politics. Everywhere! Steve also writes about the limitation of conversation in some areas such as commerce and politics where ideas become dominant and can be overvalued or undervalued and the art and flow of communication abandons the celebration of difference.

Chapter 8 gives us a sense of the conversational origins of modern humans with many fascinating examples from other countries and communities. It reminded me of a line written by Australian writer Kate Grenville in *The Lieutenant*, a novel about a young man traveling as part of the first fleet to Australia and learning to communicate with aboriginal people in 1788.

'*You did not learn a language without entering into a relationship with the people who spoke it with you. His friendship with Tagaran was not a list of objects, or the words for things eaten or not eaten, thrown or not thrown. It was the slow constructing of the map of a relationship.*'

Talking with a Map is an inspiring read and will be extremely helpful to many readers in many different walks of life who value true and expanding communication. Steve suggests we read the book as if it is a guide to another country that we know deep down but have not visited for a long time. A country where conversation is at the heart of being human and the glue that holds society together.

By Elizabeth Wilde McCormick MA psych; Dip Psych.Soc Psych, founder member and life member of the Association for Cognitive Analytic Therapy, author of *Change for the Better: Personal development through practical psychotherapy (5th edition).*

Preface

All my life I have been trying to have better conversations, whether with the people who I have worked with as a psychotherapist or with colleagues or with family and friends.

In my working life it has been a continuous apprenticeship. The people with whom I have spoken as a therapist have come from all walks and stages of life and all parts of the world. The conversations have been joyful and painful, fluent, or fragmented. It has been a privilege to help people tell, and retell, their life stories as they find their own dialogue with the world within and around them. I have learnt with them that better conversations don't just help solve personal problems or build self-worth but can also develop a relational awareness of who we are in the world.

At the same time, in my personal life I have been searching for the conversations which I need and were disallowed or disorganised in my formative years. How do we find those talking companions who can share and sustain curiosity and compassion as the world changes around us? How do we develop those wide open and deep discussions where everything connects, and words are found that are free enough to help? Certainly, at times I have found foolish and ignorant ways of talking *at*, *against* or *for* people instead of talking *with* them.

It is this mixed experience of helping others and trying to help myself that has led me to the methods of making maps of our words as we talk. For the past twenty-five years, borrowing initially on my trainings and practice in group therapy, psychodynamic psychotherapy and Cognitive Analytic Therapy, I have been having conversations assisted by pen and paper, in and out of the therapy room, with individuals, groups and teams.

So, what have I learnt?

I have learnt that conversations can bring out our finest human qualities of mutual, co-creative contact. Equally, we are very capable of getting into a conversational mess with each other. I have learnt, with others, a love of the spoken language and a capacity to be surprised at how we can compose and spin words into profound moments of personal meaning. I have recovered that first childhood delight in words when big questions are able to be asked aloud without shame. I have overcome that first teenage anxiety of saying the wrong thing and feeling mocked and red faced. I have learnt that we all have a hunger to talk in safe and open ways with space and time to wonder, assert and reflect.

I have learnt that talking earnestly about our lives and the world around us is an important defense against tyranny and abuse in our communities and societies, whether locally or globally. I have learnt that we need to talk about differences of power and influence, and we need to stand together, in among the conversations and voices, in the face of the climate and ecological emergency and continuing ethnic, social, generational, sexual and gender injustice. I have learnt that across all our differences of generation and identity we are in a continuous process of mutual translation from one local language to another local language, even when we speak with the same tongue. I have learnt that putting the significant words from a conversation on paper helps us listen, reflect and discover what we want to say, and helps us be taken seriously when we speak together.

I would not have arrived at the ideas in this book without being part of the Association for Cognitive Analytic Therapy (www.acat.me.uk) and the wider international community of practitioners (www.internationalcat.org) with their curiosity about the social and psychological forces that shape, restrict and enable conversations about our common humanity and mental health.

Special thanks are due to the 'defiant eloquence' and openness of many clients with whom I have worked over the years and the people who I have taught and supervised. Also, to friends; to Catherine – my wife and partner of many years; my family – especially little Layla and Leo; and Guy Potter who helped with edits and revisions of earlier drafts. I would not have these ideas without colleagues and those staff in the NHS in the UK and mental health professionals internationally who have tried these methods of talking with a map. Many heartfelt thanks to Darren Reed and staff from Pavilion Publishing for supporting this project.

Finally, this book is a long thank you letter to all those who have shared in figuring out the rules and methods for conversations and relationships that are sensitive, humane, and just. I hope I will not stop learning how we talk in a world which, at times, feels intent on trivializing, undermining and drowning out our capacity to be in dialogue.

Steve Potter, London 2022

Contents

Chapter 1: Setting the scene

Introduction

This book offers ideas to help us have better conversations. It demonstrates simple methods of using pen and paper to track out the lines of conversation, the patterns of interaction and the links and gaps in what we are saying. It does this in ways that engage our senses as we talk. We see what we are saying, by touching and circling words, while drawing lines and arrows between them on paper as they are voiced and heard.

Talking with a Map is a call to rediscover and heal our ability to talk with each other one-to-one, or in groups, at home, or at work, at play, through art or leisure, sport, or politics. It is an aid to ordinary, everyday awareness of how we are talking.

Talking is our most human form of relating. It is what we do to connect and negotiate. It is how we signal and establish safety or alarm. It is how we organise and evaluate. It is how we mutually influence, please, reassure and gossip with each other. It is what we do while we are doing something else. We talk and make things. We talk and decide to lead or follow. We talk as we teach or learn. We talk and play. We talk and romance and co-create intimacy and love. We talk and raise a family. We talk and resolve, fight, and repair, grieve and come to terms with what life throws at us. We talk to take heart, show defiance and give voice in the face of the continuous historic struggle with tyrannical regimes for whom talking freely and openly is inimical.

The book describes how to keep track of what we are saying by putting key words spread out on paper as we speak. This helps notice, name and negotiate not just what we are discussing but how we are talking. These conversational words on paper between us can make maps of our patterns of relating, our contrasting feelings, and actions. By talking with a map, we can develop conversational awareness and, in the process, make a new relationship with ourselves and the world around us.

The map we make while we talk can be of a moment, fragments of a conversation; or the feelings and ideas around one key word. It can map our reflections on what we do and how we cope with feelings. It can map our roles and relationships and the way we share and change our life stories. It can help orchestrate the various voices and parts to a conversation. It can help change the direction, focus or tone of a conversation. Mapping can go with the flow of the conversation or take charge of it using moments of recapping and reflection. I call them listening maps because they help us actively listen together. I call them memory maps because they extend our working memory and help us see patterns that would otherwise be too complicated to grasp.

The book shows how to talk with a map step-by-step. It does this with many illustrative maps and examples. It develops the idea of a healthy and mutual conversational awareness as the common factor to better discussions and as a protective factor against those anti-conversational forces in contemporary societies that bully, ridicule, undermine trust in language, and seek to silence us. In this context the book explores the idea of conversational poverty, and the centrality of a conversational style of language to our long and slow evolution over hundreds of thousands of years into becoming those homo sapiens who got smart and survived by talking to each other a lot. It also keeps in mind the magic and delicate self-building process of how we become conversational in the first few years of life. And in contrast, the poverty of contact and language that can arise through neglectful or harmful relationships.

The goals of *Talking with a Map* are not only better discussions and having more ability to talk about the important things facing us individually and collectively, but also being more aware of what helps and hinders us having lives that are conversationally rich, honest, and ethical.

An illustration of talking with a map

Jo and I have been talking for 30 minutes. In front of us there is a big sheet of paper with words circled and arrows and lines linking them. The map has quickly become an arena for our conversation as we talked with it and connected with each other through the words scribbled down here and there across the paper. We have now gone quiet and are reflecting on the discussion by alternately looking at each other and the words spread out before us.

It is not just the words that remind us of what we have been saying. The lines and arrows between words and circles around words tell us something about patterns, about connections and gaps. The words on paper are bearing witness and serve as a guide when it feels like we have gone astray or got lost between two different threads of conversation. As we were talking, Jo briefly rests her hand on one of the words as if to lift it off the page and get the measure of it. Seeing the words on paper helps her externalise her thoughts and feelings and make them more visible and easier to negotiate. I point at the map with my fingers. Our hands are part of the talking by linking our brains, bodies and voices with the words on paper as our assistant. What we are doing is convivial, transparent and equal. It helps us frame and share our stories and stops us talking at each other.

Jo says, 'Let's go back over what we have been saying' and with her finger she traces and recaps the conversation, 'riffing' off thoughts and feelings and memories of the conversation from the words on paper. It is like a map of the landscape of the conversation. It allows us to navigate with a visual, finger pointing shorthand that otherwise would be too laborious to describe. As Jo recaps, I am responding here and there by pointing and touching words. 'That bit is more me than you, don't you think?' Jo says. 'I am here, and you are there.' As she circles the two different points on the map, there is a circling of the words with her pen which attunes with the changing emphases in her voice and her body which leans in and out of the paper on the table. There is a relational fluency to our conversation which would be hard to achieve without the process of mapping. We can wander but we don't lose the plot. We seem to go deeper into specific feelings and moments because we can more easily zoom out again and see the bigger picture. Words rescue us, guide us, but when they confuse us, we say, 'What were we saying then? I cannot make a link to that phrase there.' 'Oh, that was when you were saying about work.' As we recap the conversation, we reshape it with the words on paper and the stories we are telling are reconsolidated in our memories.

Jo suggests we both sit back, quietly reflect and then share where we think we are on the map. We do this, and through comparing and contrasting our responses we find we are talking about our relationship between us. I say there is not enough room on the paper and Jo puts four more pieces of paper at the top, the bottom and on each side. It is a good job we are sitting and talking at a table. Jo says, 'You know, if we were a group, we could do this standing around a white board'. Jo and I talk, not just through words, but with our faces, hands and eyes. Talking with a map of words on paper between us makes us more relaxed and confident and in turn that makes us more able to be attentive to each other. We are taking the conversation seriously. But there is a playful quality to it as well. The map is like a sand tray or a play space. We are playing with the words. The conversation, like any conversation, goes in different directions. We are talking with each other and at each other. We clear up a moment of talking at cross purposes. Jo says, 'Well, you were talking to yourself rather than me just then'. The map is like a shared extension to our working memories. We are holding more in mind and our conversation is more easily enabled to jump here and there and be less linear.

As a step to finishing the conversation Jo and I use the template diagram (Figure 1.1) to reflect on how the conversation went and what general lessons we might learn from it about our talking relationship. It helped us link the content to the process as we put down our key thoughts about how we were talking and what we were doing when the talking was going well and how that made us feel. We wrote down what we thought we were trying to get from the conversation and the feelings that brought up. It was harder to own up to what we did badly, but we got there by thinking about what we did less well and how that felt. We thought we were too polite at times and could have interrupted each other more. Finally, we discussed what we had been avoiding talking about. That helped us see that we could talk about our feelings for and opinions of each other and that the words on paper might make that easier to handle. We were not sure whether what we avoided helped us or not but putting it out there on paper had us thinking about it openly. If you try mapping a conversation just do it free style and spontaneously and don't mind the mess of words because you will each, be picking out the words and links that matter to you in that moment. When you have finished then spend five minutes using the template in figure 1.1 to review how the talk went.

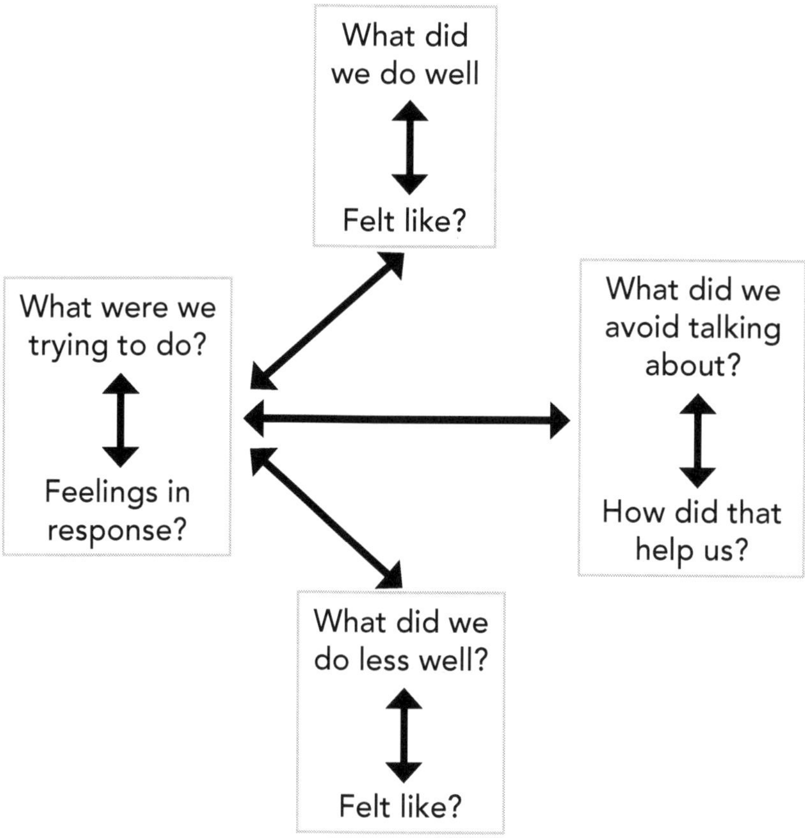

Figure 1.1

Jo and I found having the reflective map made it easier to end the conversation (it would normally have rumbled on) and go and do other things. When coming back to the conversation and the need to talk we found the conversational mapping very helpful as a memory jogger to pick up, not just what we were talking about, but also how we were talking and feeling. Jo asks who is going to look after the map and the notes to the map. We decide to photograph the maps, and both have a copy. We thank each other and fix a time to talk like this again.

Talking with a map

This idea of talking with a map can be referred to as conversational mapping, pen and paper discussions or word maps. Throughout this book the combination of methods and concepts will be referred to most frequently as 'Map and Talk'. It is a method which can bring out the main points in a conversation and look at the multiple directions and lines of sensitivity, expression and control of feelings ideas and actions.

It is a collaborative, co-creative approach to sharing our ideas and feelings side-by-side to help us notice, name and negotiate the moments and details in the shaping and direction of a discussion. It is an awareness of the 'sweet spots' of being in tune with each other and navigating the 'hot spots' of not attuning, feeling at odds, exposed or confused. It is versatile and can help one-to-one discussions, group reflections and team meetings.

Talking with a map draws upon an idea that conversations carry within them patterns and plots – we could call them templates, plans, schemas, designs. There is a 'mapping' quality to our conversations and the stories that come from them. Mapping our conversations is as good as mapping our relationships with ourselves and the world. It can help us discover, validate or renegotiate, how we see each other.

The mapping helps the talking and the talking helps the mapping. It is a two way relationship. According to Jerome Bruner, these are two distinct approaches to understanding which he calls the paradigmatic and the narrative.[1] Or to put it more simply in the context of this book: map and talk. As we map, we see more of the pattern and logic and can stand back. As we talk, we can feel the flow and be carried along by the narrative. The joint activity of talking with a map helps us explore the relations between paradigmatic (shaping, structuring, diagramming) and narrative (storying, voicing) ways of shaping experience.

Bruner was a big influence in bringing the educational and developmental psychology of the Russian psychologist Lev Vygotsky to the West in the cold war era. Among Vygotsky's many explorations of the developmental process of childhood learning was a curiosity about how language skills in proto-conversation link to skills in writing. One experiment is quite relevant to a map and talk session. Vygotsky noted an experiment where children where encouraged to remember a number of items that would be hard to keep in working memory without help.[2] The children had pen and paper to help them remember but could not yet spell and write the names of the items. However, according Vygotsky and his colleague Luria, the children found help in remembering by making marks linked to each item on paper as if in imitation of writing. These squiggle notations seemed to help the process of remembering. This rings true with Map and Talk that we are remembering not just the words but also the lines and arrows and circles that go with them and in the process we are remembering specific tones and connotations of the meaning of the words more than we would if they were just a list. It is as if the mapping element, or paradigmatic element, enhances the narrative element.

In all conversations we are looking for patterns of meaning and connection. We are telling and sharing stories to bring these patterns out. These stories seem to be finding a voice, discovering connections and making a story for the first time. Sometimes they are so burdened by retelling that connections and patterns are welden together and the story is sealed off from dialogue. Or they are fragmented and invite completion, correction or judgement through conversation. Or traced out in the barest details like a map with only two or three first signs on as with the words in italics in the following sentence: 'I was supposedly a *happy child* and then when I was *seven* my parents got *divorced* and my *father* became *ill*. I became *anxious*.' The words in italics are the markers on the map that turn sentences into paragraphs of conversation and exploration.

When we map and talk we talk of details but are searching for the bigger picture. When someone seeks to draw one big story from the many stories of their lived experience they are giving shape to a life-map. We are yearning for this meta-map: the paradigm, the grand story that gives us narrative coherence but still gives space for the detailed moments. We don't want to tell the meta-story in such a shorthand it becomes trite: 'You are born, you live and you die.'

In mapping and tracking our discussions we make something that is implicit and internal more explicit and more external. In these ways the recounting of any story is not just a telling of the story but an attempt to map its meaning cognitively, relationally and emotionally.

Roots in therapy and reflective practice

The world of therapy, counselling, coaching and mentoring is here to stay and offers a leading conversational discourse on the world. One goal of any therapeutic help should be the empowerment of clients and the wider public to discover or rediscover how to have healing conversations with each other. The aim of this book and work associated with it is to develop conversational awareness skills training.[3] Talking with a map takes lessons from the language of psychotherapy and applies them to everyday conversational life. Its pronoun of choice is 'we'. How are *we* helping or hurting each other? How are we sharing our ideas and getting things done? How you or I, she, he or they are doing comes out of how we are doing. It is easy in a conversation to go into you, you, you and an accusitive mode of dialogue, or me, me, me and an egoistic mode of talking. Map and talk stands in the verbal spaces between pronouns. I becomes you, me becomes we, them becomes us.

The methods of talking with a map have been developed in individual therapy and reflective practice with mental health teams in many contexts and countries.[4] The roots of Map and Talk lie in group work, adult education and youth work and in the relational,[5] and conversational[6] approaches to psychotherapy, and most significantly the integrative, social and psychological approach of Cognitive Analytic Therapy[7]. A full account of conversational mapping as part of therapy can be found in my 2020 book *Therapy with a Map*.[8]

Talking with a map and its encouragement of mutual aid in conversations is not to detract from the richness and value of a great deal of psychotherapy, counselling and related professional help. Long may it be available in affordable ways. Therapy can be exceedingly helpful. It is one of most researched fields in the world of welfare and care. There are an enormous variety of methods and approaches, each with their own teachers, students and languages. The accummulated evidence points to the quality of the talking relationship between therapist and client or patient as a key variable. Therapy can help solve life problems and recover self-esteem or reduce emotional distress, but in the context of this book it can also develop conversational confidence and awareness. In *Therapy with a Map*[9] I called this the unintended fruit of the therapies. Problems may still be substantial after some sessions of therapy but our ability to talk about our problems, think relationally about them and gain perspective on them is improved.

We need to talk

What might our motives be to use a map to help us talk? One motive comes from childhood and those moments of struggle and delight in discovering language and talking. Learning to talk is learning to map and make sense of our world. We need to talk to discover what we think and feel and to find our voices and be in a shared reflective space. Another motive comes from our need for each other. Talking is how we establish and maintain interpersonal relationships. It is a sensitive and refined process. We can be easily hurt and lose heart or confidence. Our talking may have no apparent content or purpose other than being in touch with each other. And yet we need to talk to name and negotiate our needs and desires. We need to talk to connect with each other and to bring together our social and psychological minds and to solve problems and puzzle things out together. We need to talk because we live complicated lives in a complex world. Or to put it bluntly: we need to talk more if we are to maintain a healthy democracy that will hear the voices that help us survive as a species and face the climate and ecology crisis[10]. We need help to talk in ways that early civil rights activists called 'speaking truth to power'[11] that challenges the deceptions and denials of those with privilege and power and helps heal the wounds of generations of trauma and injustice within and between groups because of colonialism, slavery, economic exploitation, sexual discrimination and violence. In the face of all this, we don't talk deeply often enough. The longform, extended conversations are squeezed out of everyday life by more solution-focused talk or smart, surface banter.

Better conversations

The aim of *Talking with a Map* is to achieve better discussions and better relationships by developing conversational awareness. The general view of the skills that add up to better conversation are the mutual awareness and use of turn taking, a sense of setting the scene and agreeing roles with scope for negotiating both what is discussed and how it is discussed. In better conversations, we help each other make eye contact and read each other's body language and communicate with our hands along with our voices. Better conversations can tune into our changing emotions, the ebb and flow of confidence and intent of the voice both in where it is coming from and where it is speaking to. Better conversations have flow and bring personal meaning.

In a better conversation there is a mixture of discovery while repairing previous broken ground and healing our capacity to talk. There is a sensitivity to the choice and impact of words and a spontaneity of expression with room for unexpected turns in language meaning. We take turns to hold forth and be in the limelight. There is shared control of tone, intensity and direction. There is social awareness of differences of language, of histories of silencing and speaking at and for, rather than with. And finally, there is a companionable awareness that this conversation, in this time and place, is expressing something local and unique while also carrying something from relationships and conversations in the present and past world outside the conversation. They have a sense of safety to take risks and stretch what we say and where we go with our words. Open questions can be asked, and – in the language of this book – there is room to hover and shimmer, and dive in and out, and claim a voice, and ownership and authorship as well as give all that to others (see page 12 in this chapter and in Chapter 6). All of these qualities can be enhanced and cultivated by talking with a map.

The sweet spots of conversational awareness

All of these qualities of better conversations depend on a shared capacity for conversational awareness both in the moment and on reflection. Whilst we are always partly aware of how the discussion is going, we have our blind spots and no-go areas. We have our cover stories and chatty topics that distract from awareness but there is a sweet spot in conversational awareness when we are mutually aware and in each other's zone of comfort, adventure and connection. There are hot spots when we are suddenly too aware and feel self-conscious and embarrassed and anxiety gets in the way of open dialogue. There are blank spots or blind spots that we have no awareness of what is playing a part in shaping the conversation.

We all have our moments when we are so oblivious of the dynamics of the relationships in the conversation or the ethics of turn taking and word finding that we are at the far-right end of the continuum line in Figure 1.2. In moments of talking, we may jump from being *unaware* to being *too aware* at the far-left end of the line. These sudden moments of self-consciousness are the hot spots in the conversation that are best named when they are noticed even if they are embarrassing. Negotiating them with a map can change the quality of the conversation for the better. Taking the risk to negotiate will depend on an assessment of the balance of power in the conversation.

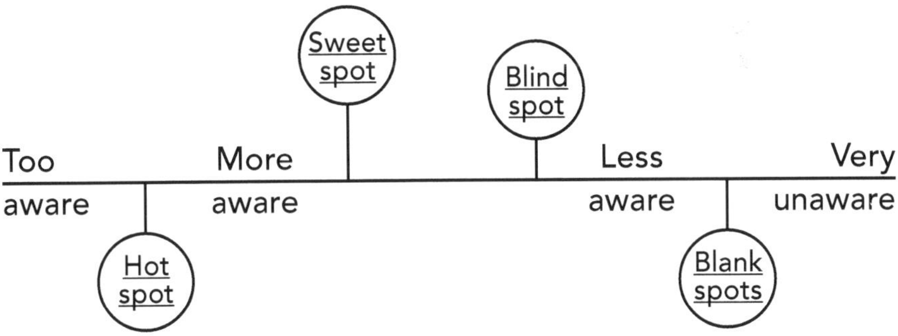

Figure 1.2

The methods in this book aim to help have more sweet spots in the conversation while keeping the flow of the content going. At the same time, they are an aid to navigating the hots spots of self-consciousness. These are the conversational equivalents of the musical experience of knowingly being in tune and on song or in harmony and spotting and rehearsing and revising things when not in tune. They are important to our personal, social and political well-being. Talking with a map is an aid to more awareness of how, when and why we choose to notice, name and negotiate how the conversation is going.

Conversational ethics

We seek to talk as we wish to be spoken to, except our needs, emotions, fears and prejudices get in the way. A conversational ethics is reality based, knowing that our awareness is not always a reliable witness and needs to be checked and negotiated. The task-driven and transactional nature of much of our talking means we tend to neglect the process for the sake of keeping up with the content.

How we talk matters as much as what we talk about. This ability to talk about how the talk is going depends on qualities of conversational awareness. This is not as simple as saying 'I know what you are thinking' or 'I get what you are saying'. It is a capacity to mutually co-create a conversation and it involves some sensitivity to multiple directions and qualities of interaction that are the central focus of talking with a map in this book.

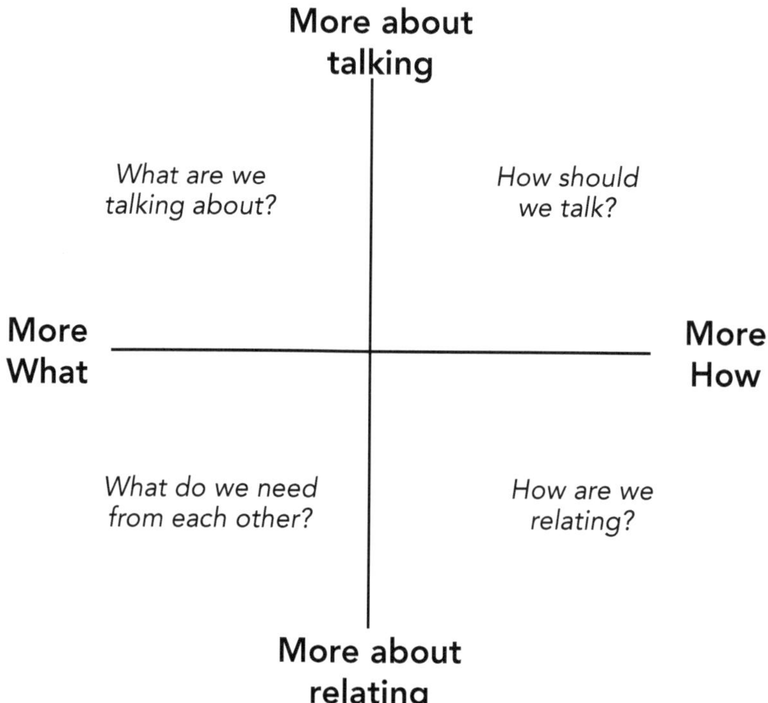

Figure 1.3

The process of mapping helps us hold simultaneously in mind much more than what we could hold without a map. It can give us a freer and extended relational and conversational intelligence. In Figure 1.3 the conversation tracker can move along the horizontal line with a focus more on what is being said or more on how it is being said. A good conversation will move back and forth along the line. Changing what we are talking about will change how we talk and vice versa. The vertical line is a conversational tracker of a changing focus on the quality and direction of talking and the quality and direction of the relationship. A good conversation will move up and down the vertical line. Check the questions in each box and think about using them in any conversation to see where the focus is and how and why it changes.

Many conversations focus too much on the upper left quadrant and then are surprised when trouble comes in the bottom right quadrant. We should not assume that negotiating how to talk is the same as negotiating how to relate. As already noted, we tend to be too solution focused, task driven and transactional in our conversation. Content pushes process aside and although we are aware of how things are going, we don't actually say. Or our talk is so conversationally reflective that *how* pushes *what* aside. A conversationally aware environment (family, school, love, friendship, workplace, politics and arts) will weave talk of the process and the content together. This is where talking with a map can help. It can help us change our part in, or understanding of, a conversation by just focusing on one angle or aspect. The map can hold the bigger picture in mind while our attention goes to one bit that resonates.

This book is written at a time when our world faces a climate crisis and is undergoing many complex transitions both locally and globally. As indicated in Chapter 12 it may be a dangerous time of conflict between open and closed forms of conversation. Between truth and deception or pro-conversational and anti-conversational forces as the world divides. We are vulnerable to those who want to undermine the delicate fabric of trust and transparency which governs our most urgent and important public conversations. Our test is to talk about our differences and to learn from each other about the generations of unspoken trauma we are carrying in different ways individually and collectively.

Four directions and qualities of conversation

At the centre of the book is an idea of conversation as a deeply human, mutual, co-creative activity which is simultaneously pushing and pulling, co-operating and conflicting in four directions (see the conversational awareness grid on page 111 in Chapter 6).

- It is a conversation **between us**: an interpersonal meeting between two or more people willing to recognise and answer to each other, not just in role or around a task or topic, but in a fully human person-to-person way. Its keynote is interpersonal encounter.
- It is a conversation **within us** which tries to establish and recognise, negotiate and navigate our own needs and responses. Its keynote is internal subjectivity
- It is a conversation **around us** with social and cultural contexts and forces. It is a process of positioning and gendering in an entangled mix of ways ideologically, ethnically, historically, locally and globally. Its keynote is social forces.
- It is a conversation that has the potential to reach **beyond us** by speaking to something that is greater than the sum of its parts. Its keynote is spiritual or existential.

These four different directions of conversation are mediated by four different qualities that can be enhanced by talking with a map. They draw on each other as distinctive lines of engagement. They might be seen as different genres and styles of conversation (more thoughtful or more emotional, more action focused or more concerned with authority).

- **Hovering** is the bird's eye, overview capacity to not go head-to-head with one idea but hold several in mind. It is the ability to see from another point of view with empathy and curiosity. It moves between big picture and detail. It zooms in and out.
- **Shimmering** is a capacity to tolerate mixed feelings and changing intensities of feelings so that we can learn from our emotional conflicts and ambivalence within ourselves and between ourselves and others.
- **Participating** is the capacity to be a participating observer in those moments when we join in, share discussion and share the roles of speaking and listening. It is a process of taking a role or playing a part. At the same time, it is something more wholehearted. Mapping as we talk can help develop the capacity to be alongside, inside and outside each other's experience. We have to join the conversational dance to know the dance and when and how to step in and out.
- **Authoring** is the capacity to own, author and give voice to our feelings, ideas and views in a way that is responsible, accountable, and answerable.

The interaction between the four directions and qualities of conversation are explored fully in Chapter 6 where they are outlined as a sixteen-item grid designed to be kept at the back of our minds more like a palette of conversational paints. The grid is the result of an ongoing research process to pin down and work with the different directions of talk and qualities of talk that are in play in a specific context at any one time.

Overview of the chapters

Following this introductory chapter, the next four show step-by-step, idea-by-idea how to learn to Map and Talk. Chapter 2 shows how to track feelings and actions in a conversation with words spread out on paper. It gives an initial feel of the Map and Talk process. Chapter 3 focuses on mapping roles and relationships that give character and structure to our conversations. It explores how these are positioned and gendered within and between us as social and emotional roles. Chapter 4 turns attention to Map and Talk as a way of tracking and drawing out patterns from stories. It highlights the value of seeing story telling as conversational and introduces some mapping templates for our everyday stories. Chapter 5 takes a practical look at setting up and managing a Map and Talk session both one-to-one or with a group or team in different contexts.

The middle chapters from 6 to 9 explore the benefits and obstacles to conversational awareness as they are made visible and tangible by talking with a map. Chapter 6 explores conversational awareness as the main benefit of Map and Talk. It offers a conversational awareness grid of sixteen elements and shows how they work as a guide in the background of mapping as we talk. They can help notice, name and negotiate the many ways that awareness can be helped and hindered. It includes reference to measures of changes in conversational and relational awareness before and after a Map and Talk session. Chapter 7 explores the contribution of writing and reading out loud and the roles that language and voice awareness play in Map and Talk. Chapter 8 seeks to give the reader a deeper and wider sense of the conversational origins of modern humans. It uses a different narrative form to speculate on the birth of conversational awareness, the integration of different genres of language with special reference to our unique need and capacity to have helpful and caring conversations and to use the awareness of this to navigate and negotiate within and between groups.

Chapter 9 gives a template for thinking about conversational poverty in our lives despite the wealth of human resources within, between and around us. The chapter focuses on the damage to our capacity for conversational and relational awareness arising from traumatising and disorganising family and social systems. It offers a simplified framework for talking with a map about the divisive personal and social narratives in our early years that can foster a divided sense of self. The positive search for self-realisation requires a dialogue or healing conversation that can take us out of these conflicts to a more integrated sense of self.

The next three chapters 10 to 12 give a wide range of examples of map and talk in action as an aid to conversational awareness whether in work, home and intimate conversations, school or arts and politics. Chapter 10 shows how the work of the book has one foot in everyday life and one foot in the therapy room. A detailed description of mapping the beginnings of a therapeutic conversation offers an angle on how we can reflect on the detailed processes of being helpers and carers using the ideas of talking with a map. Chapter 11 has examples and applications of Map and Talk. They give an everyday perspective on how it can help us have the conversational organisations; conversational families, schools and intimate partnerships or the conversationally creative lives we need. Chapter 12 explores our unmet needs for a conversational politics. It touches on the narcissistic inflation of political ideas to the extent of making them monstrous and unnegotiable. It turns the focus away from politicians and more on the way ideas are overvalued and devalued in politics. It turns the spotlight on us as ordinary citizens whether as political camp followers or the bystander citizens and wonders what change is needed for a more open and conversationally aware politics regardless of our beliefs and loyalties.

The book is not just for the talking professions for whom conversational awareness is an everyday experience and duty (whether as therapists, doctors, nurses, psychologists, advisers, tutors, teachers, carers or managers). The book is also for all of us in those moments where we wished we had the extra courage, conviviality, compassion and curiosity to try to negotiate our way through the blind spots, hotspots and sweet spots of conversation awareness. It is for artists or performers who depend on awareness of the creativity of conversations invested in and stored in their work so that we can have our conversations with the exhibitions and performances which they have produced. Finally, it is for use in steering business and political meetings where awareness of how conversations are going may help achieve better management, policy and governance. In sum, this book is for anyone who wants to review their conversational awareness and skills in ordinary and everyday transactions and relationships at work or at home. Or anyone who wants to spot when they are getting into a toxic or limiting conversational dance and figure out how, when and where to step out of the dance.

To conclude this chapter, here are two examples that illustrate the aims and range of the book: the spatial, storytelling mapping that a toddler does in the process of achieving language and conversation, and the mapping we do as we talk in our adult lives.

Where is baby?

'*We are storytelling creatures, and as children we acquire language to tell those stories that we have inside us.*' Jerome Bruner[12]

Maisie is a week away from being two years old and is being cared for by her grandparents while her mum is in hospital going through a difficult and protracted labour. Her dad is with mum. She has not seen mum for three days. Maisie knows that a baby is expected to arrive, but she has no map of time and place. There is a feeling in the air of waiting for news and uncertainty for Maisie and her grandparents. Maisie remembers often putting her hand on her mummy's tummy and feeling the unborn baby kicking.

Maisie had a recent gift of a toy pram and baby doll. It is in the small back garden which is where Maisie urgently leads grandpa by his hand while asking him 'Where is baby' and pointing to the pram with which she has been playing alone. As Maisie speaks her hands go palm up in the air by way of showing her feeling of being perplexed. She invites Grandpa to look in the pram. He lifts the blanket and lowers the hood. Maisie says, 'No. Not there.' For weeks, the pram has had a life-like baby doll tucked in under a blanket. Grandpa double checks with a theatrical gesture of searching and, squatting down beside Maisie, says, 'Not there. So where? Where is baby?'

Maisie seems to have a map of what to do and she says, 'Come on Grandpa'. And leads him by the hand to search in the garden. They go round by the bins near the shed, behind the bicycles and in and around the bushes. Maisie seems to find comfort in the conversation that accompanies the search for 'baby'. Grandpa thinks to himself that we are doing something to help, and we have a plan.

'Not in the bushes, not near the bikes or the bins,' Maisie and Grandpa say echoing each other's words through each bit of the search. They are immersed in the action which has echoes of hide and seek games they have played. They repeat the words 'where's baby' several times in a style of call and response between them. Their conversation is developing a musicality, a rhythm of its own. It is as if they are saying 'we are not going to find the real baby, but by making a story we are finding our voices – like whistling in the dark'. They have agency together, but Maisie is lead author as evidenced by the turn the conversation now takes.

Grandpa imagines baby should be here but is missing. Mummy and Daddy should be here but are missing. Grandpa cannot tolerate the uncertainty. He sees the doll – aka baby – in the house on the kitchen table and leads Maisie to the back door, 'Baby is there, look!' With some agitation Maisie resists this premature and concrete attempt to resolve the missing baby problem. It is as if Maisie is saying, 'No Grandpa, you misunderstand me. I am not looking for the doll. I am looking for a conversation that will be magic and strong enough to give shape to and 'map' my feelings.'

Can this hotspot of awareness between them become a sweet spot? Maisie says, 'Come on Grandpa' and leads Grandpa back to the pram – saying again where is baby. She wants to revisit the landscape of the story so it can continue to help her. This time they do it in a more rehearsed and assured way as if they have reached some kind of understanding of the purpose of the conversation.

Again, Maisie lifts the miniature blanket from the pram and invites grandpa to look. No baby there. Again, they go around the garden calling out for baby and looking here and there. It is as if the conversation is doing something good as an act of defiance against feeling helpless or confused. The bewilderment and uncertainty is now articulated and jointly owned. If Grandpa can use the story to tolerate the uncertainty about where is baby so can Maisie.

Indeed, it does not seem that Maisie needs to repeat it a third time. She goes with Grandpa to get the doll from the kitchen and puts it firmly and tenderly in the pram and covers it with the blanket. Stories can fly to magical spaces and come back to the ground.

It could be that Maisie is going along with putting the newly found baby doll in the pram to mollify and comfort Grandpa. In this way the purpose of the story may now have changed with Maisie now looking after herself by looking after Grandpa. Either way the imaginative conversational quality of the search for baby is now sufficiently realised to use the doll as a symbol of the missing baby and a promise that it will or can turn up.

For Maisie and Grandpa, the mapping part of the talking was in the movement and the searching the garden and the theatre of the conversation. In the map (Figure 1.4) summarising their conversation, the missing baby leaves them feeling worried and alone. They want it to make sense and go searching. In the process they are actively doing something and giving voice to their feelings. Searching as an activity makes sense and leaves them feeling less helpless.

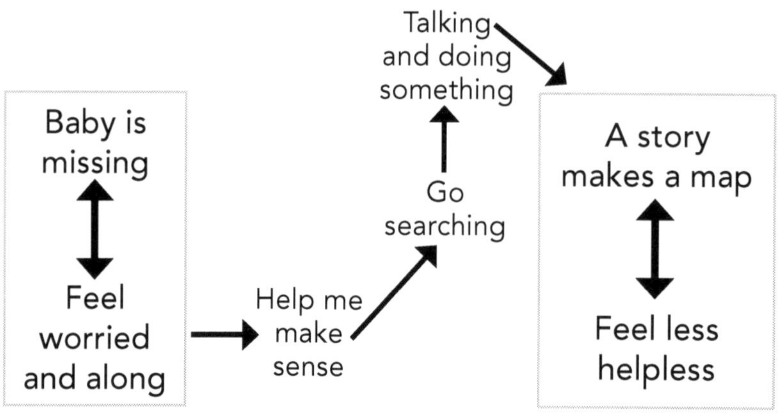

Figure 1.4

Reflections on Maisie's story

Maisie was worried and alone with her feelings about the missing baby, mum and dad. There was a comforting presence of her grandparents who were a familiar part of her life. However, there was something she was puzzling about with limited language, but a surprising amount of relational knowledge and resources about how to put minds together to make sense of something. What she did have was an analogical space, a parallel space with which she could map out a story of searching for 'baby' to see what was on her mind. The searching and talking was a conversation but it was also a mapping out of a problem to be brought to awareness. Regardless of whether it could be solved or not it was a meeting of minds. Often that is what we are doing with our deepest conversations: not finding solutions or managing transactions but giving voice and shape to an awareness, the lines of which are not defined. Our talking is a medium for relating. A problem held not alone but in shared minds is truly a problem halved and the solution must often be waited for. Maisie's purpose was not the search for the missing baby but for the missing conversation.

As is well described by Lane and others[13] the making and retelling of a story involves a process of memory reconsolidation (restorying is remapping the memory maps in search of a new meaning, a new outcome or a new relationship with the feelings involved). Many conversations between loved ones, friends, or colleagues at work go over the same ground. Each repetition reworks the memory and re-stories the memory of the experience differently. The point is not to have moments of resolution or revelation, as much as they may be valuable, but to shift awareness on by five percent or so away from helplessness to some sense of agency. In the process we may build conversational relationships that make us less alone in our thoughts and feelings and more in a world of companionship. We never outgrow this need as the next example with Sally highlights.

Sally shows them the messy middle

There is trouble in Sally's team at work. The boss, a charismatic but controlling man called Mr Jolson is not present at this particular meeting, and things are not going to plan. There are rumours and mixed feelings and anxiety about blurting things or putting their foot in it or being seen as stepping out of line. Sally is not the boss, but she has been doing a bit of what she calls 'reflective map and talk' with other teams. She has so far avoided stepping in and showing her new skill with this for fear of getting it wrong and incurring the wrath of Mr Jolson. In the absence of the usual tight controls, the conversation was getting more heated, everyone was passionate about what they were talking about. Someone said, 'What's going on. Can we cool down a bit?'

Another voice said, 'Hear me out.' Some people were switching off. One person left the meeting with their phone to their ear as a pretext. Sally stood up and said, 'Look, time out here. Watch me and watch my pen.' She went to the flip chart stand, propped it open, took the top off her pen and drew a line across the middle.

The men and the women came to temporary order at the sight of a pen and the flip chart paper. Sally said, 'At this end of the line (see Figure 1.5), I am going to put my words that describe my perception of what is going on in this discussion.' She wrote in big letters 'All shouting at once.' Then she asked, while pointing at the words she had just written, 'Is that right or does someone want to put it a different way?'

Cleo the deputy manager, a more reasonable person than her boss, suggested that 'perhaps we are not able to think when it is this heated'.

Sally drew another line to cut across the middle of the first line thereby making a cross. At the bottom of the vertical line, she wrote the words 'Not able to think'.

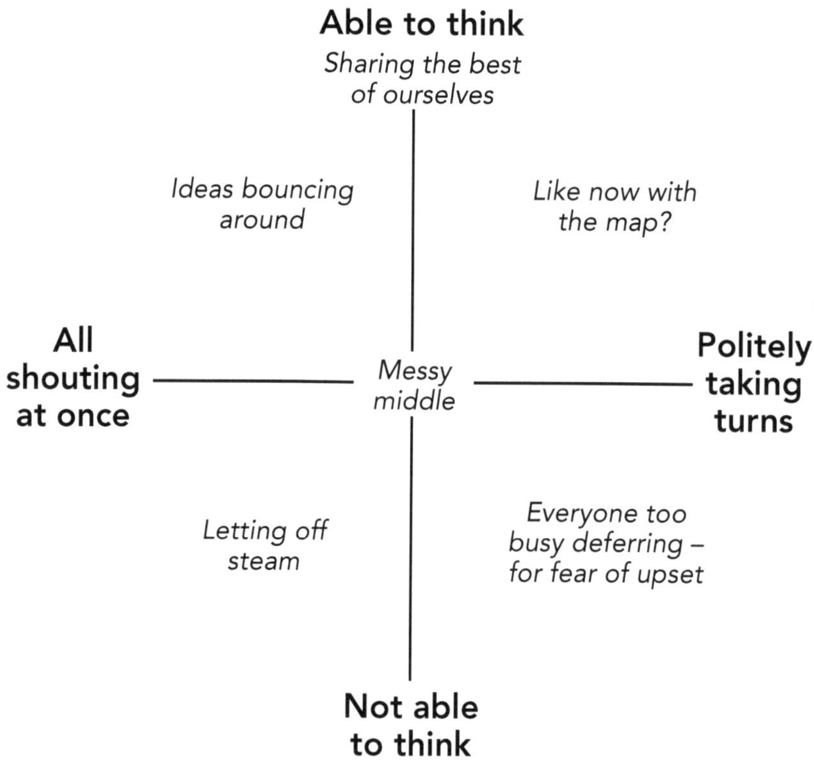

Figure 1.5

Someone said 'It is not just hard to think. I cannot think at all when everyone is letting off steam.' Sally put 'Letting off steam' down in the bottom left quadrant made by 'Not able to think' and 'All shouting at once'. This got the team thinking about the words that would go in the other three quadrants. Their minds were beginning to work together at least with the map. Their conversation was now mediated by the flip chart.

Sally said, 'This might seem a bit of a stretch but using the flip chart like this can help us make links in the conversation and see patterns in what is going on between us'. She thought to herself and chose not to say, 'Maybe it can help us be more considerate, more aware and more ethical in our discussions.' She pointed to the other end of the two lines and said 'What would it be like to be here and here? What would we be doing mostly and what would we be feeling?' Someone said laughingly as if the idea was comical, 'We would be politely taking turns'. As Sally wrote that in at the other end of the horizontal line everyone was quietly reflective for a bit. It was as if Sally was holding up a mirror to the team and also making room through the flipchart for a wider, more open conversation.

'Let me double check', Sally said as she rested her pen on the words 'Politely taking turns'. 'If we were more politely taking turns, would we be able to think?'

Someone jumped in and said to much laughter, 'Yes, but there would be fewer ideas to think about'.

'How do you know that?'

Somebody interrupted and said provocatively 'It would be boring'.

This triggered a rush of contrasting opinions and Sally asked as she waved her pen in the air, 'Look we are going over here' (pointing to and writing in the top left corner) 'Ideas are bouncing around'' Someone said, 'Well, we are talking now more about how we talk and that is unusual'. Many nodded in agreement. There was a reflective silence. Sally said to herself, 'leave it there' and put the top back on her pen.

As if in reaction someone said, 'No', and came forward and took the pen which Sally held out to him. 'We have to be honest and say that when the Boss is here, we tend too much to be down in this bottom right hand of this quadrant'. He wrote in the words as he said them (Figure 1.5) and noted that they were only his opinion. 'Everyone is too busy deferring. We are not giving each other the best of ourselves.' Sally asked, 'Where would the words "sharing the best of ourselves" go?'

'It would be up there in the middle at the top.'

Sally pointed and said, 'What here?', and they nodded, and she wrote it in: 'Sharing the best of ourselves', saying the words out loud as she wrote them to give them life and emphasis. Someone shouted out, 'But we don't, do we? Because we are too busy deferring, and we are too afraid of Mr Jolson to speak freely.' And then said to laughter, 'Don't write that down'. Sally took the pen and asked if there is a way to say it that would be the common view of the team. There was discussion which settled on the phrase 'For fear of upset' to be added in the bottom right corner. Again, there was a silence, and it was as if people were developing the conversation in their heads with the map as a reference.

Someone asked why the middle was messy. Sally said it was because it is the cross over point of not knowing and hovering and shimmering with mixed ideas and feelings. 'It is saying that you cannot go anywhere without going through the messy middle of the conversation and the relationship. Here, it is not yet clear what we are talking about or how to manage the relationship and the rules of discussion. It is the place where we can all do a bit of constructive dithering and take a breath, make a map together and see how it fits our readymade mental maps.'

Cleo said helpfully, 'Well, we need to be able to move back and forth between the top left and the top right. We need a moderator; the boss needs a moderator.' Someone else said, 'Well, we have got Sally'.

Sally replied, 'You have not got me; you have got the pen and the flipchart. Talking with a map is our moderator.'

Concluding comments

Writing is linear and conversations are not. Whilst the author has tried to write in a conversational way the reader need to bring a nonlinear conversational attitude. Read this book in the way that works for you but try reading it at times as if it is a guide to another country that we know well but have not visited for a long time. It is a country where open, lively, and sincere conversation is at the heart of being human and the glue that holds society together. It is what keeps language alive and fresh and accountable. The people of this distant country go out of their way to have conversations. They have public spaces dedicated to it. Their schooling is based on it and their lives are dedicated to the art of making conversation alongside whatever else they are doing. They know that talk can be playful and silly at times but at heart it is ready for serious discussion of the big issues that matter and are hard to talk through. Their management and politics are conversational. They spend as much time talking about how to govern as they do talking about *what* to govern. There are forces in our societies around the world that would prefer us to be ignorant or contemptuous of such a place and never visit this country again. Let this book take you there a little bit.

The methods of Map and Talk in pursuit of conversational awareness are genuinely modest, but they need practice if they are to make sense. Please think of this book as you would a book on learning to play the guitar while others sing. Such a book would not just be for reading but would require time set aside to practice the fingering and chords. There is no advantage in going for perfection or being a virtuoso at talking with a map. Just 'strumming along' with pen and paper can help a conversation find its voices, its rhythms and purpose. But practice is needed alone and with others. For video demonstrations, web-based workshops on how to Map and Talk check out the website www.mapandtalk.com.

In using this book, the reader might not need a word of warning but anyway here it is. Despite our best intentions, our most important and difficult conversations can go wrong. Mapping as we talk can help as a referee or witness. It can mediate and help pace difficult moments of high emotion. If there are intense or troublesome relationship difficulties, mapping needs to be in the hands of a third party who is trusted and neutral. And before any mapping can help, the agreement to talk compassionately curiously and openly needs to be affirmed by all taking part. This is the word of warning. Don't use the map and talk process to analyse the person or interpret their motives and values. Avoid the trap of talking for or giving a talking to someone. A helpful and creative or healing conversation is a process of talking with each other. Map the conversation or the story and keep the process centred on 'we' and what we are understanding and doing. Look for others to talk safely with. Seek to have the best kind of talk with yourself and reach for the conversational and specialist help of professionals if needed. Regardless of their backgrounds, training and personalities, psychotherapists have a common sensitivity to and interest in the conversational ethics of talking things through when it feels most difficult to talk. They can be a very good source of help.

This book is not inviting you the reader to Map and Talk your way through every conversation. Try it for a few months with some of the discussions you have and see how it helps you be more reflective, more connected, more able to stretch and deepen the conversational task in hand. Then bank it as a resource to call on when a conversation is interesting, difficult or complex.

This introductory chapter has set the scene for the book and given a taste of what talking with a map is about. Throughout this book are illustrations of Map and Talk as an aid to conversational awareness. Hopefully, they are examples that resonate with the reader; some will and some wont. Go with the ones that connect with you.

Chapter 2: Mapping what we are doing and feeling

Estragon: 'That wasn't such a bad little canter [of recent exchanges]'
Vladimir: 'Yes, but now we'll have to find something else [to talk about]'

Samuel Beckett, Waiting for Godot

Introduction

This is the first of four linked chapters that go through the methods and ideas of talking with a map. Each chapter adds a layer of skills and thinking.

With practice and familiarity these overlapping layers of mapping combine as a spontaneous and simultaneous 'Map and Talk' scaffolding to support and enhance our conversational awareness and effectiveness. These four chapters offer a guide to learning the methods and conceptual tools of talking with a map, whether with others or on your own. This first one starts with mapping the words for what we say we are doing and feeling as we voice them. The focus is on the detail of an action, its emotional impact within us and tracking out on paper one or more coping responses.

An anxiously okay kind of smile

Before we can map the big stories in our lives or the lives of others close to us and sit with the difficult emotions, we need to be at ease with the methods of talking with a map when it is something fleeting and light. Even so it may carry within its lightness a greater significance. Imagine this – you are poised with pen and paper as a conversation is about to begin.

Julie is telling you about a recent moment in her life and she says to you, 'He (his name turned out to be Harry) was smiling at me'. You, as mapper, put down the doing word 'smiling' as the action that he was doing (Figure 2.1). You add a two-way lined arrow down underneath the word smiling. The arrow is a key symbol in Map and Talk and is signalling the push and pull of the actions and the reactions in response. The mapper's assumption is that at either end of the two-way arrow, whether top or bottom, are knots of actions, thoughts and feelings with variations in power and intention that can be teased out from the conversation like the steps to a dance. The initial links and arrows on paper are inviting the conversation to open up and spread out on paper, in our minds and between us. In this spirit your pen hovers over the space at the bottom end of the arrow and is wondering about the reaction to the smiling. In your capacity of 'listening with the pen' you are imagining what it was like to receive a smiling face. Your face is enquiring. Your face is also smiling – perhaps a different kind of smile to the one being spoken of – a puzzling smile. The combination of the pen poised, and your open face are asking.

'How did you react to being smiled at?'

'I smiled back', Julie says, and she smiles at you while saying it. You write down 'smiled back' but you are also wondering about the impact of feelings and the choices of response embedded in the reaction (as in Figure 2.1).

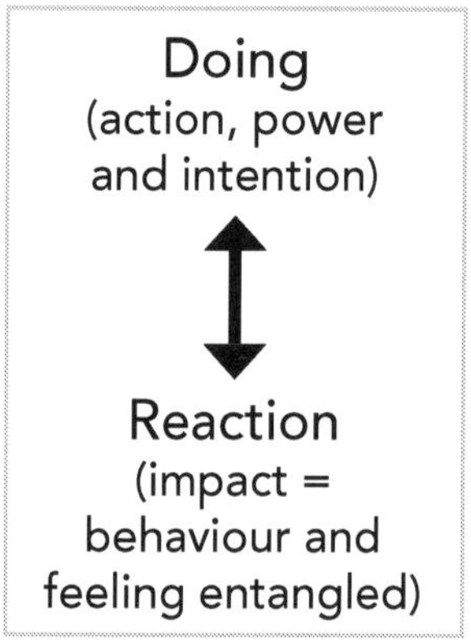

Figure 2.1

The relationship being spoken of has its echo in the exchanges between you, whether or not you are aware of it or give it attention. This is a moment of shimmering and hovering among the spaces between the words on paper, the words in the air between you and the thoughts and feelings on your minds.

These are the moments of negotiation within and between us in any conversation whether aided with paper maps or not. Julie might be thinking is it okay for me to explore this. Is it not too trivial or too fleeting? You might be wondering, as the mapper, am I going to do a good job of listening? We are always mentally mapping where the conversation is going. Putting the words tentatively on paper democratises and shares our thinking resources and makes the talking and listening relationship more transparent. Mapping a moment, however minor, in the order of things can take us to the heart of the person and their world and is also a step to building a conversational relationship.

Figure 2.2

A parallel between the pattern in the content of the conversation and the pattern in the immediate relationship often arises in some shape or form, and it is a theme we will come back to. For now, let's say the moment Julie smiles it helps you relax and trust your abilities with pen and paper in support of the conversation. You stop trying to be perfect. You are looking at the words on paper and wondering where to go next. You are not rushing. Conversationally you have already done a lot. As in Figure 2.2 you have put the words *smiled back* in the 'reaction' bottom end of the box. Putting words out there to visibly reflect the content of the conversation is an important opening step. It creates a space between the action of smiling and the reaction of smiling back. We know there is a connection but as we look at the spaces on paper we can imagine the variety of feelings, ideas or actions that might be woven in and added. Was Harry's smiling friendly, innocent or knowing; seductive or smarmy? There is room on paper to add colour and qualification to the reciprocal relationship between smiling and smiling back.

Your hand moves the pen around the words on paper, not marking them but being on the threshold of adding words. It is as if the pen and paper in the conversation are asking questions for you and you say, 'So, what was else was coming from him, or going on within you, that enabled you to smile back?'

Julie takes the cue and, pointing to the words 'smiled back', says, 'Well, it felt safe. I think. His way of smiling was an anxious but OK kind of smiling.'

You feel there is something in the phrase 'anxious but OK kind of smiling'. You feel that with the mapping you are no longer watching the film of the experience from the outside but are alongside and in it. You want to remember the exact turn of the phrase, but you are wondering where to put it on the paper. The answer is partly practical and immediate. Put it anywhere so you don't forget or lose the nuance of the phrase. If you leave it more than a few minutes the exact turn and power of the words in the phrase may have been blurred or lost. You are curious about the different directions the phrase is pointing. This is a micro moment of conversational awareness between you. Anxious but OK kind of smiling is a phrase with legs in the sense that it can take you different places. The phrase is partly saying something about Julie's appraisal of her mixed feelings, and it is partly pointing to an observation about Harry. It is also partly a response elicited by your questions. Where we put it on the map needs to be figured out by asking what the intention was behind the action and what the feelings were between the action and the reaction.

You could go down the path of asking 'What kind of smiling is not OK?' You might add, 'And how would you respond then?' Any of these questions can be asked through the pen and paper and the best option is to wait and see where Julie goes with it or even to say we could go this way or that, but which way do you wish to take it? Following the person at their pace and in their direction is important. So, you hold back; Julie pauses, and you hover. Feelings are shimmering around between you and within you both. The map can help this hesitation and dithering be a constructive conversational moment. It signposts that this conversation is on the move. Is it kept light? Does it go deeper?

One source of help for the mapper is to have a template in mind that might help guide the process of the conversation but not control the manner and content of the conversation. Have a look at the template of the 'doing and feeling' map in Figure 2.3. Actions such as smiling, or waving, or shouting, need some contextual meaning and some sense of the intentions behind them.

Julie didn't know, but she wonders in hindsight if she had first looked at the smiling man. The one action we know is the smiling. It is what is being done and for this template we put the action outside the box because it could be one of many different actions that make up a picture of what he was doing and intending along with the action of smiling. We can put in words for the background context once we know them. Now we are inviting discussion about the intention behind the smiling. We are also interested in the quality, intensity and direction of what he is doing. How was he smiling? By placing a question of the motive, or intention of Harry smiling, it opens room to think about the push and pull of power and influence.

'I am wondering if his action of smiling and his way of doing this felt safe for you?'

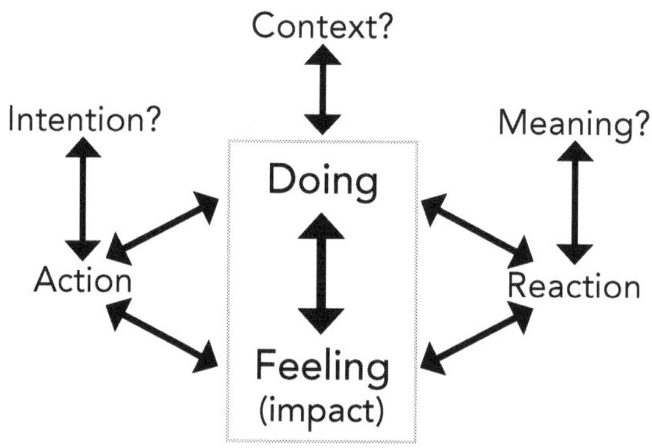

Figure 2.3

Julie says, 'Yes, I trusted him. He seemed anxious and that made me feel safe, even protective. His OK kind of smiling was trustworthy, so far as I could see. I think of myself as a smiley person, and also that it felt safe.' You show Julie the map, as in Figure 2.4, based on the doing and feeling template with trusting to trusted what is being done and felt; and smiling as the action and evidence of trust; and the smiling back in a cautious kind of way as the response. Julie gives nuance and emotional colour to the smiling. It is her appraisal and response. The map captures a two-sided judgment by Julie about the meaning of the smiling interaction for her in that moment which links context and character. It felt safe in the context and her character she feels is to be 'a smiley person'. The map prompts Julie to add that they were in the queue for the theatre, and he was in front of her, and he turned and smiled, 'He looked like someone I might mix with'.

Mapping conversations about micro-moments of interaction like this bring us to deeper and more general conclusions about how we interact as discussed in the next chapter in relation to mapping gender roles (pages 65-72)

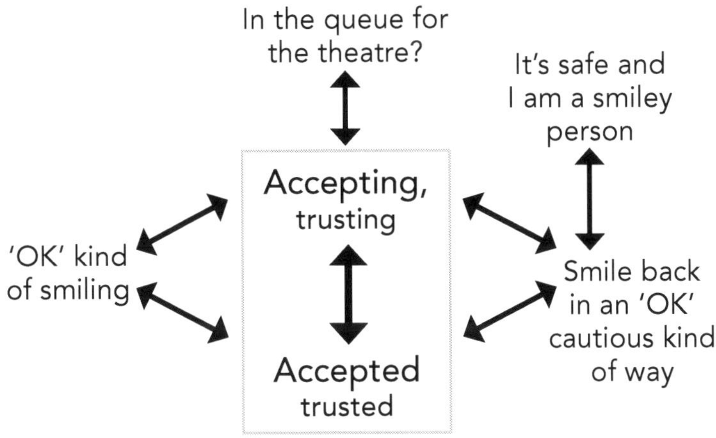

Figure 2.4

As in all moments when mapping and talking with pen and paper, we are slowing down the flow of the conversation to have moments of awareness of how we are talking. The words on paper may be from a fleeting sequence of interaction but they are dialogue buttons for thinking about roles, influences and appraisals, and more generally about the narrator's sense of self in and out of context. The map now offers a reflective aid to the conversation. Not just pointing to the smiling exchange being recalled but the conversational exchange in the moment between speaker and mapper. You might ask, for example, where are we on the map?

The conversation can go any way it wants to go from here. You are thinking that the smiling back keeps them smiling (the reaction that pulls or pushed back on the action). In this way there is a reciprocal relationship to the behaviour which is marked by the two-way arrow between the doing and the feeling words in the box. Why put them in a box you may ask? Well, they are marking out a hub on the larger layout of the map on paper. There may be several such hub positions to be mapped on paper as the conversation develops. Or it might be that just one hub covers the dynamics of the story being told in the conversation. It is a hub because it is a key position, role, or state of mind and a crossroads for coping with a variety of feelings and responses. We put a circle around the words to point out that the smiling and smiling back is a distinctive moment being spoken of. It a jumping off point, it is like a scene in a film in the sense that when we see a scene, we make predictions and judgements about the whole film and how it might go and the kind of genre it is revealing itself to be.

Try having a mapping moment of reflection for yourself

You may get a more immediate sense of Map and Talk by trying it as an aid to self-reflection. You can have a go now or come back to it at a convenient time (see also the guide to ten minutes mindful mapping practice every day on page 105). Think of something you felt in the past week at work, socially or at home such as feeling enthusiastic or bored, pleased, surprised. It does not have to be a bad feeling or a difficult feeling. It could be a good feeling. Don't go head-to-head with a big and troublesome feeling because the emotion of it might hijack the opportunity to learn from this initial experience.

Start with the feeling words

Put the word for the feeling on the left in the middle on the sheet of paper. Don't write too big, you need space for contrasting feelings around it. Look at the word (or words if a phrase) you have written down and let it talk back to you and reflect on what you are feeling and thinking.

Cover the feeling word or words with your hand for a moment and then think about your relationship with it. You might want to add or cross out words. You might have quite contrasting feelings and they could provisionally be put elsewhere on the piece of paper. Look at it again and draw an arrowed line up from it as in the adjoining Figure 2.5. Draw a circle around. You now have a place (a hub) on the paper in front of you that is inviting to know more of your inner speech and self-reflections.

Figure 2.5

Look again at the words. Do they resonate with you? Is it the wrong word in some way? Can you add some colour to it with a verb or adverb? For example, my word might be 'feeling tired', but I might now want to add 'pleased but tired', or 'more tired than usual', or 'tired and frustrated'. We could say you have externalised the feeling inside you to be also outside on the paper and you can have a conversation with it that is both internal and external. The words on paper invite you into a self-reflective conversation. It is a form of inner speech or self-talk. What could be ruminating, or introspection, is now potentially more in dialogue within you and outside you. Keep in mind the four steps of mapping: noticing then naming, then negotiating the meaning and navigating your choices and actions as described in detail on page 122.

Reflective mapping like this is making a triangle of attention between the reflective part of you, the feelings you recall and the words on paper. The triangle creates an external space for us to hover and shimmer in search of understanding. Hopefully in the process it creates an internal space. What the talking with a map allows is a capacity to work within the feelings felt in a more cognitive way and thoughts or memoires remembered or relived in a more embodied way. It is the interplay and difference between emotions recollected in tranquillity (as put eloquently by Wordsworth)[14] and those which make their presence felt physically.

Similar feelings go together, contrasting feelings are set apart

When making a map, if the feeling words seem closely allied, put them together in a cluster. If one or more words feel that they are a reaction to each other – like anger to hurt or shame to blame – then put them slightly apart, separated by a question mark. If the feeling words seem quite opposite like happy and sad, proud or shamed then put them apart so there is room to eventually track out the steps that link them.

Put the positive or highly valued feelings at the top of the sheet of paper and the painful, feared or dreadfully avoided feelings and states of mind at the bottom (see hopes and fears template on page 84). Seeing feeling words from the conversation written out here and there on the map is inviting the mapper and the person (or persons) talking to look for links, see gaps and patterns to draw out the shape or structure to the discussion. It offers a touch stone to moderate the intensity of the feeling as originally felt, as reverberating across the years of similar experiences and as rekindled in the moment of recollecting and rewording.

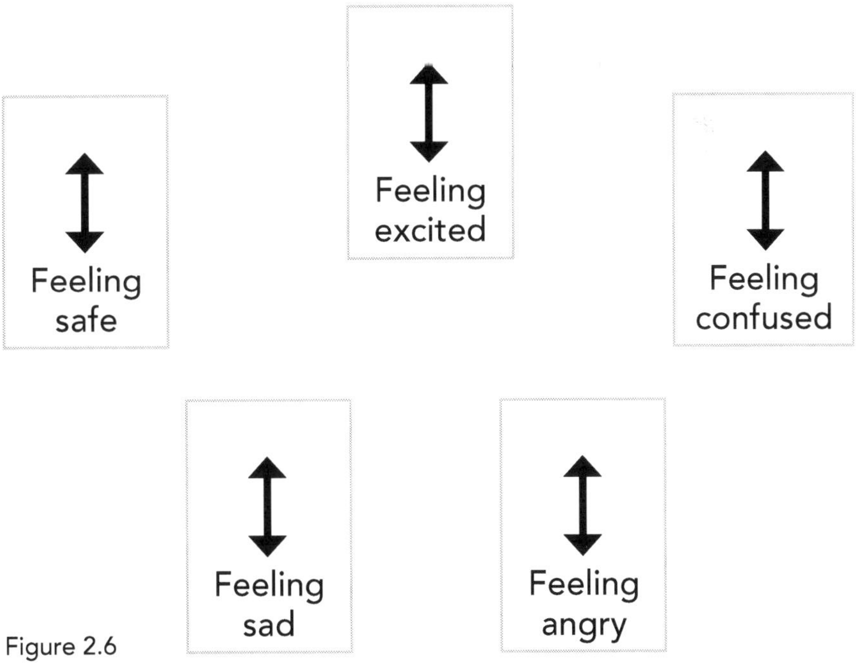

Figure 2.6

Feelings words spread out on paper help extend our working memory as they mediate the exchanges between early experiences recollected in the current conversation. Finding the words for what we feel is a negotiation. The more conversational the process the more chance of sharing a fuller sense of the feelings. We can go over the words and wonder what we were just saying. What was the word for that? It is helpful to stay with feelings. The mapper's feeling response may offer an important additional source of emotional and conversational awareness. The mapper can more easily check the relevance or validity of her or his feeling responses by pointing the pen to them on paper and wondering with the person speaking how they fit or not.

As different feelings are discovered, there may be need to make another map that just investigates one feeling and the hub and spokes of actions and reactions around it. An extended conversation may involve several sheets of paper each with a detailed map of the push and pull of actions, feelings and reactions. In addition, there might be a map of the process of the conversation as detailed in Chapter 5.

Or start with the doing words

Figure 2.7

If you were mapping with and for someone else, their conversations are likely to start with the actions done to them rather than the feelings aroused by these actions. Perhaps when we are reflecting for ourselves on our own experiences we are inclined to start with the feelings. However, follow where the conversation and the reflection goes and start with the doing (action) end or the felt (feeling) end. There is no hard rule or governing principle. Start where it starts. Some of our memories are led by feelings and others by actions. When we make links between actions and feelings, we also meet gaps. We need to mind these gaps and leave a question mark rather than force a feeling word out of them prematurely. For example, I might quickly say as someone mapped my conversation that I felt angry when someone was teasing me. As will be explored in the next few pages the anger might be seen as the quickfire reaction to the action of teasing. But the idea of minding the gap between the obvious links might make it easier to explore what I felt before I reacted with anger. Did I feel hurt, humiliated or stupid? The process of talking with a map in this way helps us ask questions about the more hidden feelings beneath or behind the conscious feelings.

Now back to the words for feelings

Now go back over the experience for which you have the feelings and add the action or doing end of the two-way arrow. It is a moment for sensing the intensity of the doing words or phrase. Its intensity will resonate with the feeling words already there. You may want to change the doing words to make them stronger or softer as you recall and feel the call and response between the action and reaction. The kind of example I have in mind might go like this: 'I was very angry when he was teasing me. No, now I see the word angry on paper I feel I was angry but even more I was hurt. Then I was angry with him but also with myself because I let him see the hurt.' These are moments of hovering and shimmering described in the first chapter of the book and covered in more detail in Chapter 6 on conversational awareness.

The next step in using Map and Talk for a conversation with yourself is to look at the first feeling word you put down and ask if this is what you are feeling (circle the pen around the feeling word(s)) because that is what was going on (circle the pen around the doing words) how did I cope or manage myself and my feelings. This is put on paper with words for what I needed or wanted at the time and what I did to deal with the feelings. It is a bit like a chain reaction. Feeling this, I appraised my choices or fell into automatically responding in a familiar way and assumed others would respond in such and such a way. The end point might tail back to where you began or it will take you to a new position.

The map is an aid to listening and self reflection. We are constantly using the words on paper to recap and review our understanding and make the work of being aware of what we are saying a joint activity. We may change the intensity of words or add qualifying words the enrich their meaning or just to jog our memories about the context we are mostly referring to such as in the teasing example.

Between the action and the reaction is the emotional impact

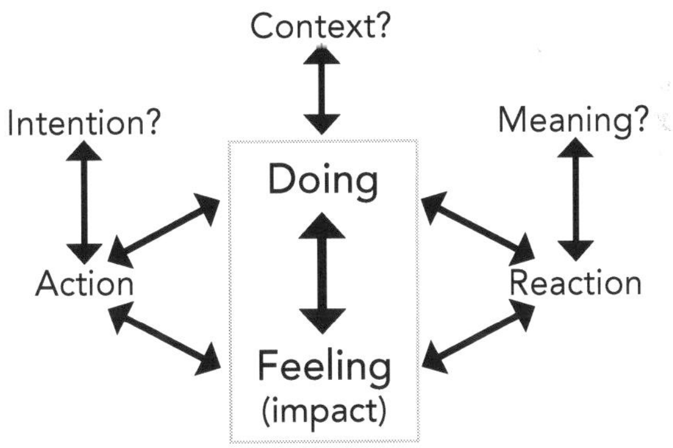

Figure 2.8

As already indicated, the emotional impact of what someone is doing is often the first focus of conversational mapping. This is the feeling end of the doing and feeling relationship. Someone is shouting at me, and I feel hurt and upset. My reaction could go three ways. I could submit which might lead me back to feeling hurt and upset (though I might feel now I am choosing this as the least frightening option). Or I shout back and follow the arrow up to being at the doing end of the box and doing to rather than being done to. This might feel better in the short term but in another way, I am joining the *shouting to shouted* at dance and am likely to be caught at both ends of the two-way arrow. Or I might run away or take cover (that would need an arrow taking me off somewhere else on the map. As we are tracking the conversation with the words and arrows on paper, we can have this basic template in mind to guide us but at each word choice we can have a question mark asking what is or are the right words here?

Several things are in the air at this point. As the doing words go down, there are questions to ask. Does this change how I would describe my feelings? Would I put stronger or softer words? Have I discovered other feelings lying on top of or underneath the feeling words already written down? What was going on that gave rise to this action? In the next chapter we look at the same process in terms of what role was being played and what were the intentions behind or the context to it. If this pattern of interaction is a familiar and important role I play, or a big part of me, then where did I learn it from? Who in my life responds now or used to respond like this?

The person speaking may only recall the action and the reaction. He hit me (action). I ran away (reaction). These might be seen as the specifics of what was going on, but we want to use the mapping process to wonder what the person was intending by the action. Around the action is a position someone is taking or was taking towards us and behind that position is an intention which if we can get our heads round it gives us some help in making meaning both of their actions and our reactions.

Dino makes the link only when his brother cries openly

Imagine this. Little Dino, a seven-year-old boy, is being shouted at again by his teacher for being late for school (he has to care for his brother). In reaction, Dino lowers his head to protect his face from hurt and shame. The teacher shouts at him more, 'Look at me, boy'.

But Dino won't raise his head. His body and neck are contorted by a battle of emotions mixed with shame, rage and hurt beyond the range of his capacity to regulate or negotiate. The teacher, who cannot bear the gap in their exchange, raises his hand as if to slap Dino. Through the day and all the way home Dino carries the emotional wounds in his body. The feelings are there without words and without conversation within himself or with others. As he walks home Dino is trying to voice his feelings to himself, but they are unspeakable. It is too much for him. Once in his house his little brother Marco rushes up to him with the pleasure of having him home. Dino shouts at Marco and pushes him away for what seems like no reason. Marco does not hold his head down in shame but looks straight back into Dino's eyes and cries. Marco's hurt is innocently, defiantly and tenderly in the conversational space between the two brothers. It is as if Marco is saying 'you are usually my loving and protecting brother what is this now?' His tears are conversational and there is no escaping the action and reaction. Dino is faced literally and symbolically with his brother's hurt. Isaac Newton is also famously quoted as saying 'I can calculate the motion of heavenly bodies, but not the madness of people'. By madness we might say that for every emotional action there is not an equal emotional reaction.

There is a moment for reparation. Dino cannot resist the dutiful voice within himself and the call for comfort from Marco and he comforts his brother and in so doing the interpersonal act soothes his inner self and make the world around him also seem less hostile. Here is a space which can be mapped, can be negotiated to fill the gaps between the actions, intentions and feelings.

In Map and Talk the idea is to put something important in between the action (shouting in this case) and reaction (crying). This missing link is the emotional impact of the action which in turn is also the emotional origin of the way of coping. To the extent that he does sustain empathy for himself and for his brother he can only do this with some kind of map of the dramatic events he has been through.

One of Freud's more enduring formulations was of the compulsion to repeat a pattern of interaction in the hope of making sense of it by unconsciously recreating the drama of it in the present (therapeutic) conversation. I would say, it is done in the hope of bringing a conversational awareness to it out in the open where our responses might be mapped out and renegotiated. The more Dino is shouted at by his teacher the more he may shout at his brother, or he may make the link and cry openly in front of his teacher and not internalise the interaction. Our struggle is to get unresolved drama and trauma out in the open where we can notice it and renegotiate it. The compulsion to repeat a pattern is a cry for help and a search for meaning. Marco offered a meaning for Dino by not joining his dance and showing his own hurt. If Dino could see this, it could offer him a way forward. Mapping it on paper helps the process of remapping it in our heads and in the embodied repetitions.

Doing and feeling are related

We can end up with a map with several key 'emotion and action' words linked and connected by patterns of relating. It is necessary to first have an aside about the tense of verbs when using mapping to help bring conversational awareness to our talk and our story telling. We are listening for **doing words**. Words that imply some action, and in putting them down on paper we mostly bring them into the active present tense and call them doing words such as loving, hurting, caring, neglecting. Doing words get added colour as they are spoken with adverbs and qualifiers either spoken head on or as asides: 'She is loving but smothering; he is neglecting but carelessly'.

Often the doing is the active end of the exchange, and the feeling end is the done to and subjectively felt end. In some Map and Talk moments it may be the reverse and the power of the feeling is in the live and active tense: 'He insulted her, and she was raging in response.' In contrast to 'He was raging at her, and she felt insulted but kept quiet'. In making word maps it is helpful to create a space between the doing words and the felt words. It is a representation of the gaps between the links we are making. By creating space on paper, we are creating space in our thoughts.

Asking what we are doing is one of our favourite conversational questions. What are you doing? Where are we going with this? Such questions help us figure out the intentions behind the actions and make better sense of my own actions and responses in a reciprocal relationship. Just as I am making my response, I am making sense of what we are doing. We are using the Map and Talk process to gather a background awareness of intentions and actions. That takes us into the detail of finding words for feelings and tracking a spread of connected or contrasting feelings in the example of Julie, then Dino and Marco.

To go back to the example of Dino, we might ask why Dino didn't shout back when his teacher shouted at him? Or why did he hide the hurt and anger on his face in shame? Looking back, he thought he already had an ideology drummed into his child mind of soaking it up, and cutting off, and appearing to be strong. Why could he not show his hurt feelings like his brother did? Perhaps when he is older, he will shout back at his teacher. Or in a world that set the rules of gender and gendering positions differently (see page 65) he would allow his tears and show his hurt. The mapping process, even with a few sparse words on paper invites and encourages this openness of dialogue with different options set against choices made or assumed ways of thinking and feeling. One thing we are listening out for is what in Cognitive Analytic Therapy we call a 'response shift' which is when a familiar, almost habitual, pattern drummed into us in the early years of childhood does a marked shift (such as from submissive to defiant) because the balance of power or the context changes. As Dino talks of his childhood experience, he may remember when his response changed. As he got taller, older and stronger he started to talk back defiantly to the teacher (a response shift) and the teacher stopped telling him off or picking on him. He may compare times now with times then and see how the context has changed. Perhaps, he reflects now as an old man that teachers don't shout at children like that anymore. And then he

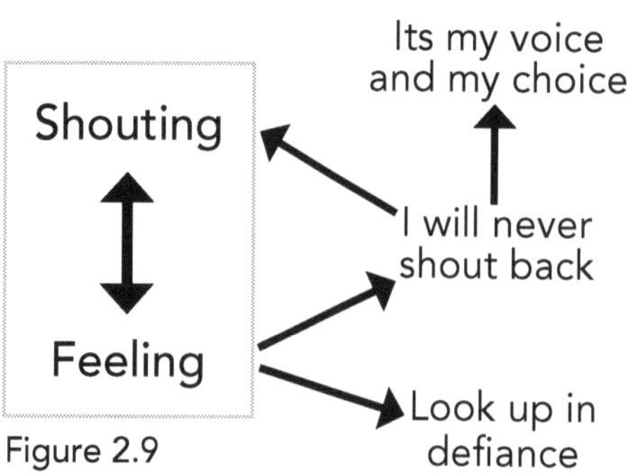

Figure 2.9

remembers, and it is mapped out on paper (Figure 2.9) – 'What changed when I was ten years old is that I looked up at him in defiance and I knew I will never shout back. And why? I can tell you why. It is my voice and my choice what I do with it which is more than he ever had.'

As in the example of Dino, there may be more than one way of coping. They may vary in their intensity and direction. One way of coping may backfire and just make the person feel worse about the situation. Another way of coping may take them to the other end of the reciprocal relation or doing to others what is being done to themselves. Another way of coping may take the person in the story to a completely different place or state of mind.

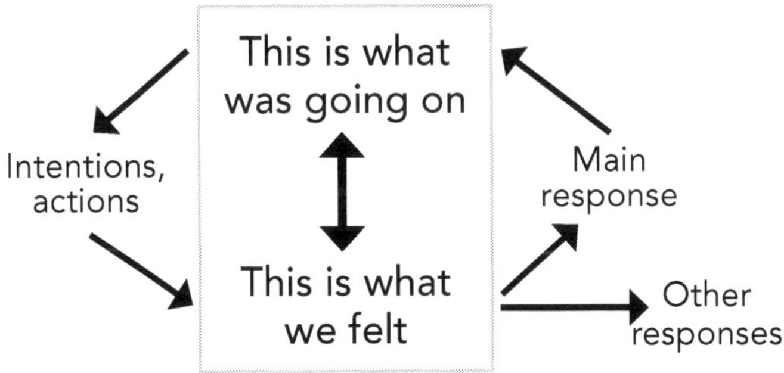

Figure 2.10

The conversation needs anchoring by a tentative link on paper between the active doing and the reactive feeling. Once it is down on paper, we can hover and shimmer and develop the conversation around it. Once the skeleton of words are there on the map, details can be added and questioned and revised until there is a sense of something being on paper that helps the conversation.

Coping with feelings

A key mapping moment in any conversation is to hover over what the person wants, or the situation needs when faced with the impact of emotion which may be unsettling or challenging or painful. It is a key point for wondering if there are choices of alternative procedures for coping internally or managing the situation interpersonally and socially. Mostly what we want or need as a way of coping with a feeling may be healthy. If I feel scared, I might want protection. If I am feeling bored, I might be looking for stimulation. If I am feeling guilty, I might be looking for atonement.

It might be helpful to take a step back and map out what our basic relational needs are when faced with our own emotions in a specific context. As in Figure 2.11 there are always choices that drive our motivation and intentions. Sometimes they align and other times clash. We may want gratification but need meaning. We may need connection to find gratification and meaning.

In the world of philosophy and psychotherapy, our deepest existential need is for meaning. Gratification is our biological or instinctual need for survival and balance. Other primary needs might be a mix of these such as the needs for care and love, for agency and a sense of ownership and authorship over the situation around, within and between us. This might link to a need for control and safety. One of the legacies of Maslow's hierarchy of needs is to think that some needs are more basic than others. From the point of view of Map and Talk and the development of conversational awareness the interesting question is how these different needs are orchestrated in relation to each other and which one is dominant may vary with the context or according to the response from others and the intensity of the initial feelings.

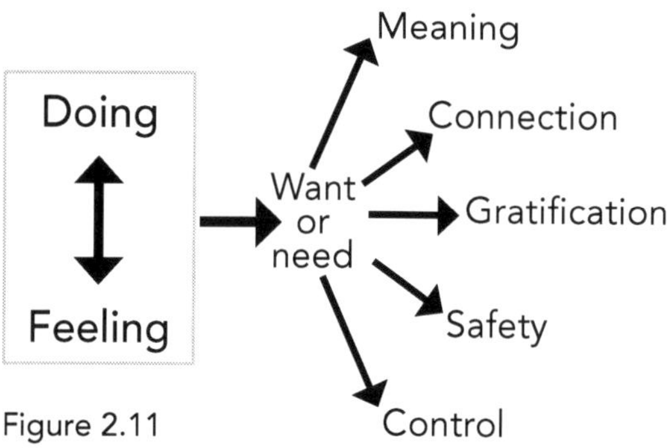

Figure 2.11

For the Freudians our needs and our conversations and thoughts about them are driven by a longing for instinctual gratification. It could be that needs for food and shelter or safety and care fall within this. A need for meaning might be judged the ultimate need that gives agency and purpose to the others. It is an existential need for a coherent life story, and a sense of an understandable purpose.

The relational dimensions of these needs are richly explored by Ruthellen Josselson in her highly readable book *The Space Between Us*.[15] She uses the metaphor of space to explore the interplay of action, response and orchestration between eight kinds of relating to self and others. Her first four are primary: holding, attachment, passionate experience and eye-to-eye validation. She writes:

'They are present either from the beginning of life (the need to be held and the need for drive gratification) or shortly thereafter (as in attachment and awareness of eye-to-eye response).' Ruth Josselson goes to describe her other four dimensions of relating:

"The second four require cognitive maturation and may not develop until late childhood. Idealisation and embeddedness require a concept and experience of the self, as the capacity to think about how one is positioned in regard to others. Mutuality and tending, also very much concerned with responsiveness to others, require development out of egocentrism and into a world of others.'

Talking with a map whether reflecting on childhood or looking at and linking to present life at home or work can catch the interplay of these different relational needs and the presence or absence of space to express them and own them.

The reason for spelling these different needs out is that they may be alive, and work alongside each other, or be separate procedures in response to the same core feeling. Some of these needs will be at the fore of attention and others deeply hidden or disassociated.

The conversation about needs and wants in relation to aims can pivot around various questions, each helping elicit a different perspective from the map into the conversation. 'So, if this is the pattern what were the aims?' 'What do you or the others want?' 'How conscious were they?' 'In hindsight, as we reflect in the conversation now, what did you want?' 'What was your desired outcome and what did you fear as dreadfully avoided outcome?'

Mapping all the elements together

Mapping with words on paper is helping language do what it is good at doing, which is puzzle solving.[16] It is a joint activity linking feeling thoughts and actions. So far, we have been looking in detail of how to map the push and pull between what is being done and felt in the story or process of a conversation. Now a fuller template can be introduced which gives sight of the bigger picture of a whole map. The movement around the map (Figure 2.12) begins where it says: 'starts by doing'. This is the question the mapper has in mind as the speaker is talking. He or she is mapping the conversation – or a story coming out of the conversation. Here is an example to follow through using this template. Imagine I put the words 'Pressure/demanding' where the 'Starts by doing' words are. You are mapping the conversation for me, and I am telling you that someone at work is putting pressure on me to get a job done. So, I might put 'get the job done' where it says 'Intention?' The action that follows from this is the boss is constantly checking up on me. As I look at this on the map you might ask whose voice is that saying, 'Get the job done!' and I would wonder (hover and shimmer) and say, 'well the boss of course but is it me to myself as well?'

We work out as we talk with the map that the feeling this leads to is 'Pressured'. The map is following two tracks in the conversation, one within myself to myself and one from my boss to myself. Then you as mapper may ask me, 'So, what did you want, or need given that you were feeling pressured?' I say with my hands touching the relevant words on the map, 'I want to get the job done and get the boss off my back and have no more pressure'. And that points to the choices I could see. This is where there may be more than one choice and more than one outcome. I might say one option is to submit, knuckle under and work really hard.

And I respond by doing that, but it takes me to the top end of the box where it says: 'starts by doing.' Except now it is not just my boss putting pressure on me it is me putting pressure on to myself.

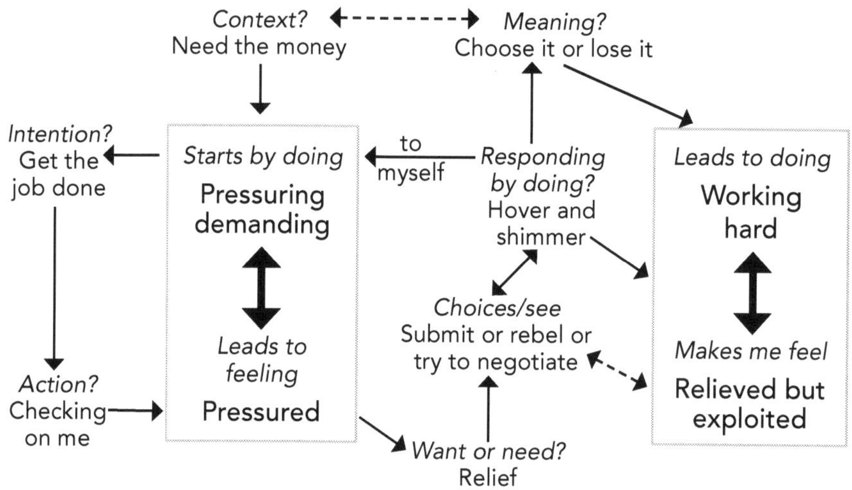

Figure 2.12

Seeing this pattern of doubling up on myself is one very useful aspect of mapping out the patterns and seeing the different layers to the story. I might respond by giving myself some slack and taking it easy. This might mean to me that it is too much, and I respond by taking the pressure off me and that takes me to the top end of the second box where it says, 'leads to doing' which is 'taking it easy'. At this point you are hovering with the pen and wondering with me what 'taking it is easy' feels like and this is where shimmering with the conflicting feeling and responses comes in. I may say well it did not help me relax because I still felt guilty and afraid about letting my boss down, letting myself down and afraid of failing. This in turn pushes me back to the choices I see before me and a feeling that there is no escape from the pressure.

The next arrow in the box points up to the choices I see and the meaning I make (submit, rebel or try to negotiate) and what I end up doing on the basis of this implicit or explicit appraisal (in cognitive terms). We may not be conscious of this, but one part of mapping is to bring it out into the open. The choices I see are across all the points on the map. I am making some sense of the action and the feeling it provokes. As you and I retell the story with the map over and again with compassion and curiosity, I may be reliving some of emotions and having some of the bodily sensations. The map helps me see what the pattern of response was and what it alternatively could have been. Seeing patterns helps to think relationally about the choices.

Jessie's magic bus moment

Jessie and Rania were friends and were learning to talk with a map together about stuff that bothered them. They met when they could at Rania's home, but Jessie was often late which Rania ignored until Jessie had to mention it one time because she was very late, and she felt it was disrespectful.

'I missed the bus,' Jessie said and added that she was often late for work or social events - even family events. 'It does me no favours and I feel guilty and embarrassed by when it is happening, I am lost in the drama of it.'

Rania suggested while it was a hot point of awareness for them, they map out the push and pull dialogue of what she was doing and feeling for herself and her world by being late. They started with the moment that led to being late today. Map the little moment in the here and now and frame the bigger problem thought Rania.

Jessie recalled that earlier when she was running for the bus, she felt excited - as if in a race she was going to win. She knew she was late. When the bus pulled out from the bus stop too soon for her to catch it and the driver caught her eye and shook his head without stopping, Jessie said she swore at him.

'I felt angry with him. I blamed him for all my problems.' Rania raised her eyebrows and Jessie said that she now felt some of the mixed-up feelings of excitement, competition and anger coming back as she retold the story of the experience. Rania had put a sequence of feeling-words spread out on a big sheet of paper. 'Excited' was in the middle on the left of the paper. She had put a circle round it to make it stand out and added question marks above the two-way arrow to leave open the question as to what Jessie thought she or others were doing to give rise to these feelings. Rania said to Jessie while pointing at the word excited, 'Is that it? What you were doing was winning a race and that made you feel excited?' As she spoke, she added the words 'winning a race' to the map.

Jessie studied the words and arrows on paper as she listened and cast glances to Rania. She was feeling uncomfortable as if Rania was getting close to something she wanted to run away from. Jessie nodded and Rania asked if it was okay to do this mapping and talking. Rania nodded again this time more emphatically and said definitely okay, and Rania then pointed to where she had written and circled 'Not stopping for me - feeling angry, blaming him [the bus driver]' (Figure 2.13). Jessie prodded the words with her finger, as if not wanting them to be there. She blurted out, 'He didn't stop for me!' She then shook her head, and it was like she was in two minds.

'It was not fair of me. He couldn't stop, there was traffic behind him. I feel embarrassed. I love finding other people giving me reason to be blaming them.' Rania put down the word 'embarrassed' as another feeling in the sequence and asked, 'Is that what you also feel now?'

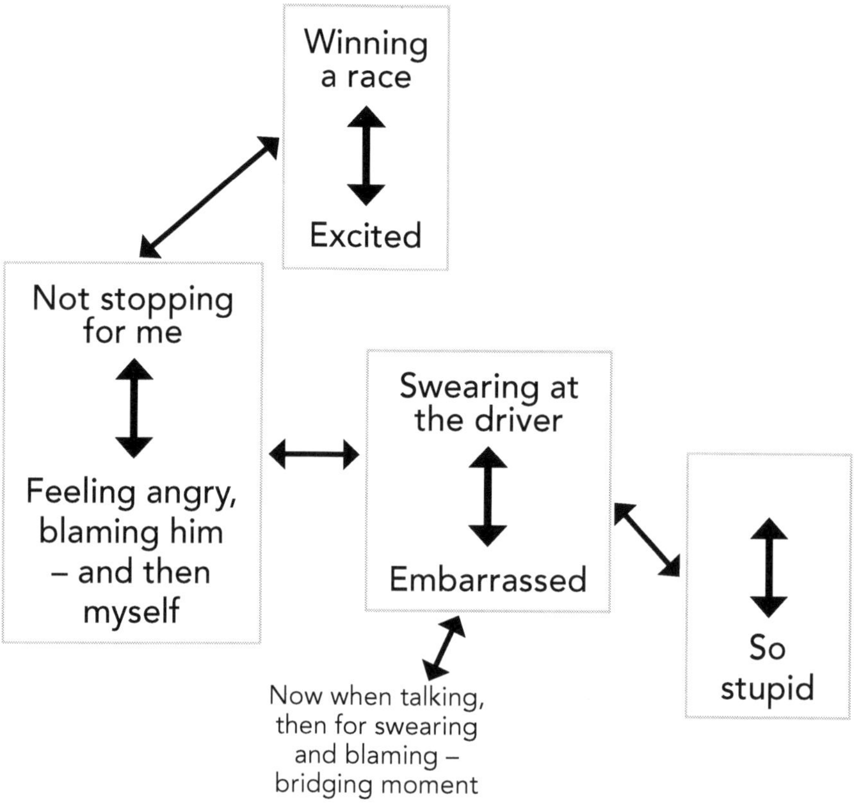

Figure 2.13

'Yes' Jessie went back to the 'feeling angry' and 'blaming' words that Rania had put in a box with an arrow going up from it. I am angry with myself for swearing at the bus driver. I am angry with and blaming of myself and I am sure you are angry and blaming of me for being late now as well. Rania said she was angry a bit and it was easier to discuss with the words out there on paper. They smiled at each other. Jessie said that what is on the map is in her now. 'I can feel embarrassed and angry churning in my tummy, and I see from the map how it carries me from one context to another. It is my dance.'

'Yep, but we all do dances like this', says Rania. 'I suppose our challenge is to see and touch them out there on paper and by talking directly to them, and then notice them kicking in and change the steps.'

Jessie said, 'Well, these mixed-up feelings are a mush of emotion inside me, and words touch them but don't separate them out. Seeing them on paper laid out like that apart from each other does something I cannot quite describe.' Jessie hesitates and they both stare at the map and Rania waits in silence. 'It is like I can swim in, and among the feelings and get my head around them'. Jessie hesitates again. Rania says, 'It sounds like there is a 'but' coming – a doubt.'

Jessie says, 'Well, first I have got to stop feeling so stupid with myself.'

Rania made another box with the word 'so stupid' and wondered if it should go with the angry and blaming words but thought to herself that it might be a different moment and more a kind of self-accusation. Rania explained that she hoped they could use the map to capture the shimmering between these feelings and added, 'I like what you say Jessie, the spaces and arrows between the words on paper might help create space and separate links in our heads'. She wanted Jessie and her to have room to hover over the feelings and their implications and think more openly about the way they divide up and merge with each other. 'Perhaps that is the only way you cope?' Rania spoke while surveying with her hands outstretched towards the spread of feeling words on the paper.

Jessie said, 'I don't usually stay with these feelings. I get so entangled and confused that I run from them.'

'What happens? What feeling goes with running from them?'

Jessie points to the word excited. 'I need to get excited again.'

'How?'

'I don't know.' Jessie pauses and looks at the map as if for inspiration. 'Oh, yes, I do. I knew there was not another bus for ages, but I do this weird thing. I imagine a "magic bus" turning up at any minute. I look for it in the distance coming down the road. The magic bus will be nonstop and will catch up with the other bus and overtake it.'

Jessie was smiling – almost grinning with delight, and as she spoke the thought of the magic bus cheered her up just as it did at the time. Rania was hovering over the ideas and feelings in the conversation with the help of the map. She drew a picture of a smiley faced bus and wrote on it the magic bus.

'So, what is the magic bus doing for your feelings?'

'Getting me there on time?' Jessie said defiantly, knowing it was not the answer.

'Yes, but what is the idea of it? What is it doing for your feelings of "cross" and "stupid" and "embarrassed"?' (Rania points to the words and circles them).

'I feel safe dreaming of the magic bus. It comforts me but I guess it stops me changing.' Jessie looks at the map. 'I never get to grips with these feelings.'

She looks up and around her as if there might in some shape or form be a magic bus in the room now.

'I don't know if I like your magic bus,' says Rania. 'Maybe I envy the way it lets you escape responsibility.'

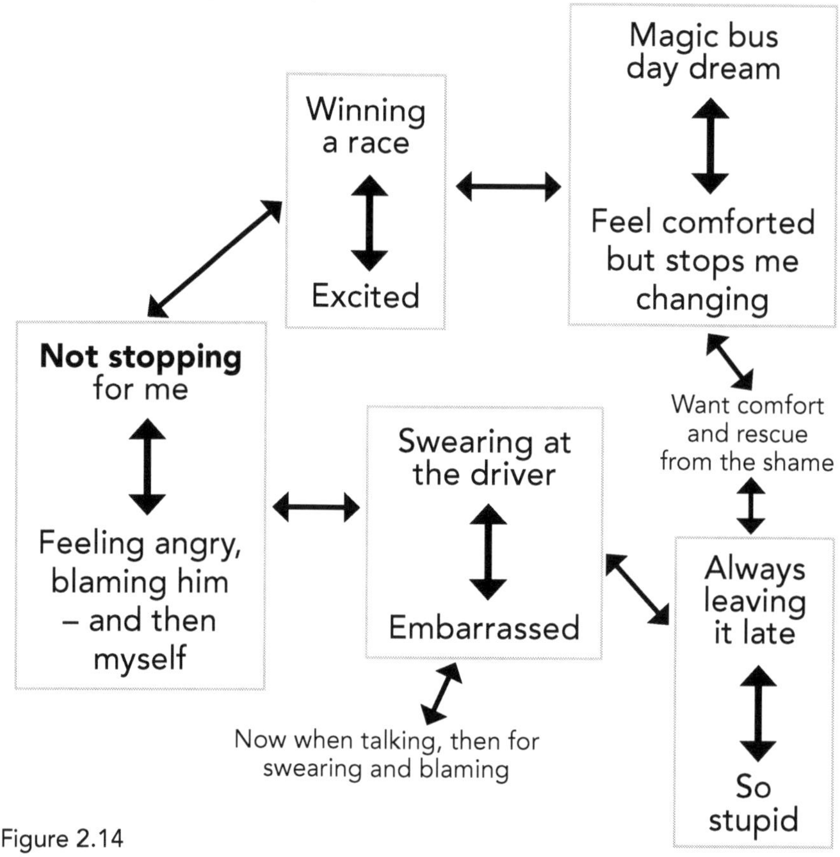

Figure 2.14

Jessie says defensively, 'Well in my head, I was winning a race.' Rania writes this in and Jessie laughs. 'Stupid me, I am addicted to leaving it late. I get high on the excitement.' Jessie then added that the words on paper in front of her made it feel less mad and she was less judgy of herself. Rania and Jessie filled out the map linking actions to feelings so that the map as it was in Figure 2.13 developed into the map as in Figure 2.14. Now looking at the whole map made Jessie a bit upset, and she jabbed her finger at the 'Magic bus daydream' words and said defiantly that sometimes a magic bus does turn up. 'Like when I found my boyfriend. I thought there would never be someone okay whom I could rely on but then he turned up.'

Together Jessie and Rania are reliving her experience and reliving some of the feelings. By recapping where their conversation and understanding has got to, they are building shared use and ownership of the map. They are talking with the map. They agreed to watch out for when they have magic bus moments in the conversation. I have got a question for us. Where are we on the map? Are we a real bus or a magic bus?

The tidy map

The final map at the end of several stages to the conversation was the one in Figure 2.15. Its purpose was to lift out the pattern of interaction in the running late and magic bus story and apply it more generally. Jessie looked at it and said, 'It is breaking the mould of previous conversations I have had about this part me'.

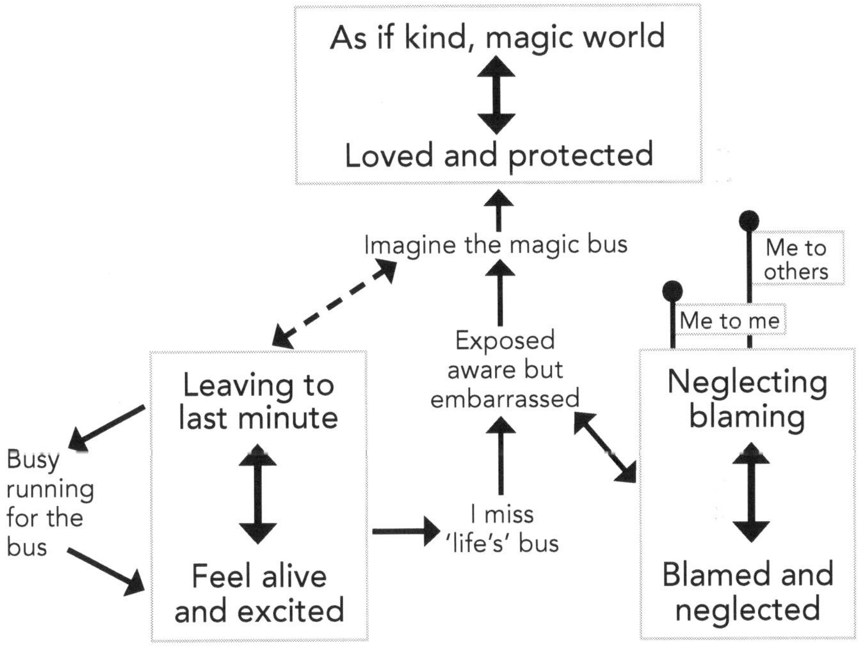

Figure 2.15

What they added to the tidy map was the hidden starting point to the sequence which is 'leaving things to the last minute' and 'feeling alive' and 'excited' in the crisis that results. In contrast to this, there is a dream place of being rescued, 'loved and protected' at the top of the map by the reality or the dream of the magic bus. This serves a purpose of an idea of rescue and comfort whether it is fulfilled or not. What it hides is the box on the right side of the map and the feeling of being 'blamed and neglected' by self or others. Jessie and Rania had several conversations that were richer with the map making than without it. They swapped roles and Jessie made a map of Rania's version of a magic bus pattern.

As will be described later in Chapter 7, it can be helpful to the process of conversational mapping to write to part of the pattern coming from the conversation. For the sake of completion in this chapter here is a letter to the conversation. It shows how combining the use of words mapped out and words written in prose form and then read out can take our discussions about ourselves to different levels of awareness. The letter is from Jessie to the magic bus pattern, but it could be accompanied by a letter from Rania to Jessie or a letter from both of them to the mapping and talking style of conversation. Writing the letter was an aid to discovering new feelings and meanings.

Dear 'magic bus' pattern

You are a big part of my life. You are very seductive because you are always there to get me out of a hole that is usually of my own making. You represent a loving world that will protect me. I long for it. I hide in the magic bus moments. You are my imaginary comfort place but what you bring is short-lived and also mostly in my mind though you would be surprised how often those buses turn up. Ha, ha.

Now as I write to you, I can see that you are the cover story (see Chapter 7) that takes the sting out of my problem of being late, you help me dismiss my need to take responsibility for managing my time and my commitments to other people. It is like I am thrill-seeking and daring myself to fail and be rejected. I could live dangerously – like running for the bus and being excited – and reassure myself that if it all went badly, I could count on the magic bus turning up in some shape or form. So, stop seducing me magic bus! You are a big snag in my life. I am going to spot when you come to mind. Because when you do turn up, I think I am lucky and instead of thinking about my efforts and achievements or qualities I put it down to magic. I think I am the child of generations of men and women waiting for the magic bus and not having their feet on the ground as a result. I am not ready to give you up entirely though I am now curious to see when in childhood you became a part of me.

Your old but reluctant friend Jessie.

Conclusion

Mapping out the patterns of interaction on paper helps us reflect and gives us a paper extension of our working memory. It allows space for mixed and conflicting feelings. As we are listening to the conversation and teasing out a story from it, we can follow the feelings as the impact of the action, or we can follow the action and find out who is doing what and the intention behind it. The mapper does not have to get the words right or lay them out neatly on the paper. They use the process of putting words on paper to show the effort of listening and the intention to join supportively in the puzzling and meaning making nature of conversations.

The map tracks the changing focus of attention and the changing journey of the conversation. If in a group, or one-to-one, when there is disagreement about views expressed, the map can act as a witness.

As will be shown in the next chapter, once we have mapped the push and pull between doing, feeling and coping then talking with a map becomes a scaffolding for exploring roles and relationships.

Chapter 3: Mapping roles and relationships

'We build too many walls and not enough bridges.'

Isaac Newton

Introduction

This chapter describes how to map out roles and relationships that arise from what we talk about. It helps show how our stories and conversations are shaped by intimate and powerful relationships with others and the dance of power, freedom, and restriction within, between and around us. It helps put names and faces to what we do and feel described in the previous chapter. It prepares the ground for using Map and Talk to tell and retell our stories in open conversational ways that are co-creative and healing.

We can see how social roles such as mum, dad, teacher, boss or friend tie up with the emotional roles such as caring, bullying, neglecting, idealising. A role is a versatile idea and sociological and psychological theorists give it hundreds of meanings and uses. Its use here is practical in drawing a circle around a distinctive cluster of interactions within and between us that have become a familiar and habitual part of us.

Mapping out the roles and relationships in our conversations can show how we make a sense of self from a mix of social identities which in turn are shaped by gender, generation, class and ethnicity and other social forces positioning us in relation to each other. Mapping can make it easier to see how these roles are powered and driven. Are the roles tightly or loosely held? How are they spoken of in conversation? Are they overt or covert? Are they named with contempt or awe, with irony or delight? Are they owned up to and morally framed or denied and weakly held by ethics and values?

A role can be such a familiar part of us that it is inhabited as a second-nature way of being ourselves. I am a nice man, I am the good girl, he is a bit of devil, she is adventurous, my dad was always the hero. Naming a role is always relational in multiple ways. It positions us inside or outside the role and in contrasting relation to another role. For example, 'I see you here as being strong as the boss, but I could imagine you here feeling weak when you feel like the disappointing daughter or son'. Mapping out the patterns that roles make in relation to each other at different moments in our lives can help us talk more consciously about them and renegotiate them. We take our given roles in childhood and carry them into everyday adult life. They are as ingrained in us as our names and accents. In childhood it is parents and family who are usually the powerful role models and invite us to fit into gender roles, family roles, sibling roles and point us to roles in our local society and culture. We also take roles from films and other media.

Roles give or restrict agency, power and influence. To change our lives for the better we need to change the roles. Map and Talk can slowly build awareness of interplay, origin and power of roles and their identities at the heart of what we are doing and feeling. It helps by self-consciously generating a more reflective kind of conversation about them.

As we map roles in a conversation with a spirit of reflection and mutual awareness, we get closer to seeing how we inhabit them. We are looking out for moments when voicing the role relationship changes in the process of mapping and talking. Do we speak of them in the third person? Does the voice shift from being accusative as 'you are this' to one that is more authoring and owning 'I am that'? Are roles cast in binary ways between us and them, you and me? Are the roles familiar and tie in with traditional gendering or are they breaking new ground or showing evidence of resistance? Are the role changes that are yearned for farfetched dreams or real possibilities? Mapping as we talk also keeps in mind the roles in the conversation. As the mapper what role am I being pulled into? How does it frame my response? Does the role I feel I am being pulled into by this conversation mirror or clash with the role someone else is taking or enacting?

One way to think about the interplay of roles and relationships is to think like a choreographer. Every word for actions and feelings on the map is like a dancer without a partner. Or a role without an appropriately responsive relationship. When we are mapping and talking, we are thinking of roles as heuristics: short cut working tools that help picture things and navigate our way in and out of the small steps of stories and conversations. The role of wife or husband are locating devices for making a bridge between personal and social experience. But the specifics of the choreography will vary from context to context, generation to generation, gender to gender. Roles are dynamic and alive. Just like the role in play, however fixed it might be on paper it can come alive in a thousand different ways according to the personality and presence of the actors in the moment. As we remember roles, we recreate them and relive them. How did my dad take to the role of being dad? How did my mum take to the role of mum? Was it choreographed by the neighbours, by the church, by society or by unresolved trauma from earlier in their lives? Or parts of all of these. Mapping can help our conversation measure up to these complexities.

Tony Ryle, who developed the versatile and collaborative psycho-social model of therapy which has shaped the thinking in this book, used the idea of reciprocal roles as a conceptual tool for therapy. He wanted to capture the richness from psychoanalysis about the way we internalise relationships with powerful intimate others (whether caring or abusing) and use them as templates for relating to people and the world around us. The richness of Ryle's thinking cuts across the various approaches to psychotherapy and can be summed up (see Figure 3.1) and paraphrased as: 'What others did to me, I do to myself and then do to others or get them to do to me'. He called his approach Cognitive Analytic Therapy, but it might just as well have been called 'role relationship' therapy. He was interested in the idea of role as a bridging concept between the micro details of what we do and the bigger picture of self and identity in society. This relational way of thinking resonated with the developmental thinking of infant researchers in the Vygotskian tradition (Bruner, Trevarthen, Stern, Reddy).[17] From the moment of our first cry at birth we are gesturing our way into the roles that will become us.

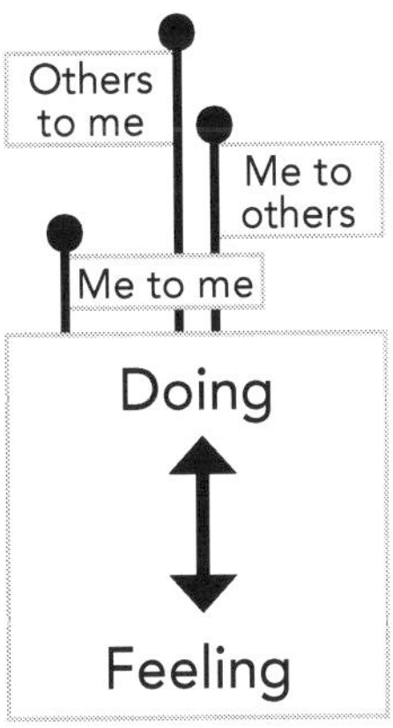

Figure 3.1

Ryle equally had a contrasting version of this sequence that is very relevant when we consider conversational poverty in a later chapter. It goes for Ryle like this: 'what others **don't** do with me, I **don't** do with myself and **don't** learn how to do with others.' His flexible, elastic idea was to think in terms of roles as reciprocal. If the mother is caring the child feels cared for and reciprocates by caring back, by trusting or by wanting to play or explore or show hunger or pain with the expectation of a caring response. How the chain of reciprocations develops in the context of the initial caring role is what is made visible and open to dialogue through mapping. For example, in the previous chapter the changing role reciprocations between Dino and Marco were born of a specific context of big brother, little brother, absent dad, protective mother and cruel teacher.

As the patterns of reciprocation of roles is brought to life in a conversation the mapping of them on paper is an invitation to shared discovery. Do we respond to each other with role reciprocations which seem in tune but can make a chaotic interaction to those around us? Do we bring different role systems in our heads from different childhoods and different local cultures when we meet to relate, live and work together? I thought we were doing the waltz. You saw it as the tango. Where there is pressure to align and fit in with the other, but attunement and negotiation is absent then social and emotional roles get entangled. We lose our relationship with ourselves, with each other and with the society and culture around us in the process. Map and Talk can help more accurately track the push and pull of these roles and give time, space and voice to disentangling them.

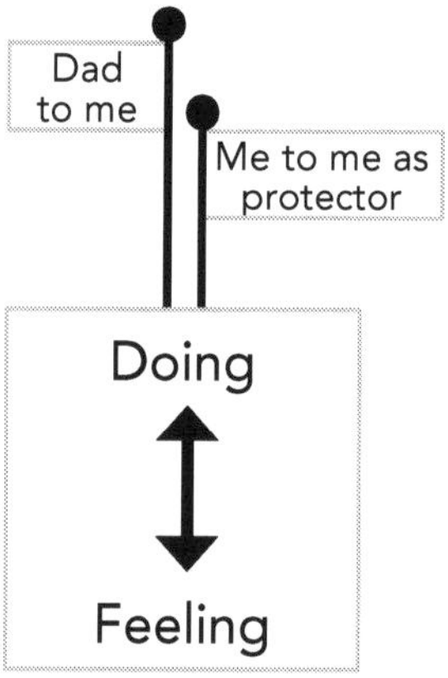

Figure 3.2

There is something else we can do at this point which is to put names and faces (if needed or wanted) to the source of the action at the doing end of the reciprocal relationship. We can tag the doing words with a distinct person or role (historically or currently) then flag it up as in Figure 3.2. The idea is that then we can think about the specifics of who I learnt the role from or with and who I am replaying the role now. We can also move from a more general view of the role relationships as played out within me as well as between me and others. It can also be possible to flag up the quality of these roles as the bedrock of a social identity or an expression of the demands and controls of surrounding society and culture.

Wendy shakes loose of her mother and daughter orchestration of roles. Wendy thought she knew her role in relation to her mother. She was loved and loving back. That was how it had always been. Now with her own children growing up she was aware of difference across the generations. Wendy was not so demanding of her children and wanted them to enjoy their independence and have an easier time of separating from her than

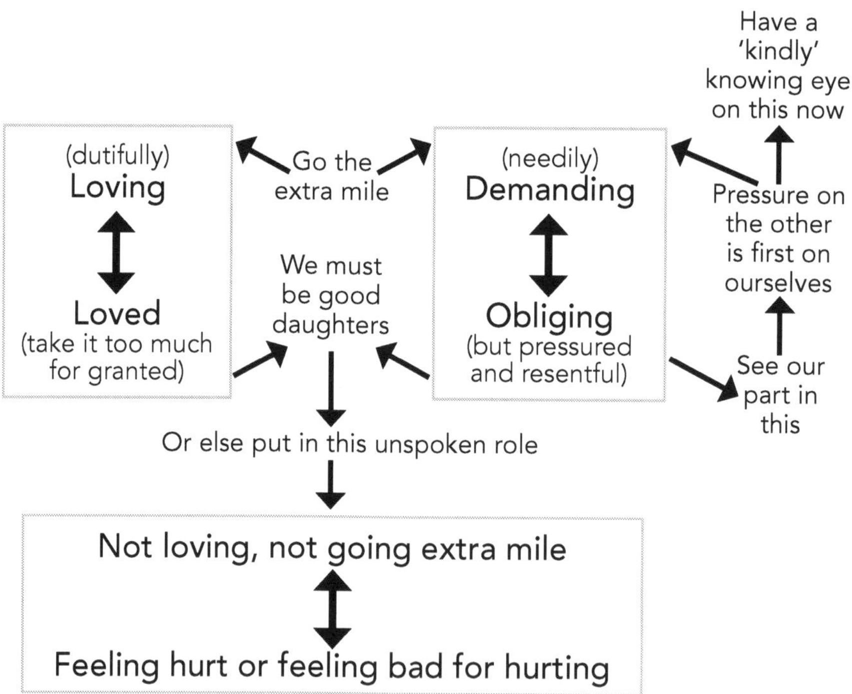

Figure 3.3

she did with her mum. She was surprised at noticing this and indeed only really noticed it when she named it during the mapping process. Her friend mapped it out as an entanglement between her and her mother. On paper it could be negotiated in a new way. Wendy wagged her finger at the words mapped out in front of her.

'I have always been the loving daughter to a very loving mum, but we never once had cross words.' Wendy wondered to herself why they never rowed. 'We always went the extra mile to be nice. Now I want my daughters to be less compliant: to rebel.' Wendy was immediately clear she would never challenge her mother but the mother in her head was not the mother in real life. The mother in her head needed the map to separate out two densely woven emotional roles that had been lived as if one. They are separated out visually in Figure 3.3. Wendy called the demanding role a silent intruder. A moral pressure to speak and behave in a certain way. There was a neediness in it that had a hidden side, voiced like this: 'If you are not obliging and going the extra mile with a smile, then you are not loving and not good. And if you are not good and loving then you will be hurting me.' In giving voice to this in the conversation, Wendy could tease out this entangled knot of lovingly demanding with the map: 'This is in me. The change I want is for me.' She didn't think her mother was aware of the demanding element to the role. It was something buried in her marriage and the gendered fabric of the culture. 'I put pressure on myself, and I end up responding or reciprocating to myself in ways that are more demanding than loving at times. I take it out on myself and then I resent it which further wears me out.'

Wendy's friend asked, 'What do you need?'

'I don't need to rebel, though I will delight in watching my daughters rebel. What I need is a kindly eye on myself. I need to soften the dance within myself. Seeing it disentangled on paper is a huge step in making the thought of a kindly eye possible. I can choose to be put upon and/or respond lovingly to my demanding mother. The point is to have the choice to do my own dance.' In reading this take a moment to go over the map Figure (3.3) and consider how it helped Wendy have the conversation she needed.

The emotional element of roles are modified dramatically by adverbs

Our descriptions of interactions can be dramatically transformed when we begin to qualify the intent or meaning of a role relationship. See how the original emotional and interpersonal meaning of the verb is modified by an adverb. For example: what is the changed meaning of inspiring if it becomes 'terrifyingly inspiring'? Wendy's mum was lovingly demanding, and she needed to separate the loving from the demanding. Is trust very different as a response if it is felt to be naïve as in 'naively trusting'. In Figure 3.4 demanding and

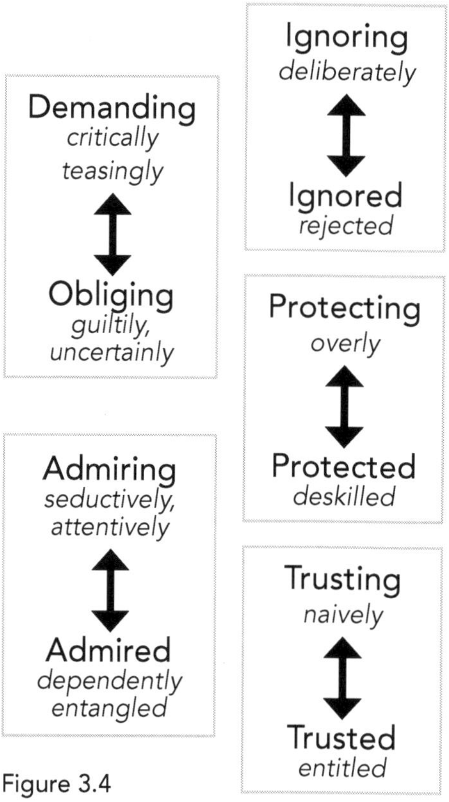

Figure 3.4

obliging could be qualified by any number of adverbs. To be needily demanding gives it a clinging attachment quality. Look at the examples in the box and see if you agree with the reciprocal matchup between both ends and whether you would change the wording. Or what would change at one end if the wording was changed at the other. This openness to rework and play respectfully and creatively with the power of the push and pull between words is an important skill of conversational awareness mapping.

When we are mapping, we are listening for these nuances and asking about the quality of the emotional role relationship. How we remember it from childhood may be through rose tinted glasses or by overlooking some of the positive aspects. In Figure 3.4, ‘ignored’ might be different if the fuller account of the doing end was ‘busy earning money, then ignoring’. Or ‘protecting’ might not feel so good if it was overdone and led to the person feeling over-protected and lacking self-reliance. Whatever the general or dictionary meaning of a word, they also have local and unique significance when we use them in the context of a specific story. As an exercise for yourself, put down an emotional role relationship with a two-way arrow connecting the doing and feeling ends of a role in your world and then see what changes for you if you add adverbs at either pole of the role.

The riot policeman: conflicting roles and threats to a sense of self

The value of having roles in mind as conversations and stories are shared is illustrated by the discussion around this conversation with Tony, a young riot police officer. As already noted, conversational awareness depends on holding in mind mixed feelings and conflicting roles and their implications within self, between self and others and the surrounding context and situation. The conversation is being mapped as Tony is debriefing about a moment of crowd control when things got out of hand and some officers some protesters were hurt.

The role needs mapping in relation to the person and the context. Let's imagine that Tony is holding a line with his fellow officers in the face of demonstrators. He is anxious to do his duty but is feeling scared and emotionally disturbed to the extent that he is desperately hanging on to his role. Let's say that in his case he is hovering and shimmering between feeling sympathy with the cause of the demonstrators but also the pressure of loyalty to his colleagues. He also wants to do his civic duty and at the same time keep himself safe. If he loses sight of his role, he fears he might lose it emotionally and get carried away. Somewhere deep inside Tony a muted voice says, 'I want my mum'. His colleagues are chanting to each other 'Hold the line'. Tony relates his experience of critical messy moments when he and a protestor got hurt. As Jack, the debriefing counsellor, tracks the conversation, Tony is saying, 'Don't waver, feel scared. Up for a fight, do my duty, want to laugh, should have chosen another career. We should pull back, want to run. Guy next to me is losing it.' Jack with his pen and paper does not know where to start, so asks Tony 'So, what in all these feelings is the one we should build the conversation around?' Tony stops and thinks and looks at the blank sheet of paper.

'I was scared,' Tony says and Jack puts down the word scared.

'And we were scary. We wanted to, had to scare people into backing off to stop things getting out of control.'

Jack put 'scaring to scared' inside his first box (1) with a two-way arrow linking them. This was the first feeling hub in the conversation. It was not the only feeling but maybe it was the key feeling around and against which the others circulated. Jack has a bigger picture in mind of mapping a conversation about the police officer's conversation about his role, then in the thick of the action, and now looking back.

While pointing with the pen to the word 'scared' on the paper Jack asked Tony what he wanted or needed when feeling scared.

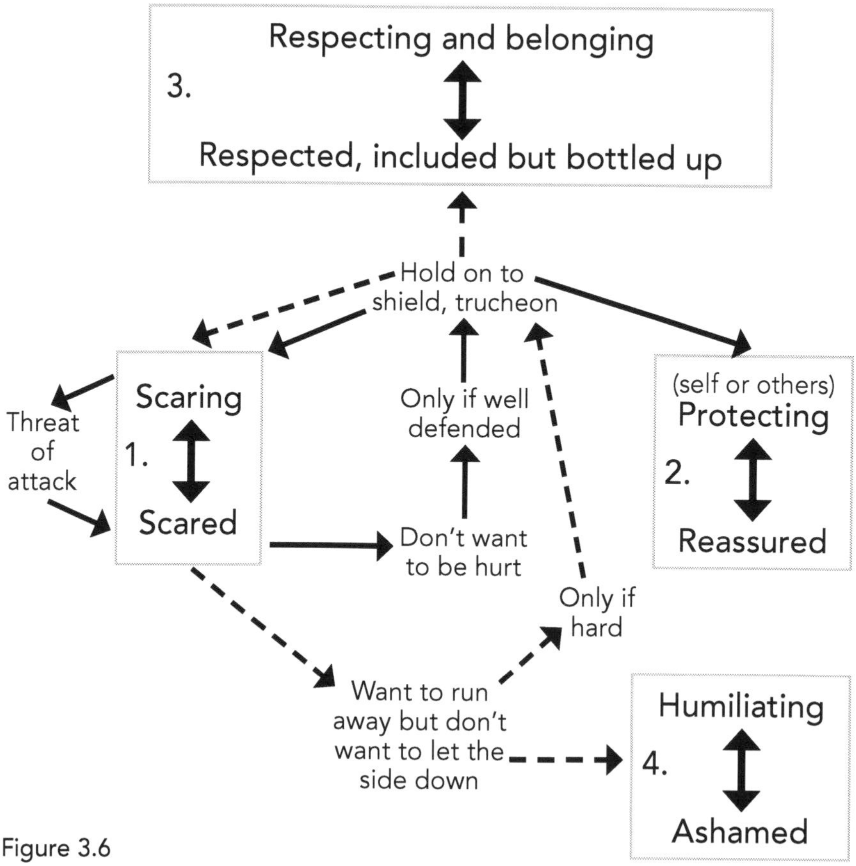

Figure 3.6

'I know what I didn't want. I didn't want to be hurt. I didn't want anyone to be hurt. I guess it helped to look well-defended. So, there I was with the big man on the outside and the scared-little-boy inside me, holding on to the shield and the truncheon.' Tony looked at the way Jack was making the map in front of them as they talked. He was having a reflective conversation now about the fragmented conversation he was having within himself and hearing from around him at the time of the riot. His fingers pointed to the scaring and the protecting boxes. 'I was doing two things at once.' He could see he was in a scaring role and a protecting role at the same time. One was directed outwards to scare others and the other was directed inwards (partly) to protect himself.

Once the hub feelings of 1 and 2 were on the map, Tony and Jack sat back and looked at it. Jack led Tony through a recap with the map. 'You were scared you might be hurt and protected yourself with the truncheon.' Jack wanted to stay with this moment of conversational awareness. His guess was that Tony knew the scaring and the protecting pattern of coping and he could orchestrate them and voice them. He looked at both ends of the protecting to protected reciprocal role and said to Tony, 'So, you wanted to be protecting of others and be protected.'

'In theory,' Tony said, 'But also, I was wanting to use it to scare people off and to protect others. I did feel reassured, but I don't suppose the protesters felt reassured.'

Jack said, 'The map can help us see more than the conversation can tell. Do you think in not wanting to let the side down you had to play the role of the hardman?' Jack pointed to the words on paper and asked, 'So as to be included and respected. And that was another reason for relating to the truncheon, the shield and the helmet?'

'Yes, but I never feel like the hard man. It is a pretend role.' Both men were working the conversation through the map and Jack asked Tony, 'What does the map do for the way we are talking?'

'It opens my eyes. I am surprised at how much I was carrying emotionally and managing to keep a lid on.'

'I don't know where to put "keeping a lid on"' Jack reflected and searched with his pen for where to put the phrase. 'Maybe here', he said pointing to the protecting reciprocal role. 'Nah', said Tony. 'Wait a minute, it is all over the map. The whole thing is keeping the lid on. Me, them, the protesters, society? I know some of the guys can lose it in these moments because the feelings are bottled too tight, and it can feel like they are going to explode.'

Jack nodded as if he understood and looked at Tony and then at the map as a prompt to have another look and pointing to the 'scared' place on the map and asked what else Tony could have done to cope with feeling scared.

'I know what I wanted to do. I wanted to run away.'

Jack wrote down the beginnings of another pattern: 'Want to run away but' (in a different coloured pen shown here with dotted lines and arrows). And Tony interrupted him 'But ... but I don't want to let the side down.' Jack looked at Tony directly.

'Is it okay to ask you what it would feel like to let the side down?'

'Sure, it would be humiliating. It is a no, no. Can't happen. I'd die of shame. I would rather be dead.'

For Tony this is his nightmare place as described on the Hopes and Fears map on page 84. It immediately invites two things. One is the challenge of staying with these feelings which are so hard to manage, so routinely unspeakable, that they are pushed out of mind and out of conversational awareness. The process of mapping as we talk gives them a chance to be explored indirectly in an emotionally manageable and more socially acceptable way. Jack had an idea that what would help is to get on the map the opposite position to letting the side down.

'What is totally not letting the side down Tony?' Jack wanted to put this at the top of the page and pointed his pen there and Tony came straight out with the answer.

'It would involve being respected and included by my mates and colleagues.'

As Jack filled the words 'respected and included' out at the top of the map as a desired role relationship, Tony added something. 'But to be up there you cannot show your vulnerable feelings. You must bottle them up.'

They were near finishing their discussion and Tony said it was helpful to open up discussion in a safe way with the words out on the map where they seemed less out of control and crazy like they were at times inside him. He wanted to have the map and go back over it and have a conversation about it with himself.

'You could write a letter to it or some part of it,' said Jack. 'Like write to Dear Scared, or Dear Shield and Truncheon, or Dear Mum, or Dear Protesters.' Writing to something outlined by the map or to one troublesome part of it can help keep the benefit of the conversation by keeping it fresh and open. It can take it further.

Tony interrupted 'I would write to what I am missing out on. Dear kids.' He went on to say that although he valued the variety of the police work, he felt he needed the balancing influence of another side of himself. Reflecting on the map he felt that it had helped him step back from a difficult experience and see it from different angles.

Reflecting on the value of mapping a conversation like this it may be true that when we are talking without a map, we may limit our awareness because we are more likely to get lost in the twists and turns of the conversation. Having a map of the key lines of character and roles and relationship located in one event can help choose the direction to go in the discussion and how far to go emotionally. It extends working memory and offers points for linking to other experiences and roles.

Role awareness

Use the awareness grid in Figure 3.7 to think of a role you currently have and wonder where it is along the horizontal axis. Is it a relative new role or one deep within you? On the vertical line ask is it more familiar and navigable or strange and uncharted? New roles can be familiar and navigable and even if we have never been in that relationship before we take to them with some ease. It may be that the emotional and social aspects of the role are in alignment with the other person, or that a role deep within us maps onto it. Some roles are deep within us but as in the top right quadrant of the grid they are familiar and navigable. We say to ourselves and the world: this is me so take me as I am. If a new role is strange and uncharted, in the sense we have no personal maps for navigating it, then we need to make allowances and take time in assessing and incorporating this role into our sense of self. Maisie in Chapter 1 was finding her way into a new role. Finally, there are some roles which we might sense, or feel the impact of, but are a hidden force within that we have never consciously negotiated or formulated. These are the roles that are often the focus of our more troublesome discussions. An example is at the end of this chapter in the story called Stormy Weather.

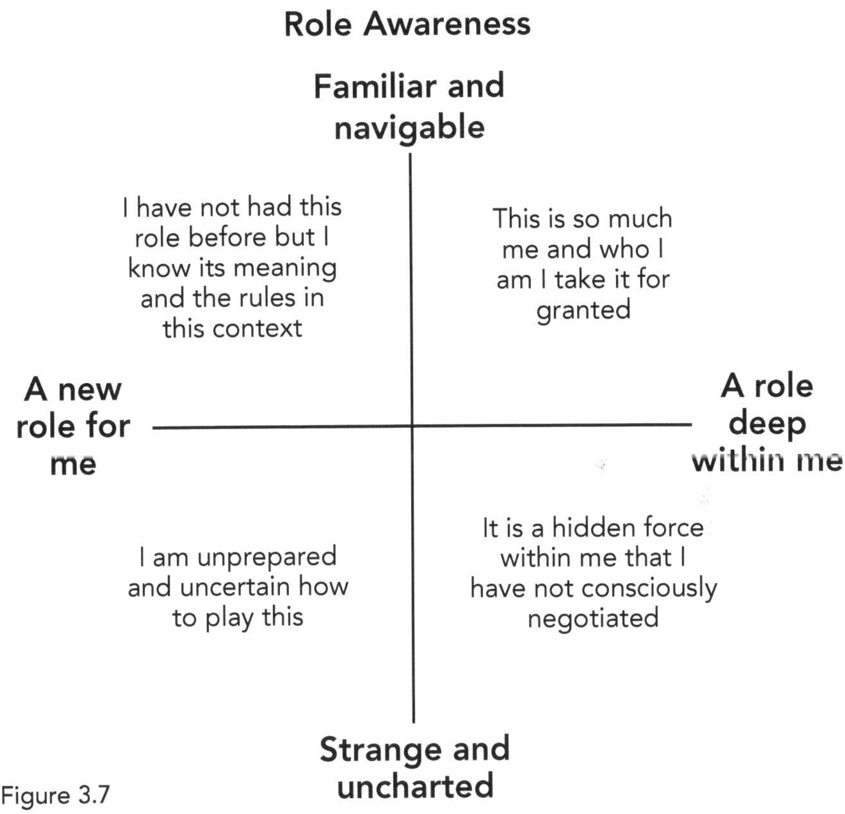

Figure 3.7

How we handle roles and build up a more or less enabling repertoire of roles through which we find and express ourselves, will depend greatly on the emotional and social capital available to us. Limiting or oppressive roles and a general absence of role security is a direct threat to our mental health. A society should be judged by its capacity to offer role dignity and security and avoid role poverty. There is no reason not to have an abundance of roles so that each of us has more than one role as a source of worth, security and esteem.

Me and not me

Another way of approaching role awareness is to see our sense of self as composed of a repertoire of roles that are orchestrated well or badly within us, with others and with the world around us as the situation changes. Early family life and school life is a 'schooling' in orchestrating and conducting conflicting roles. For Ryle, in his development of Cognitive Analytic Therapy,[18] roles were ideas that could help you look at society and the individual at the same time. The focus could be on the interaction and its outer impact between people at the same time as its inner function for self. A useful exercise draws on the ideas from Harry Stack Sullivan[19] a psychiatrist in the US during the middle decades of the 20th century who made the rich but simple distinction between what was *me* and what was *not me* and what was *bad me*. He saw some of our ways of coping with anxiety as a form of dissociation. If something is too unsettling to think about or feel because it does not make sense or hijacks my stable sense of who I am then I make it not me. I don't go there. And I resist allowing anyone else to take me there or raise the possibility of going there. I do this in large part without knowing and it lands me with what Donnel Stern calls unformulated experience.[20] A contemporary of Sullivan's, Karen Horney, a founder member of the Berlin Psychoanalytic Society and a refugee from Germany in the 1930s, made a significant contribution to a more social and relational approach to psychoanalytic thinking. Towards the end of her long and varied career, her work looked at how the ways we cope with the gender and other social pressures in early life cause conflict and anxiety to which we respond by various coping procedures which in turn can produce more conflict. She describes in rich analytic detail how we move inward, away, against, or towards our self, others and our world in various limiting and conflicting role responses (Horney. K, 1945 Our Inner Conflicts). At the heart of her work in contrast to Freud was an optimism about the innate vitality and search for fulfillment in both the childhood and adult self.

There are times when we should hold on to our roles and follow them tightly. The centre forward approaching an open goal with the ball at their feet should stay tightly in role and give all themselves over to the task. The young tennis player Emma Raducanu, when asked how she sustained her extraordinary run of straight wins out of nowhere to win the US tennis open championship in 2021[21] said she just took one shot at a time and stayed focused in the present moment. Performers who give their all to a performance must give themselves to the role and inevitably there is an adjustment to be made after the applause has died down in recovering a fuller more rounded sense of self. The risk of such focused attention is that we lose our sense of self to the role. It hijacks us. This can be appropriate in contexts where a role must be performed at all costs. The actor becomes the performer on stage, the police officer on duty, the therapist in the room.

But we need a kindly observing eye to know when to loosen the knot of our ties to the role in the context of a specific time and space and recover a wider sense of self. The challenge in an age of identity politics is that certain social positions become lived out as 'all or nothing' roles and we lose any conversational space to negotiate (see also Chapter 12).

To reflect a step further on the barriers to role awareness in figure 3.7 now look at the grid in Figure 3.8 with two dimensions. The vertical axis touches on the relationship between my sense of myself and the roles relationships that make up me and my life space. At the top end I take them to be very much part of me. The 'Open' end is the idea of any one of these roles being so strongly associated with me means that no other perspective gets a look in. If you ask me about my football team, my hometown or my national identity or my politics I may say this is me. How I say it will depend on how open or closed my negotiation with it is. In the top right corner of the grid in Figure 3.8 it is not negotiable and absolutely me. In the top left corner, it is part of a repertoire, and I can adapt to different sides of me in different roles and contexts.

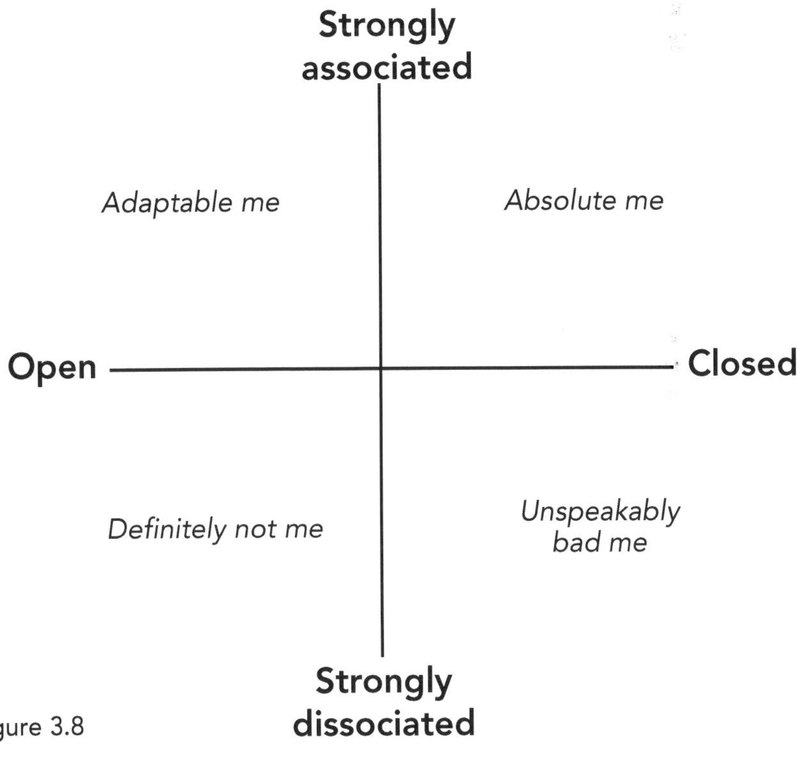

Figure 3.8

In contrast, at the bottom end of the vertical line my relationship with part of me is completely dissociated, disowned, or repressed. This is either a known part of me that is so shameful in its history or possibilities it cannot be acknowledged as in the bottom right corner, or in conversational terms it might be the unspeakably bad me. In the bottom left corner are qualities that might be seen as part of me which I declare to be 'definitely' not part of me. Rather than repressed but known as in the bottom right corner (like Freud's unconscious where repressed thoughts will keep bubbling up in some shape or form) the bottom left side is pushed away as just not part of me. It then shows up as fragments of unformulated wordless experience. Or if I say, 'It is a life and death, all, or nothing relationship', then you might put me in this respect in the top right-hand corner of this two-dimensional grid. If you see me take the last piece of cake at a party and accuse me of being greedy, I might so dissociate from the greedy person role that I completely deny that I took the last piece of cake. In the language of Sullivan, I repress any knowledge of this bad part of me. It is in the bottom right-hand corner as the unspeakably bad me which is disowned by being strongly dissociated. In contrast, if you notice me being quiet in a group and you encourage me to speak, I might say I prefer talking one-to-one. I might say that being talkative in groups is not me and in may be part of unmet needs and untried skills described in chapter 9 on conversational poverty.

The horizontal line moves from closed roles and positions to open ones. The top right corner of the grid is a place for tightly knit, rigidly held roles and identities. A young man's support for Manchester United was non-negotiable and on match days it took over his life. He said, 'When I am in this role and cloaked in the identity that comes with it, I cannot see another side to myself. It is all or nothing.' It becomes 'absolutely me.' Roles that are strongly associated with the self and held in fixed and rigid ways might be functional for a short time in certain contexts, but if they become part of an identity, they limit our ability to be in dialogue with others, and the world around us and, most importantly, within ourselves. Teenagers can set up a very tightly knit group life with identity conformity and fixed roles, which is fine as a transitional experience of finding themselves but not as a fixed identity solution for life.

In this context, the helpful conversation with a young person going through such a journey is to not put all your role and identity eggs in one basket. To value the attachment solution derived from the group conformity and to identify with it, but to see it as a piggyback ride to another perspective, not the final destination of the self. Such group identity solutions are tested by how well they can be negotiated with and whether the top left corner has the power to call them over into a more adaptable and flexible version of me and the different sides to myself. These struggles are more easily edged into an open and reflective conversation with a map.

In contrast, at the open end of the horizontal line roles and identities can be more loosely knitted together and can be strongly identified with but negotiated according to the context. It is a feeling of having several sides to oneself that are flexible and dispersed and loosely orchestrated in different combinations depending on the situation. Conversational awareness is more likely to flourish here and be an important help in finding the sweet spot of role reciprocation in day-to-day interactions with others. Inevitably in our personal and work lives and in our conversations about our experiences there will be movement around the four parts of the grid in Figure 3.8, but with a sense of defaulting back to the top left area.

The roles we give to things

Tony's relationships were with things such as the truncheon and the shield. Things as objects can have roles in our lives that are almost as alive as our relationships with people. We invest ourselves in things, give value and meaning to them. Toys, clothes, jewellery, flags and banners, homes, cars and all manner of things are extensions of ourselves and become aids to and part of our inner conversation. They may help or hinder open dialogue with people. They are objects in our lives with distinctive signatures of space and time. If we can make a conversational map of our relationship with things, we can open a conversation with ourselves. This may be a steppingstone to more open and conversational relationship with ideas, feelings, and most importantly, the people in our lives.

Figure 3.9

The object is both a thing in itself and an imaginary role relationship. A simple example is when you go to sleep and want to wake up early so you set the alarm on the clock. The idea of the clock helps you get to sleep but the idea of the clock is not what wakes you; it is the real clock sounding the alarm that wakes you up. We externalise our worry about waking and put trust in the clock. And at the same time, we internalise an idea that it is there and reliable. The trust depends on the battery not running out and the idea of the clock giving us peace of mind. Where our relationship with people is different is in the complexity of the negotiation and the conversation to mediate the inner idea and the outer experience. We can talk to the alarm clock but the attachment to its reliability is very direct and simple. If we become anxious about our relationship with the clock, we can check whether we have set it correctly. With a person we are negotiating through a variety of activities and levels of engagement. We may have very simple and transactional role relationships almost on the same level as the alarm clock (such as buying a ticket or going online to make a purchase) but the presence of an interpersonal and role relationship in the transaction open it up to complexity and humanity. One important aspect of the conversational awareness that can be awakened by talking with a map is to recover the humanity and personality in things and to be conversational in those routine transactional moments.

One way of learning about roles and relationships is to focus on the role of some of the important things in your life and map out what they do and how they make you feel. How we use a car or a home, or the tools of our working lives or books in our schools and homes may point in the different directions and ways we organise our lives and have a sense of self. If most of the things that matter to us are privatised and in our possession, what is our relationship with the communal and collective things in our shared worlds: the parks and trees, the buses and trams, the libraries and the presence of particles in the air?

Things have a role relationship in our lives. They are on our maps and in our conversations as symbols and pointers and participants. We work, talk and live with them tangibly, literally and imaginatively. They are part of our language, our embodied sense of self and intimate space. They are carried with us and signal who we are or not. We can learn relational thinking and develop our conversational awareness by mapping out our interaction with these things and the patterns of activity that go with them. You can judge how a person might talk with you by the way they 'talk' with the things in their lives. We can judge a society by its conversation (or anti-conversation) with its common and shared heritage of natural resources and manufactured things.

Hubs are positions for roles on the map

A hub is an anchor point on the map for the roles coming from the conversations we have with each other. A map is likely to have two, three or four of them as the conversation develops. A hub is marked by a circle to indicate it is a key position on the map and that it has an inside and an outside. Inside the hub are two sets of words separated by a two-way arrow indicating that they are in a reciprocal, push and pull, cause and effect relationship. The words at the top end of the circle are the doing words and are the source of influence and control. As already shown, they give rise to the words for feeling evoked at the bottom end of the circle. Outside the hub are sequences of response; beginning with wants and needs (and what is not wanted or needed). These wants or needs are the drivers, consciously or unconsciously, of a pattern of coping with and managing the feelings triggered inside the hub. They lead to some response within self or some action towards others or society.

For example, 'I feel lonely' fits into the bottom end of the hub because it seems like others ignore me. I cope by seeking company but assume or predict that I will only stop getting ignored if I do nice things for people. My appraisal of the situation leads me to do nice things, and, in the process, I ignore my needs and feel empty inside. This is the conversation I have with myself that the map can help tease out. It circles round a hub of emotion. It anchors one role relationship, and it tracks it out as a familiar and habitual part of me. It is how I have learnt to handle myself in relation to others. It can feel automatic and self-evidently a fixed part of my character. Carefully mapping this pattern around a hub on the map can be the platform for a variety of conversations. One hub of emotion and coping might be an entire map in itself.

Positioning to positioned

The word role does not translate easily into other languages with the same looseness of connotations which it has in English. Position is another word for role that flows naturally from placing words on the map. This is visible, so when pointing at the map and asking, 'when you were in that position, in that place, what was keeping you there?', we are pointing at a place on a piece of paper, but symbolically and analogically we are pointing to a space and time in the person's life as position both within the self and with the world.

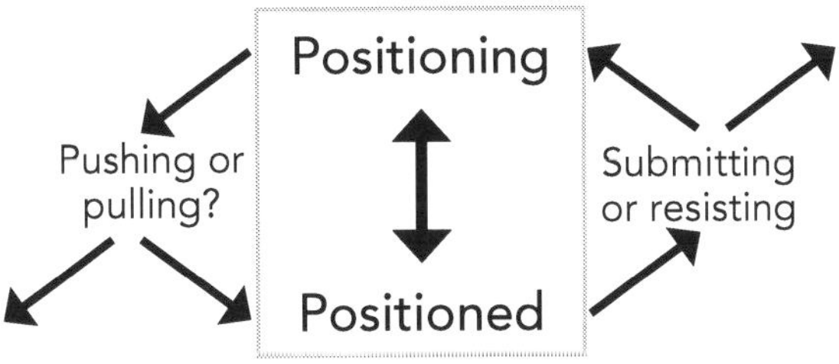

Figure 3.10

We use the phraseology of positioning in our everyday speech, and it reveals a kind of geography of power or an implicit mapping of power dynamics. 'I am placing you in an impossible position by casting you in this role.' 'His mother always kept him in the position of child.' 'His father could never let him occupy the top dog position or even an equal position.' As in Figure 3.10 the gaps between what we do and feel with ourselves, and with others, is a gap between our positioning and our subjective experience (or other people's experience) of being positioned. The positioning is enacted with varying shades and intensities of enabling or restricting 'push and pull' as on the left side of the figure. You positioning me as inferior or as not belonging may be intended to harm me but at the same time be going off somewhere else to buy favour with another group or person. From the subjectively and socially positioned end of the two-way arrow I may be forced to find myself or accept the position given, but equally I might choose to submit or resist. That would partly take me into a reciprocal or counter positioning of you and or at the same time be taking my actions and intentions somewhere else.

The positioning within me or between us is coped with also by various shades and intensities of reciprocation, resistance, refusal or submission. For example, in the Stormy Weather example, Simon is positioning Janet as female by the way he is positioning himself as male. The key element is power: the power to control, to resist, refuse or subvert; to know, to voice and negotiate. This shows up in action, and body language but also in conversation.

Mapping moments in a conversation is also about mapping the push and pull of power and control. Earlier it was suggested that every role is an invitation to a relationship. A dancer in search of a dance. But the call to relate is often pointing in more than one direction. What I am doing to position you in relation to me or you are doing to position me in relation to you depends on how we simultaneously are positioning ourselves. Talking with a map helps us see how we are at the same time in varying degrees agents, captives and authors of our situation. We are being authored and positioned by others and the world around us and we are authoring and positioning ourselves. As already described the movement of power and control is inward and outward at the same time. We need conversations about the role that is too tightly held may be loosened enough to leave room for ourselves to renegotiate our participation in the role and others' reciprocation with it. Roles that are fixed and embedded can become second nature to us. Sometimes we can simultaneously say that 'I am my own worst enemy' and 'I was being treated badly'. The process of mapping and talking gives us a chance to stand back and disentangle our agency from the positioning woven into us or stamped on us.

How to give each other freedom to change involves a conversational awareness of these power dynamics. As we look at the internal power and workings of the role, we are also looking at its external status and influence. We can use maps to track out the dynamics of power and the workings of difference in authority and the legacy of racism, sexism and other forms of oppression, exclusion, and harm. In every society there is a class positioning, or a gender positioning along with positioning of groups, generations and lifestyles. It is a central part of the legacy of colonialism, slavery and empires to understand and show answerability to, and reparation for the exploitation and dehumanisation of ethnic and racist positioning of superiority and inferiority. Whilst it is not in any way the whole answer to injustice, it is an aspect of conversational awareness from which all can benefit. Mapping is one of the most helpful ways of talking about this in a compassionate and enlightening way. It gives us more chance of seeing the dances of power and control between us. We are less likely to go head-to-head and lose the conversation to hurt and blame before we have made any progress.

Drawing a line between positions

Sometimes, before a map can be made, it needs a simple line between one extreme or exaggerated position and the contrasting equally extreme position or role. For example, I might put at one end of a horizontal line 'prouder at work' and then at the other end 'more ashamed at work.' We could then mark where I thought I was last week and where I am today and where I would like to be. In such a conversation I can begin to negotiate my positioning and the roles and relationships behind it. One readymade question for any conversation with a map is to have in mind the counter position to the one that is at the forefront of discussion. If I am being humiliated, what would it be like to be validated? If I am being protected, what would it be like to be abandoned? If I am being admired, what would it be like to be slurred or disparaged?

Gendering to gendered

Gender is a central and universal form of positioning in our emotional and social role relationships. Despite the dominant and reductive narratives of recent centuries, the psycho-social dynamics are complex and varied. There are a thousand nuanced ways of gendering each other and of weaving gender dynamics into our sense of who we are emotionally, sexually and politically. As with all 'map and talk' ideas we turn the noun gender into a verb. To gender and bring out its power by bringing it in to the active present tense as 'gendering'.

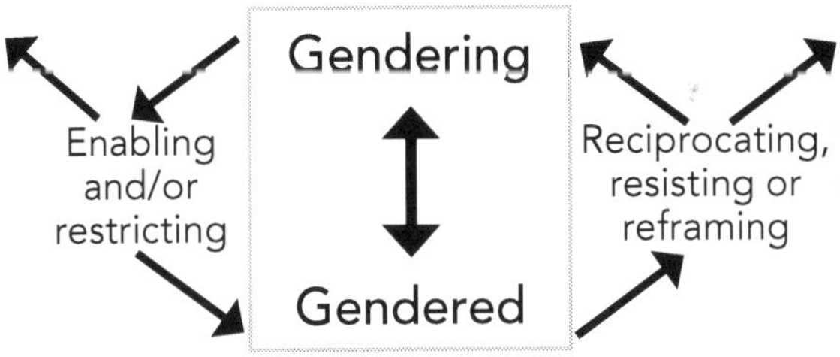

Figure 3.11

When mapping, we are looking at reciprocal roles from the doing end at the top to the feeling end at the bottom in terms of gendering to gendered or doing to and done to and felt. It opens the spaces to explore the detail of how gendering is routinely enacted and internalised in our formative years and how we negotiate it in teenage years and adult life. If I am at the receiving end of the binary gendering me as a boy or girl, I experience it consciously or unconsciously as being gendered.

In Figure 3.11 each of us will have individual words for mapping the gendering and gendered ends inside the box in different contexts and with different people. The arrows outside the box point to patterns of relating that are enabling or restrictive or a mix of both, and on the other side patterns of coping, resisting or responding to the gender positions that have been cast on to us. If you have an interest, use this simple template to map out your own gendering-gendered dynamics and the explicit and implicit conversations that went with it. As with other exercises in this book you can also write a short personal letter to one part or aspect of the map or maps you make. Read Chapter 7 on writing, mapping and voicing words though before you do.

Gendering is always combined with generation, class, ethnicity and other contextual factors. Among feminist and social justice thinking and writing, it is richly understood in terms of intersectionality[22] as the combined impact of class, ethnic, gender and other status and power dynamics. Talking with a map can catch these multiple dynamics both in their personal and institutional power to position people in relation to themselves and each other. At a societal level there are big common forces positioning us but from an individual view it is important to hear how varied and personalised our gendering experiences are. They vary within and between generations, over a lifetime and according to interactions with intimate others and surrounding micro-culture. In Chapter 8 on Cora the 'mother of tongues' there is a speculative illustration of how the uniquely human experience of language and conversation may have been powered by the inter group dynamics of gender.

Gender is both simultaneously deeply psychological, socially fixed, biologically primed and embodied. We know it through our roles and identities, through our words and outlook but in our relationship through our bodies above all. As we learn to notice, name and negotiate knowledge and control of our bodies and learn the names for its parts, we enter into a gendering and gendered position to ourselves, within ourselves and to others.

At the same time as this gendering to gendered process is taking place and being mapped in all its complexity in my brain and body, I am being met as a person, as a presence in a family, school or community. Some of this meeting underscores or distorts my emerging gendered self and some of it contradicts or transcends it.

In reciprocal role terms, gendering is enacted first from others to self as an implicit role relationship. We then adopt the roles we are cast into as actions, self to self, of our own volition. I position myself with the signs, gestures and language that others use to position me. This becomes the familiar boy/girl orchestration of me. I assume my place in the same instance as I am given my place. It is intersectional in terms of class, generation, ethnicity and other social dynamics of status and power. Mapping can help see and give compassionate and conversational voice to this intersectional process.

How I am given the role and how I reciprocate – respond, or react, or rebel – is always contextual in the sense that I am given this role at this time, in this context. I then look to elicit from others the dances which I have been given. I expect to be gendered in line with what is given and familiar to me and will draw others into these dances and me, and my body will act as if I am in these dances whether they allow or limit spontaneity and vitality of expression. Once we have laid out the idea of a dynamic and central relationship of gendering through mapping our roles, we have an external space that can help us think about diversity and difference, agency and authorship.

Lucy takes an assertive role

Lucy, a four-year-old girl (with her mother, aunts and brother in tow) is approaching a small but narrow run of steps over a wall to the beach at the seaside. Lucy is skipping, happy and playful and assertively steps in front of strangers to go first up the steps saying, 'Me in front'. And then with her hands in the air says, 'Ladies first' and then Lucy pauses, looks round and adds, 'Always.' She is on the threshold of not just imitating a phrase but finding a conversational moment for voicing, owning and authoring it. Lucy does it with humour, with conversational and contextual awareness. She has an audience but is also speaking for herself. The idea of 'ladies first' is one she has heard from her aunts, but she has never said it before. She now embraces it, and it embraces her. Lucy owns it more by adding 'always' for emphasis to herself.

Such fleetingly, possessive use of ideas is essential to negotiating meaning and connection in the world. The meaning of the idea is both culturally embedded but also locally and uniquely activated by her. The accumulation of conversational moments of this kind become live 'gendered' personal mapping and voicing moments to be added to an individual repertoire of ways of becoming a person in a transitional and changing world. Are such delicate transitive moments of self-discovery and authorship routinely discounted or cherished and incorporated or dismissed, crushed or teased out of us? We need an open and positive eye and ear for them and mapping as we talk and reflect helps develop those eyes and ears.

Mary lost her faith when she felt unfairly forgotten

Mary stopped speaking when she was two and barely said a word for two years. Then she became a chatterbox, but there was an unspoken gap of conversational poverty that was never addressed. As the first-born child in her extended family after the Second World War she was the delighting and delighted centre of the world for her mother, her aunts and grandmother. This blissful state lasted for two years until the coincidentally big day her dad came back from the army and her little brother was born and the focus of delight changed its gender and went elsewhere to Dad the hero and his new-born boy. Mary went from the apple of everyone's eye to overlooked and felt confused and forgotten. It was impossible to get any of the limelight and she found no way of getting attention until she stopped speaking. It was as if she was saying to herself, I once had a leading role but now it is only a walk on part. So, I will have nothing to say and will stop speaking. Mary became a silent observer. After two years her mother, who by now had three children, became concerned. Mary was a bright child and learned much from the observing position of her silence. The world swept around her, and she developed a great eye for details of shifting attention and injury or neglect. School began to change things and she started walking the dog with her grandfather. As she remembers it some sixty years later Mary became chatty on those walks with her grandad, and she rejoined the growing conversation of the family as if nothing had happened.

In her life there have been two places from which conversations can grow. She could feel these two places deeply embodied within her. Her mute place – hurt, outside, forgotten, and her chatty place – talking superficially, randomly to hold some attention. There was a third place, but it was so early in her life she had no conscious memory of it. It was the princess place: the focus of attention and conversation, but she was mostly talked of and at rather than with. She realised looking back that in those first two years of being the spoilt princess of the temporarily 'matriarchal' family she was so smothered with attention that there was no room for her to find her voice anyhow.

She was raised a catholic and went to a catholic junior school. At nine years old she was top of the class. She benefitted from her observing eye for detail and the analytic powers of children who listen a lot. She was a good, talented, quiet but sometimes chatty child. One day her form teacher Sister Theresa was called to the headmaster and needed urgently to find someone to be prefect and take charge of order in the class while she was briefly absent. She put the two boys with the top aggregate scores in all subjects for the year (they were second and third to Mary who was first). Mary immediately noticed the choice and the bypassing of her claim to be in charge. He claim to feeling special was bypassed. She put up her hand saying, 'Miss I was top, I should be in charge'. Sister Theresa looked at her and, saying nothing and showing no feeling, looked away. After a while Mary put her hand back down. She never wanted to be given the prefect role again. The two boys relished their roles and patrolled up and down the rows of desk. Mary decided that if the church and God put boys above girls, it was not fair and either God does not exist or is not as good and wise as he is made out to be. Mary knew from that day as the boys strode up and down the aisles of school desks that she no longer supported the church, or the school. A private and invisible conversation with herself had taken place. In looking back and talking of her experience we made a map of feeling dismissed and it seeming unfair. It pointed to a longing for good authority that could be trusted (figure 3.12)

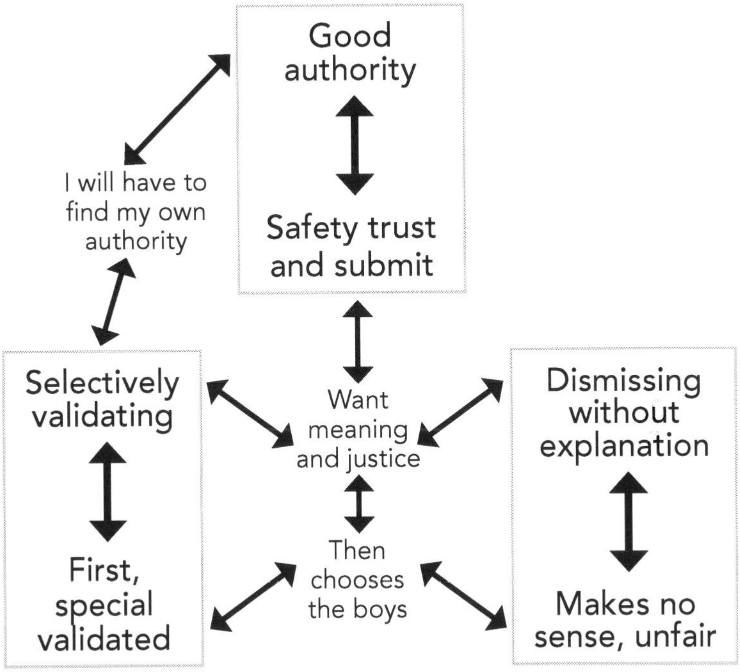

Figure 3.12

Stormy weather and messy moments of conversational awareness

Simon shouts at Janet: 'The weather forecast is wrong. I know those mountains.' They are talking about checking the weather forecast which Janet thinks is predicting a storm for the mountain walk they are planning the next morning.

'You're shouting.'

'I am not shouting; I am making my point. There won't be a storm.'

Janet suggests quietly, 'Let's check the weather forecast anyway to be sensible together'.

'You are doubting me. I have walked those mountains with my dad. I know those mountains; they are my mountains.'

'It is not about you. It is about us being safe,' says Janet and they fall quiet. Simon's bullying, entitled and self-important tone is intimidating. How he is talking is spoiling any chance of progress or understanding between them. Janet's need to have a voice is being brushed aside but so are their shared needs for a safe hike in the mountains. Janet says to herself, 'He has control issues. I am in trouble with this man,' and says out loud to him, 'You have not got a clue about what is going on between us have you'. Somewhere deep down in the soft underbelly of Simon's body these words from Janet cut through. He knew he was hurtful and violating a conversational ethic. He smiles like a naughty boy, but his need is for admiration from her – just as he would give it to his dad and his dad in turn would give it his granddad. Janet looks away from him, saying to herself in a quiet voice, 'why do I bother?' Their eyes meet for an instant and then are averted. They were stuck in a position defined by a role that Simon felt compelled to play.

There was though in hindsight a flickering moment of conversational awareness where they could have talked about the process, shared feelings and allowed a change in tone and roles to meet different needs. Simon looks at his phone. His problem and conversational poverty is a mix of his exaggerated entitlement to have an opinion and his deep well of disavowed male vulnerability. Janet and Simon both know his story. They have seen it replayed at the dinner table when they visit his parents for family gatherings. Simon is the youngest, they call him 'Tail end Simey' and point to the dining room wall with photos of older siblings graduating and no space left for Simey. He needs to bully his way past any vulnerability which he feels. The role awareness that Jane brings is that she was cherished and encouraged in equal measure by mum and dad but on condition of not making a fuss. Thrive but thrive quietly.

She is surprised when Simon says, 'I know I can be an idiot – all of the men in my family can be idiots'. He looks away from Janet when he says this. It is as if he talking to his own world rather than to her heart. It is like a practised way of soaking up criticism and any vulnerability in the moment by making it a fact of life beyond his control. 'Hey ho,' he says to himself. Simon can dimly sense he is hurting Janet and creating a painful mess in the middle of their conversation and their relationship, but it is external to him and that is better than it being inside him and him feeling all messed up.

Janet says with some annoyance and sarcasm, 'Let just go walking, I don't mind it if it's a storm. I love walking in storms.' Simon feels Janet's scorn and briefly again it touches an inner void. But he cannot get off the content hook of thinking about the weather. His body sends him a trauma signal from somewhere back in childhood 'I am hurting, what if I am hurting Janet?' He has a flash of shame, then guilt, but won't go near it because it would expose him to unknown emotions. He says to Janet, 'Okay you win [who's winning?, wonders Janet]. I will check the weather forecast.'

'No, no,' says Janet, emboldened and now trapped by her scorn. 'If you know the weather Simon, let's do it your way. I will remind you when we are freezing to death on the mountain tomorrow.'

The next day lost and in danger, sheltering in the mountains – cold and shivering they had an opportunity to go back over the conversation and map it out in their heads. Simon – soaked through without any waterproofs admits that he was an idiot and a know-it-all. His template of masculinity has him by the throat. 'I come from generations of men who know it all.'

'But you don't notice it hurting me and hurting us. It makes us stupid. Look at us soaking wet. And in danger. You don't talk to us but only to yourself.'

'I know, I know, I am an idiot. Beat me up.' Simon was beating himself up in a way that felt hysterical and fake to Janet and suddenly something clicked for Janet. She said, 'First you were opinionated about the weather and now you are opinionated about yourself being an idiot. It is the same. Your stories are always already storied and sorted, there is no room for a conversation about them. Whatever the topic – your family of great men, your stupidity – you make it all yours. I am always on the outside trying to get in. Even when you are apologising.'

Simon was silenced by the defiant eloquence (page 180) coming from Janet. She spoke on: 'There is no room for me, or for us. What would it be like to share a conversation with me rather than talk at me? What would it be like to share a conversation with yourself rather than talk at yourself? You would begin to have an interior life of your own with the world as it is now rather than ruled by generations of Dads. You would need to not know the answer and be willing to be lost and vulnerable and be open to the mix of feelings that have to be faced.' Janet then laughed with delight at her courage and its impact. (She felt she was breaking into new territory – a messy space outside her own childhood system of roles and outside of Simon's closed and imposing system).

Simon shivers in the cold and ponders, 'I don't know, I have never done that. Been vulnerable with someone. I guess it is in there inside me all the time.' His eyes reach directly to Janet's, and he looks at her as a person. They hold each other to ward off the cold. What Janet and Simon needed is not far beyond their reach. Both have areas of conversational poverty (see Chapter 9). They need to allow and connect with different layers and directions to their conversation. If they could have had the kind of mutual-aid conversation (as mapped in Figure 3.13) that they needed, they could have had some time in box 1 instead of being hijacked by Simon knowing best and going to box 2, thereby putting Janet in box 4. In struggling with the dilemma in box 3 of avoiding conflict or being challenging she ends up silenced and hurt as in the bottom end of box 4. Simon is both agent and a victim of a conversational poverty ('irritated and silenced' on the map) arising from the narrow relational world of his male upbringing going back generations in one form or another. In his turn he is inflicting his conversational poverty on Janet. It was a poverty that put their lives and their relationship at risk in ways that are all too common.

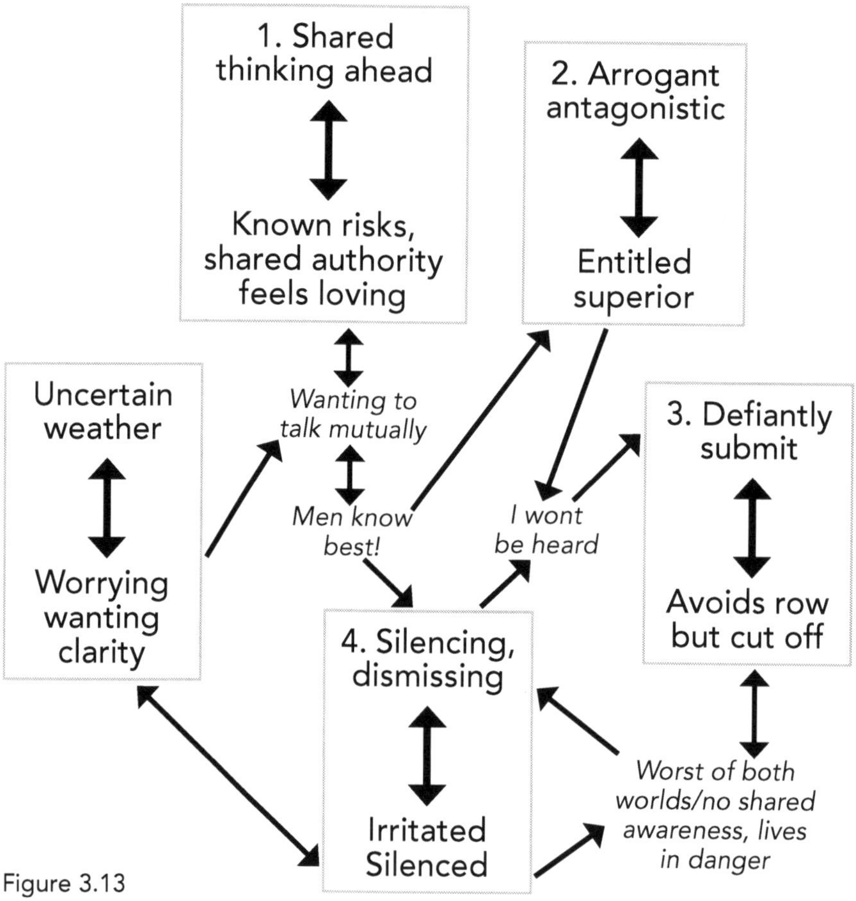

Figure 3.13

Chapter 4: Conversational story telling

Introduction

For this chapter, in the context of talking with a map think of stories as the product of conversations. Stories grow out of conversations. Stories need to be conversational. we need to tell and retell the experiences of our lives in story form in a conversational way. Making it conversational gives scope for the story to be told and remembered differently and for several aspects to come to the fore. Conversational story telling helps us sit with each other in among the multiple stories of our lives. They are open to be rediscovered, retold and relived when the story telling is conversation. The links and gaps become visible. There is the possibility of an open relationship between the story and the telling.

Some conversations become story telling relationships instantly. It is how they begin.

'Hi, what's new?'

'I cannot wait to tell you.'

And off the story telling goes until it is told, shared and ends.

Some stories are chopped off by the ending of the conversation before it is complete.

'Sorry I have got to go.'

'But you never finished telling me what happened.'

'Oh, another time.'

Other times there is no story and the proposal to talk is a call to relate and connect.

'Can we talk?'

What do you want to talk about?

'I don't know just things. Just chill.'

The conversation has to have the capacity to become the story. The masterpiece of a conversation which is the story is the widely acclaimed play by Samuel Beckett, *Waiting for Godot*.[23] The story of the play is the casual and compulsive use of conversation to help pass time until the mysterious Godot arrives (see Chapter 11, page 218 in this book for a more detailed treatment of the play).

In the opening chapter of this book the search for the missing baby and the conversation that was built around the search was both serving the need to be in an open and enquiring and validating conversation and to have a story to peg these needs on. In this way some stories are piggyback rides for the conversation in affirming companionship, or passing time, or establishing a pecking order. A piggyback ride is a temporary, empowering relationship. Within a conversational framework, stories can give each other piggyback rides as one story grows out of another. And conversations get piggyback rides on the back of stories.

We can tell stories in a plodding and closed way. Then it is hard to find a conversational quality to them wherein there is a sense of participating and negotiating our roles and involvement. There defining emotional and somewhat magical moments in conversational story telling when we are suddenly no longer outside the story talking about it, but inside it living and feeling moments of the story as an experience also interior to us. We are engrossed. Such moments need noticing and sharing.

All too frequently the conversational life goes out of the story, and we are talking at each other rather than *with* each other. There may be the appearance of conversation because there is turn taking, but like a group of friends telling jokes one after the other, there is not space for analogy and transference of feelings. It may be entertaining and meet a performative and group building need. Perhaps at such times there are hidden self-to-self conversation going on, unspoken and tacitly assumed like the conversation Mary had with herself in the classroom in the previous chapter.

A good story is conversational in the way Bakhtin[24] meant when he introduced the idea of the modern novel as novelistic (Dostoevsky as the prime example) which is to say, in the thick of the story, you are in the middle of several threads of plotlines and characters, and you are open to being surprised since you have some idea of the way the story could go but no certainty. Bakhtin contrasted this novelistic and dialogic form of literature with more monologic, epic or heroic forms where the plot is fixed, and you know the destiny of the characters and the morality of the story. This line of thought is pursued more fully in the final chapter of this book, with the example of narcissistic inflation of political ideas into fixed and closed stories which confuse and destroy a democratic conversation.

Mapping makes the story conversational

The art in mapping and talking is to hold the story and the conversation open to each other. The challenge when we are talking and listening at point 1 on the map (Figure 4.1) is to keep an open mind, and this involves keeping the conversation and stories going long enough to make links and see and feel gaps by hovering and shimmering (pages 117-119) between different feelings and ideas (point 2). This process is exposing and challenging (point 3) in ways that may feel good or bad, or a mixture of both good and bad at the same time. To share and discover we need some exposure and to be challenged but too much can shut us down or cut us off from each other. The process of mapping helps as a mediator of our need to have our lives sorted with stories.

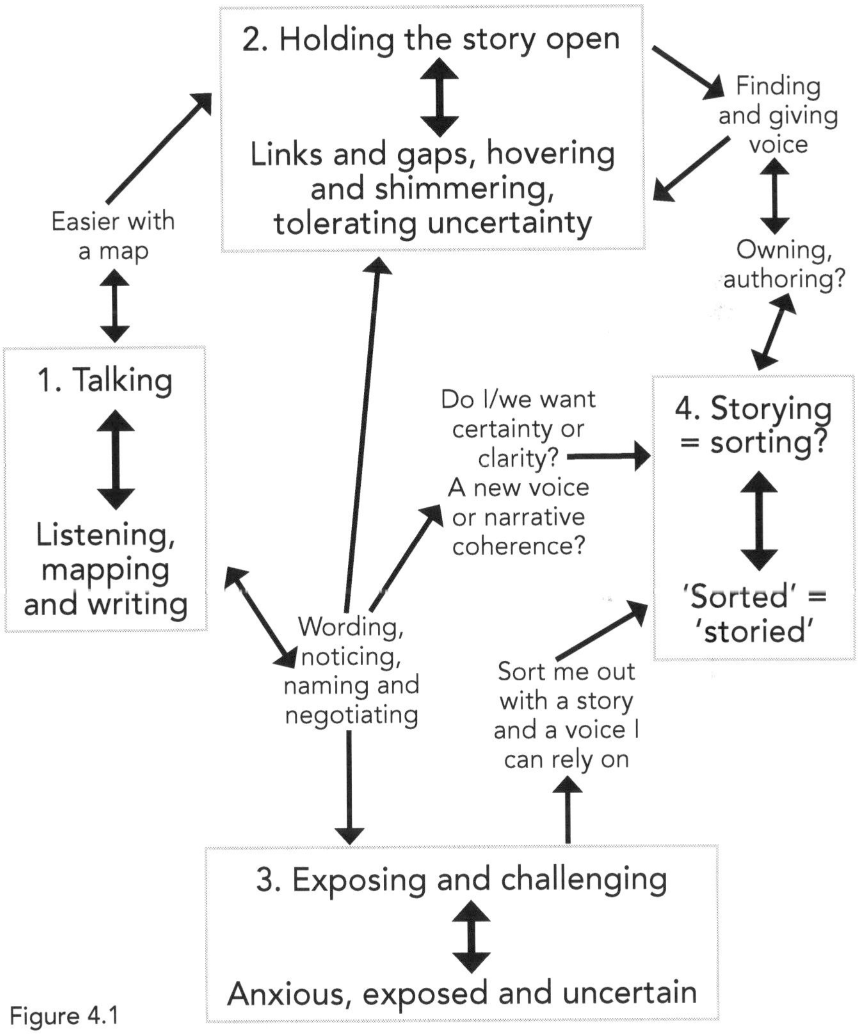

Figure 4.1

The role of mapping and talking, or of any conversation, is to do the three Ns (see page 122) of noticing, naming and negotiating together so that we can navigate our way through the conversation and stories. Most of the time this is easier with a map, and it is working to hold the story open while acknowledging the need to story the story and test or feel the benefit of something being sorted out because it has been successfully storied (point 4).

Tidying up a story and in the same breath tidying up a conversation too quickly around a story is one of the enemies of conversational awareness. 'I have got you; I know what you mean.' We do it through pressure of time but also because we have what might be an innate need for narrative coherence and to see things fit together.

We use Map and Talk to create a space, hold a space open for the words and the patterning of the story to emerge. Of course, eventually it must be concluded and storied. Our deep longing for narrative coherence (the story storied) bids us sometimes to resort to familiar narratives. It is surprising how much we hold on to bad stories or ones that limit us because they are familiar. The award-winning Nigerian novelist Chimamanda Ngozi Adichie warns in a popular TED talk of the danger of living by a single story.[25] Her point is that we are made of many stories that intersect. In the context of talking with a map we need a conversational approach to get inside and alongside the intersection of these multiple stories. At the other extreme, we are also at risk of being lost in among too many stories. Do we prefer to relate to a bad story out of fear of otherwise having no clear story at all? One way we hold stories open is by telling them repeatedly and each time giving ourself and others a slightly different relationship so that our interaction with the story and its meaning is slowly changing. Perhaps in this way we are repeating the familiar contours of an old story and clearing the path to a new story at the same time. Freud described this in his own way as the powerful compulsion to repeat the emotionally charged and unresolved parts and roles in a story to relive them in the therapy conversation in the hope of some escape from or unconscious validation of them.

The storyteller can run away with the conversation by 'holding forth', leaving no room for the person(s) who has now been cast in the role of silent (silenced) listener. In the context of therapy, I have called these dog stories (Potter 2020)[26] The conversation can undermine the story by having a discordant tone such as being cruelly light-hearted when referring to something tragic. There are endless variations on this juxtaposition of tone and content as actors, playwrights and comedians know only too well. They need to be noticed and indicated on the map. Mapping can helpfully interrupt a storyteller who is running away with the story or challenge banter or digressions by focusing on the features of the story. Of course, we may at times like the repetition over and again of familiar stories as they indirectly reaffirm roles and bonds.

'Have I told you this one before?'

'Yes, many times but go on, it is always worth a little run around.'

Some of the best television comedy is where the story keeps changing but underneath it is the same familiar plot, pattern or map of interaction. We map conversations to be ready to track the stories as they arise. 'Can I map out the main lines as you talk?'

'Yes. It will help me understand what is going on.'

Stories are more easily nurtured and held in the conversational roots and harvested for their wider meaning with a map than without one. Even without pen and paper we are mentally mapping the story. We are getting the measure of it; seeing where it has come from, where is it going and who is involved.

Links and gaps

In the previous chapter when thinking about how we are positioned, we are making links, but equally coming across gaps. Most of the steps to Map and Talk so far have been geared to tracking out links and getting the shape of pattern of interaction. We like our experiences and our relationships to fit together and make sense. That, after all, is the essence of a story. As just described, our tendency is to go for closure and get the story told and sorted out. But an important accompaniment to mapping out links and patterns from the conversation is to meet gaps. In terms of conversational awareness these are the blank spots and the blind spots rather the sweet spots or hot spots. When we make a link, we are crossing a gap and we should be equally curious about what is not connected. Gaps point to gaps in the stories of society and gaps in ourselves. They point to unstoried experience and the fragments of hurt that have never been figured out. They point to areas of poverty in our language and talk as explored in Chapter 9. It is moments when the conversational flow is interrupted, or things don't add up. Something is being denied or hidden. We have an ethical and political duty not to fill the gaps with cover stories and not to fudge the gaps but wonder about them.

The Shakespeare scholar Emma Smith[27] highlights the importance of gaps (she calls it gappiness) in plays such as Hamlet. The play has few staging instructions, and each director and actor can bring their own narrative to the events and richness of language in the play. Even then there are gaps which can only be filled either by the performance of the actors or by the imaginative participation of the audience each in their own way. Our appreciation of theatre, of music and literature and all the arts is partly through filling out our own patterns to join the dots and link the across the gaps. This quality of gappiness is at the heart of our best conversations too. We notice and seek to fill in the gaps with each other. We find and fill some of the gaps in our stories by being conversational, and mapping can give us some signposts and marker points.

Let's just stay with this idea of gaps for a moment. We like seeing patterns and they meet our need for a complete story and narrative coherence. Gaps are what is not noticed, named or negotiated and as a result not storied. Gaps may be pointed to by asides, looks and catches of breath. It is useful when following the lines of an emerging pattern to put down in the margin words 'to come back to' or words that point to another map or another pattern altogether.

The unique contribution of Map and Talk is to give external space and form to both the links and the gaps. The gap between naming and wording something and it being named and worded is a gap we can open further. Holding the process open is done with the pen and a capacity on the part of the mapper to constructively dither and not rush things.

Talking about gaps is a gentle and delicate process which touches our defences and difficult feelings. If at any time the mapping becomes an obstacle, it can be put aside, and talk continues in its own way. However, in such situations it can help to wonder what processes might be involved in making the mapping an obstacle as they may be symptomatic of other factors restricting the conversation or the story. Mapping should never be an imposition or a runaway machine. It is a tentative background process that comes to the foreground to recap and review the conversation. Tolerating gaps is a step towards tolerating difference. There are the links we make once a map of the current moment is visible and accepted. Does it apply to this element of my life, or does it have echoes elsewhere or in earlier life stage? Is it a pattern of relating which I learnt early and deeply in life or is it a local response more unique to the situation? These more detailed questions are considered in later steps.

Storying our own and others experience

Story is another word for pattern. In telling stories we are recomposing and reorchestrating experience. Our stories are patterns and maps of our experience. The templates in the preceding chapter give us room to range around the story in a conversational way and to see where it goes that is new in the telling of it. As we listen, we are listening for a pattern. Just as most fictional stories have a plot so most of our life stories have patterns which we can take from them. This is not always true. Experiences which have involved traumatic relationships and disorganised interactions may lack any coherent pattern or story. Even then we try to get some sense of the story by seeing a pattern to what is being recalled and described. It can be a challenging or revealing experience, and as in Figure 4.2 we need to be in dialogue as compassionately as we can between the storying and the feeling of something being storied. We need to open the story slowly with curiosity to help us to see links and thread them together in a narrative that offers a well-enough patterned story. With the spontaneity and immediacy of the conversational moment of mapping together it can feel like it is being mapped, told and storied for the first time. In one important way the retelling in this relationship with these words, currently, is a fresh telling. Retelling is reliving. We may tell it with the repetition of the emotions and roles of the experience in mind. I don't want to feel the hope or feel the shame again like I did. We may bypass the messy or shaming or confusing bits of the story. These issues are explored with much more attention in Chapters 6, 7 and 9.

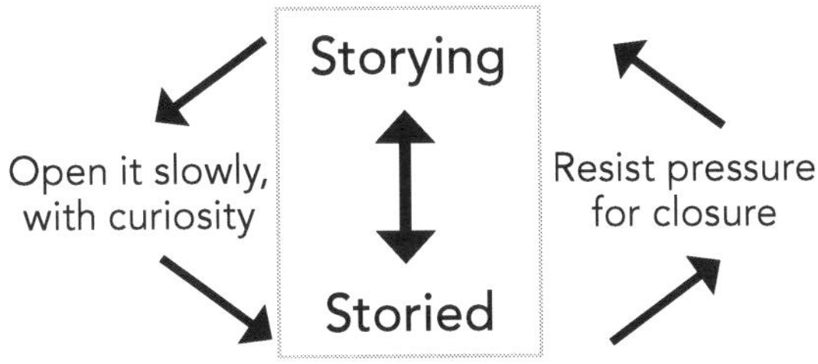

Figure 4.2

Templates can help the Map and Talk process

The chapter ends with two templates and examples that give a sense of how mapping can help keep a conversational feel to the experience of storytelling. The template map is more like a guideline. It is scaffolding for the story and the conversation and dissolve into the background once the map and the story telling relationship is established. Mapping templates can help shape a story and keep it alive conversationally. The same template can track out the content and the process of the story telling. Each of our stories and each of our conversations are unique but there are plot lines that have a familiar feel. We should listen out for their likeness but not impose them in a ready-made way.

Hide and seek with hopes and fears

This template has proved useful (in therapy and reflective practice teamwork) because it mirrors patterns common to many of our life stories at home or work, and it tracks the way our conversational storytelling struggles to make sense of events that carry within them a mix of hopes and fears, dream and nightmare outcomes combined with approaching or avoiding them.

The start of the *Hopes and Fears* template map is the box on the left. In Figure 4.3 there is something challenging me that I either face up to or avoid. It might be something going on around me or something being done to me. This template can equally serve as a guide to a group discussion. There is something facing us or challenging us. The bottom end of the box is the feelings I, or we, have in facing the challenge. (To work with this map, create your own blank version and fill in your own words in the face of a challenge.) We are likely to be in two minds (hovering and shimmering with ideas and feelings). In one mind we are hoping to get to the top box on the map described as 'what I want me or others to be doing if things are going well'. In this box it might be helpful to fill in the words for what 'doing well' might feel like. There may be several answers and the words on the map invite the conversation to explore the different responses and different ways of wording them. The push and pull and the call and response between doing and feeling described in detail in Chapter 2 comes in here. Also, the role reciprocations and responses described in Chapter 3.

Alternatively, we may fear and want to avoid the bottom box on the map wherein something is harming or hurting us and I, or we, may feel harmed. We are trying to catch on paper the shimmering and hovering yoyo between hopes and fears as we explore what we want and don't want.

Often, we are juggling the opportunities and risks between going for the good outcome and avoiding the feared outcome. In our conversations and in our storying of experience we may find the map helps us pinpoint the risky moments wherein our seeking of the good outcome is overvalued and overreached, and we are describing in the story and the conversation a fragile but desired place with the risk of being flipped or dumped into the feared outcome. Whether we fall to the feared place or not the anxiety about the fragility of the desired place may be the dominant element in our reflections on our experience.

In the top right of Figure 4.3 it can be helpful to name the extremes of what we really, really want as our dream outcome or the bottom right place what we really, really don't want as our dreaded outcome or nightmare place. This is the place that may only rarely happen but the fear of it dominates our behaviour. At the top it is evocative of a yearning for a magic solution and its role in the template is to see how this yearning helps (it motivates or inspires us) or hinders us (it stops us getting on with realistic activities or relationships). It could be that our dream place is so overvalued that, if achieved, it feels so risky and fragile and demands emotional attention and self-inflation to maintain (thereby taking emotional energy away from more routine concerns). There are many aspects of our societies that push us into this split position and for more clarification of how this can limit conversational and relational awareness see 'brilliant or doomed' on page 206, in Chapter 11.

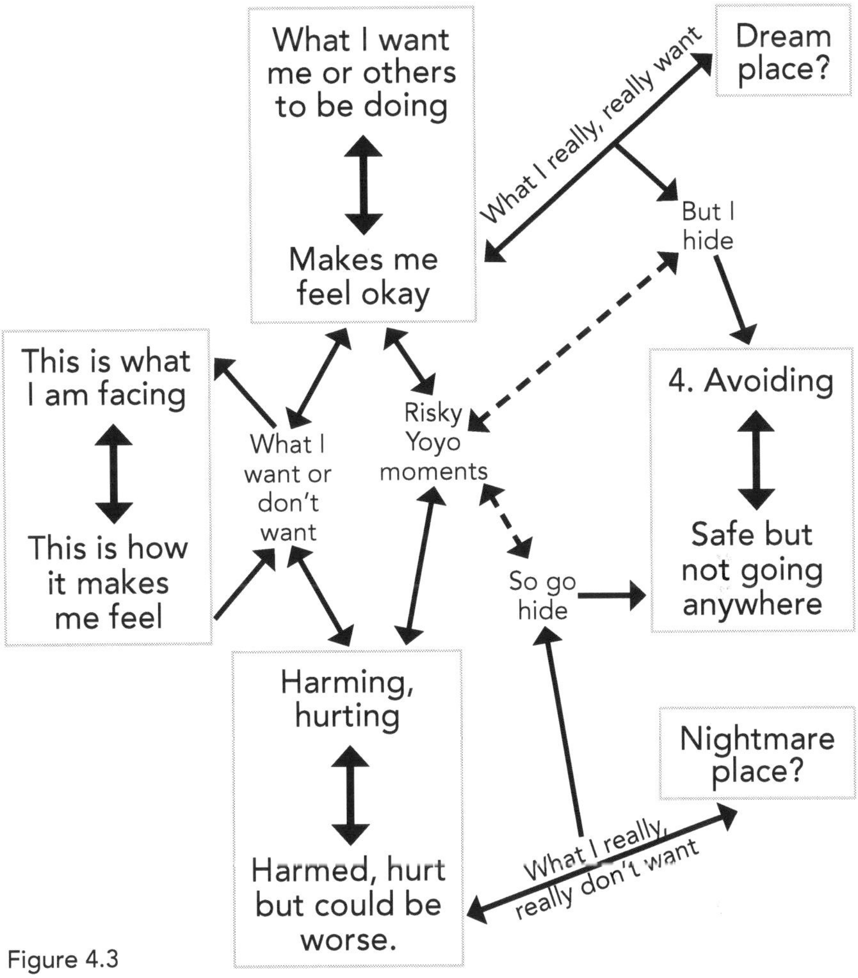

Figure 4.3

There is one further box on the hopes and fears template map. It refers to the hiding and avoiding place where we might hide from or feel safe away from the yoyo of hopes and fears. This could be a place where we hide from what we seek, and we can move this box around the map as we may hide in our dreams or nightmares or any number of more detailed patterns that might get written into the parts of the map. It may have been a place of retreat or comfort we learnt early on in life and while it worked in part in childhood as a desperate or the only available measure, its value now is less clear.

There are a thousand ways to avoid challenges. These range from putting things off, not thinking, having sour grapes. They all work in part to provide some temporary relief. Once we have found a good, safe place, we can settle there and take time out to figure out what the options are. The risk in being in the safe place is that it is also an avoiding place that provides comfort but limits exposure to the good things as much as the bad things. We may not get to balance realistic achievement or happiness against the dreamlike version. We may not get to test whether early fears of real danger as children are still the same now as adults. Or whether we still need the same response because we don't go there and both the extent of the threat of the 'nightmare' now and our capacity to cope differently now go untested.

Many conversations have an element of hopes and fears in them. With this template there is scope to work out the movement between extremes and to add in the seesaw between seeking to engage with the 'yoyo' between hopes and fears and avoiding engagement in search of safety, even if the price of safety is isolation or lack of involvement.

The sense of being inbetween a hoped for and feared place is a risky and potentially creative moment for self and others. It can be the hot spot or the sweet spot in our conversational awareness as we talk. It is the point where we need to be able to hover, shimmer and constructively dither to reflect on our inner choices and conflicts, the push and pull from others and the systems around us. Illustrations of the versatility and value of this template are on pages 10, 60, 116, 203, 232 and in the thwarted and hurt conversation of the couple in the example that follows.

The unhappy couple

A picture tells a thousand stories. Look at the picture of the couple. Let's call them Andy and Doreen. We want to help them by mapping out the conversation they have just abandoned, or the conversation they fear having or long to have. She is accusing him from behind the safety of the sofa. Is

Doreen fearful that Andy might switch from sulky and depressed to agitated and aggressive? Or is she holding herself back? Is Andy crushed by the world and by himself and despairing? What role is he taking? Is he hiding, withdrawing, passively rejecting and abandoning? Where does Doreen find space and dignity? What does she hope for?

Each viewer of this picture will see a different pattern of interaction. Doreen and Andy with help have the possibility of choosing and changing the conversation. What map emerges will come from the couple trying to talk together or separately about their feelings, perceptions and needs. There are many individual stories for them condensed into this moment. As much as we want to relieve their suffering the key benefit of map and talk might be an increase in conversational awareness and or a decrease in the conversational poverty within and between them and with the world around them.

We, as partners to the discussion with a map will bring our own perspectives of gender, social injustice and what might or might not help and who might respond to help. The process of mapping can partly help us not get in the way of their thinking things out together.

Going around the map in Figure 4.4. it might start at the bottom of box 1 with Andy speaking of how he is feeling shamed and worthless by Doreen's indignation, demands and criticism, but even more by those coming from within him. At the same time, for Doreen, the finger pointing at Andy is a cry for action and connection but also an attempt to get away from feeling the despair that Andy is embodying in his slumped position and putting onto Doreen. Andy feels useless so sinks into himself and in a self-effacing way, as in box 3, ignores his partner and his own inner feelings. Doreen feels ignored but senses or fears it could be worse and guides her behaviour to avoid a more dreaded nightmare place where either or both of them might be out of control and affected by unmanageable feelings. To cope, Doreen hides in her familiar place of box 4 feeling neglected and sad but relatively safe. In both their minds is a lost yearning for the top box 2 of respectful recognition and care. On the one hand Doreen feels that challenging Andy is the only way to get his attention to make some moves in that direction. On the other hand, she and Andy hold it in mind passively as a dream of care and love that could be recovered if circumstances were different.

The importance of roles mapped out in this way is they can show that what others do to us now may have echoes in what others did to us in childhood. If one of my parents was always threatening me and insulting me then feeling threatened and insulted would become a way of being for me. It would be my role and my template for the world. Most importantly and painfully it would be how I treat myself in my internal conversation and it would quite likely be what I would expect as treatment from others. I may even elicit it or find the comfort of familiarity in it, however painful. It becomes the only conversation I know about intimacy and care.

An additional value of mapping a story with this template is it helps create a space between the dynamics of the story and the dynamics of telling it. The person telling a story of yo-yoing between hopes and fears is also likely to relive the various emotions involved and equally the listener (as the mapper)

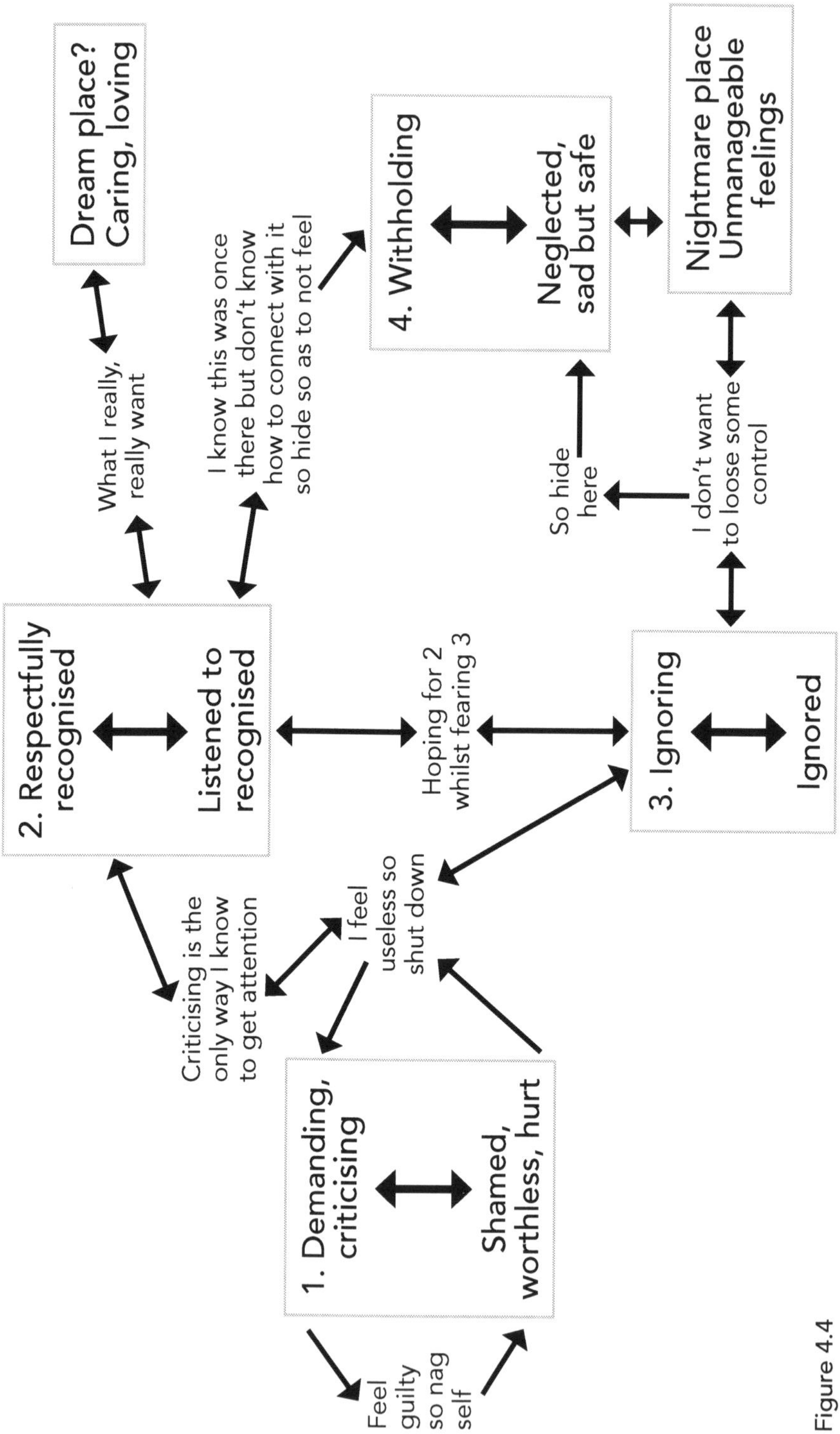
Dream place? Caring, loving
What I really, really want
2. Respectfully recognised
Listened to recognised
I know this was once there but don't know how to connect with it so hide so as to not feel
4. Withholding
Neglected, sad but safe
Nightmare place Unmanageable feelings
So hide here
I don't want to loose some control
Hoping for 2 whilst fearing 3
3. Ignoring
Ignored
Criticising is the only way I know to get attention
I feel useless so shut down
1. Demanding, criticising
Shamed, worthless, hurt
Feel guilty so nag self

Figure 4.4

is likely to get caught up. If the mapper can use the map to notice and name the push and pull of his or her feelings in the story, it can be a possible model for Andy and Doreen to be open to new ways of responding and talking. The mapping activity helps both be involved and somewhat able to be detached at the same time.

One of the roots of this way of thinking is the work of Mardi Horowitz[28] who talked of desired but fragile states of mind (if they are achieved) and feared states which may be dreadfully avoided.

Loving, inspiring and validating

In the context of parenting, education or mentoring, it can help internalise the positive and empowering elements of conversations to have a template that tracks patterns in stories of caring, inspiring, delighting and validating. Or the parts of a story that have these qualities playing in and off each other. In Figure 4.5, box 1 starts with attentively caring and the recipient of the care feeling attended to and cared for. The map helps wonder if the child or mentee internalises the external care and attention and gives it to themselves. It may depend on taking in the other positions on the map.

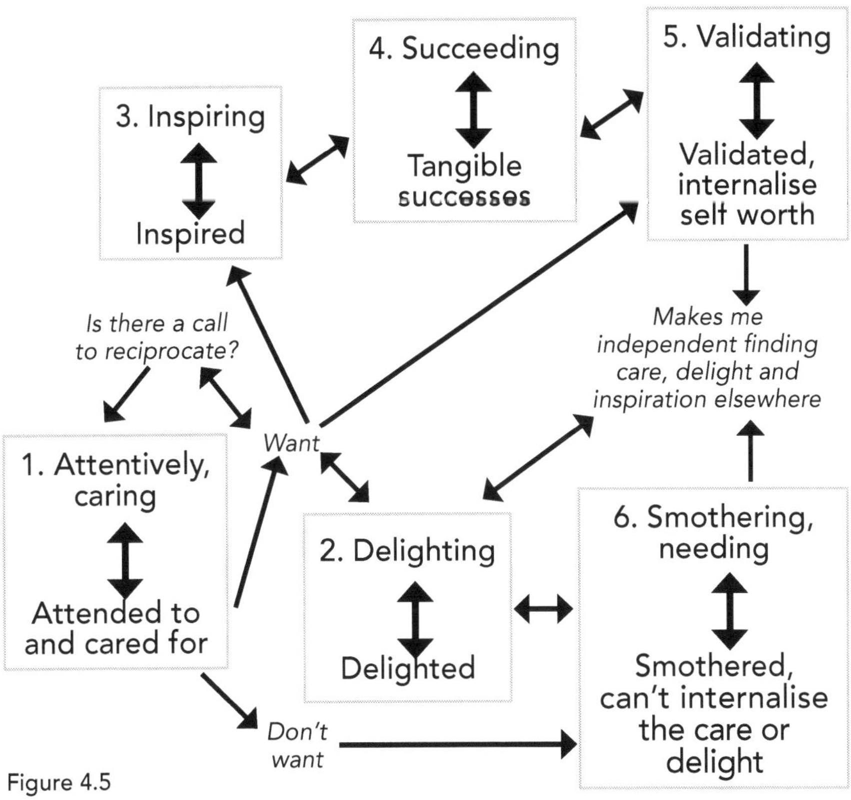

Figure 4.5

The challenge is for the inspiring figure and ideas to be within reach and able to bring tangible success and validation. Often boxes 3, 4 and 5 on the map are entangled and assumed to be one single loving and caring emotional role. Separating them out makes it easier to take them in their best proportions. We may need validating even if we don't succeed. Or we may feel smothered and deceived by an excess of 'false' validation if we don't feel we have succeeded. The base note of delight in box 2 which we hope for at the beginning of our adventures in life may always be needed. As any parent, partner or mentor may know, the delicate task is to separate patterns of delight in box 2 from feelings of being smothered (box 6) or performing to succeed and be validated for the sake of the caring and inspiring 'other'.

Bill's risky moment

As you read Bill's story see if you can make a map of a reflective conversation with him using the hopes and fears template. Make it in your mind's eye or with a pen. I have put some words in italics that I think Bill and I might find have resonance if we put them on a map to help see the patterns in the story. You might highlight other words though.

Bill was talking about a moment when he was at risk of beating himself up. We later called the map we made his risky moment map. He had started talking hopefully about where he wanted to be with the job he was doing. He was busy making a kitchen unit for a customer and it was not just any kitchen unit but the first sign of him branching out on his own and working for himself. His wife had made him a website. He was tired of his work 'jobbing' as carpenter for a large building firm.

We used the hopes and fears template (4.4) to as a reference to map out what he would be doing if things were going well. He had said 'getting the unit built on time' and that he would be feeling good and feeling proud. His wife was being 'encouraging and supportive' which on the one hand he valued but he hid his self-doubts from her and was terrified of 'letting her down and failing'. He was in the thick of it. He could feel the sense of achieving something in the air. It was within 'touching distance'. He put his hand on it on the map. His risky moment would be getting stuck. He was waiting for the preferred worktop material that had not arrived. He expected it two days ago. Why was that 'risky'? I was asking him. He looked blankly at me. 'Because I would get behind and I would beat myself up. I would feel stupid.' Bill said that stupid is a familiar place.

We wrote out a paragraph to take away for the sketchy map we had created of the conversation. The paragraph went like this: 'I cannot wallow in feeling stupid. It is as if when I get into the risky place, I cannot tolerate the uncertainty, so I kick something to provoke a crisis to distract myself, beat myself up and fog up how other people can respond. I started telling my wife the work top is not good enough. She said I should compromise and use materials I have already got so you can get things finished.'

This short paragraph when he read it out helped in finding a reflective voice outside his anxiety and his voice that was dismissing of his own worth. He got the job done on time and to his surprise, the couple he was doing it for were exceedingly grateful. They loved the different colour of the worktop even more. The customer that was hard to please was the one inside his head. The real battle was not with their criticism, which didn't exist, but with his anticipated failings. He could see how knowing and sharing the pattern in his story with his wife or with others could soften his internal critic. How we talked about his story and how we reframed it as a story allowed us to stand apart from it.

Joe turns the tables

Joe had a 'zero hours' contract working in a bar. He'd had lots of bar jobs and people said he was good at it. He was a conversational barman. He could chat, banter, and lend a sympathetic ear when needed.

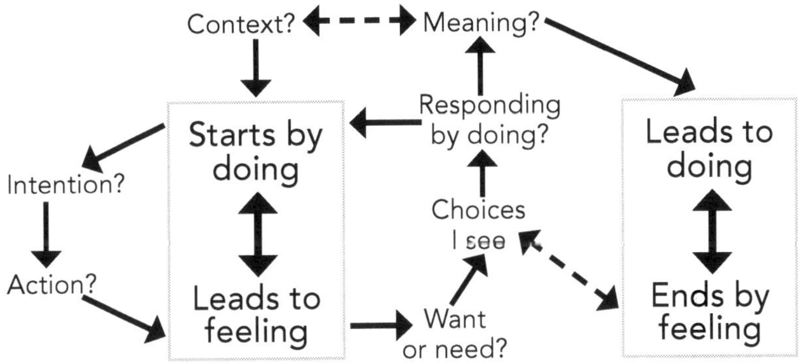

Figure 4.6

His story and our Map and Talk discussion (following the template of Figure 4.6) began with him describing the start of his shift the day before, in the early evening at the quiet time. As we talked Joe knew that my plan was to keep track of the conversation with a spread of words on paper to help us listen to his story and get to the heart of things. I drew a margin down the side of the paper. Joe saw me put 'quiet weekday, early evening' in the margin in small writing. I didn't think it was going to be the main point of the story, but I wanted to have it in mind. 'That's just background context. I am listening out for how your roles got negotiated,' I interjected, as Joe continued talking.

'So, there I was checking the beers were on tap and cleaning up a bit more and Frank, the manager, comes over and says he is letting me go. "When?" I ask. "Tonight," he says.'

Joe looked at me. His voice was indignant as if in that moment of sharing the words and remembering the experience he was reliving it. He repeated, 'He was getting rid of me.'

I wrote down 'Getting rid of' in the middle of the page and put an arrow down from it. In my mapper's mind was the following run of questions. If this was the action what was behind it? What was the manager's intention? What was the reaction he expected from Joe? And what in fact was the emotional impact and how did that show in his expressed feelings and the way of coping? Whether I need to ask these questions in a plodding way or not (they are surely in the air between us) depends on how the conversation goes.

The impact for Joe, as he remembered it, was that he felt stunned and gutted. Joe thought Frank's motives were to save money while business was slow but also to keep his friend (another barperson) in a job rather than Joe.

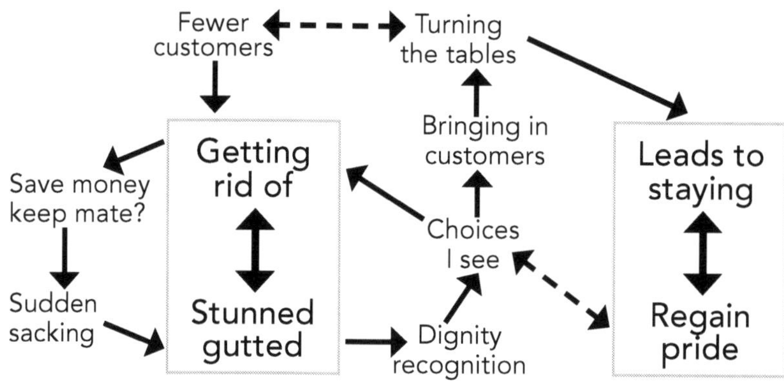

Figure 4.7

The context can be a pointer to many factors leading to the action. Joe may talk of many things, but the skill of Map and Talk is to initially track the threads of one story on paper. What is relevant is how Joe appraises his choices of response to the impact on his feelings (stunned and gutted). What does he need or want? What options does he have? Is he aware of what he needs or wants or is his response carried out on automatic pilot, or driven by a need deep inside him from previous similar experiences?

Joe looked at me and then at the emerging map for a response and says, 'What was he doing? Getting rid of me without a care in the world.' Joe sounded angry and indignant and prodded the words on the paper between us. It was as if he was talking now to the paper.

'I wanted my dignity back.' I wrote down dignity and recognition. We discussed other ways of responding ranging from retaliating, walking away and dwelling on it fruitlessly. This led to Joe to see choices of negotiating with Frank rather than being stuck in the stunned and gutted role. Joe explained to me that he told Frank that he would be mad to sack him. That he really loved this place. It had a vibe. That he knew how to get the customers in and spread the word. That he knew so many people and can draw them in. Joe told me, 'I pleaded with him and sweet talked him. I thought I was crazy. What was going on? I should have walked away but I turned the tables.' I put down the words 'turning the table' as his response to 'wanting my dignity'. He touched the words on the map as in Figure 4.7.

'Did I turn the tables, or did I lose my dignity?' Joe asked reflectively. I said, 'Well maybe the map can help us. Let's just recap where we have got to with the map of your story. I wondered out loud if turning the tables was a way of not getting angry or storming off. We put the words 'getting angry' and 'storming off' as the path not taken. Joe said, working his finger around the map, 'Well, that would have just made me more stunned, and I would end up sacking myself'.

Joe continued, 'Frank went away and then came back later after one or two customers had come in and said as an aside to Joe that they would keep him on, which made Joe smile and Frank wince. Frank then said sorry which surprised Joe.

How does the mapping help the talking with Joe? It helped him see that he didn't rise to Frank's bait and get emotional and turn on himself by sacking himself. He found it validating and gave him a wider perspective that might be useful in other situations. 'I was not confident Frank could be influenced, but I knew that the worst-case scenario was I would have got some of my dignity back. Even if it had not led to staying, I would have with some pride rather than self-blame.'

Chapter 5: Managing a session of talking with a map

Introduction

The book so far has introduced the methods of Map and Talk as a way of developing conversational awareness and talking well with each other. Now the focus is on how to set up and manage a Map and Talk session. While mapping can come into any kind of talk however casual and improvised, the focus in this chapter is the kind of discussion intent on building a capacity to reflect on how the conversation is going. This could be for a variety of educational, therapeutic, organisational, welfare, political, civic or creative purposes.

One ever-present chicken and egg question is 'are we making a map of the conversation or making a conversation with the map?' The answer is alternately both. Sometimes the conversation leads, and the map follows, and other times the map leads, and the conversation follows.

Map and Talk can be a constructive and helpful companion to the conversation. It puts the conversation in view whether for fifteen minutes, half an hour, an hour or more. It can be more, or less formal and structured in its arrangement. It may be a one-off discussion or part of a series of meetings. It may be a chance to stop and reflect on business as usual, or it may be an open exploration of personal needs and values which feels like a step out of the ordinary. In using the mapping process to focus on various topics of conversation we are never far away from checking on how we are talking.

'Let's Map and Talk' is a way of saying 'Let's have a more reflective and thoughtful discussion.' Even before any words are shared, or put on paper, the participants have a sense of an intention to take each other seriously.

Map and Talk can use pens and paper at a table, or on our knees, side-by-side, one-to-one. Or it uses flipcharts and white boards as a group. In the era of and after COVID, and talking online, there are ways to share the process of mapping and talking with a second camera, virtual white board or holding the paper up to the screen. Even without any of these resources, it is surprising, when working remotely, how useful the unseen, offscreen process of mapping out the conversation is as a source of evidence of thoughtful and active listening.

It is the immediacy and spontaneity of moments of mapping that is valuable. With the pen and paper, we see some of the words just voiced on paper between us and can touch them (and visualise making links and moving words around) and at the same time be touched and moved by them. The layers of meaning, analogy, metaphor that are part of any conversation are mirrored with the words on paper and the circles, lines and arrows separating and linking them.

We start by agreeing and staging some rules and ethics about how to talk. We then focus on what to talk about and begin talking about it. Mapping helps keep track, sometimes on two separate pieces of paper, of what we are talking about and how we are talking. Here are some tips in setting the stage for a conversation.

Give the conversation a title or caption (a chat about life, a reflective practice meeting for the team about X. A neighbourhood group meeting). For first efforts at mapping, work with someone who has had some practice but if this is not available then it helps to start with someone who you trust, value and enjoy talking with.

Whether it is two people, five people or twenty, the process of mapping and talking needs introducing, owning and leading by someone. There is a leaflet on what to expect from a Map and Talk session to download at www.mapandtalk.com/downloads. The person offering to be the mapper needs to be willing to take a hand in navigating and noticing the process of discussion. Sadly, we are often wise after the event about the direction a conversation is going. Mapping can bring moments of choice of direction, tone or pace more quickly to mutual attention.

Like any deliberative and personally creative activity it needs framing with boundaries of time and place where it is safe to talk. It needs time to get into the spirit of talking openly and time to wind down and reflect on how it helped or not.

Don't start learning to Map and Talk with your nearest and dearest, tempting as it may be. There is likely to be too much at stake and not enough mapper independence or neutrality.

Remember that the aims of Map and Talk are modest, and the process is messy. Don't try and make a beautiful map, just one that gives some pointers to the conversation. It can always be tidied up later.

Checklist for a Map and Talk session

- Agree a time and place.
- Give the session a working title.
- Agree how long for and rules of joining and leaving.
- Agree terms of participation such as confidentiality, mutual consideration and co-operation.

→

- Agree any rules specific to the context such as only for community business, team building, sorting out finances in the marriage, or exploring the meaning of life.
- Share welcomes and introductions and gather items or topics for map and talk.
- If just two people, agree who is mapper and who is talker. If more than, also agree who are the main participants in the chosen topic for map and talk, especially if the group is too big in number for all to take part.
- Make elements of this chapter available for reading.
- Agree to take time at the end of one round of Map and Talk to review the process and assess progress and benefits or setbacks.
- Reflect on how the session went: share lessons learnt, and chances missed.
- Agree ownership, anonymity and confidentiality or use of the map if to be kept.
- Go to the next Map and Talk item or discuss if wished for or needed for another time to talk in this way.

The steps to Map and Talk as detailed in the previous three chapters are not like steps on a ladder just going in one direction, but more like steps in a dance where there is room for variation and improvisation of movement back and forth. There are videos of each step on the Map and Talk website (www.mapandtalk.com).

The terminology used is *Mapper* for the person or persons doing the mapping and *Speaker(s)* for the person, or persons, doing the talking. There will be times when the role of mapper and the role of speaker will be so fully shared that it is experienced as both mapping and talking simultaneously together. This applies whether the mapper is helping the speaker explore a personal concern, or both partners are mapping and talking about a common issue each with their own take on it.

Initially Map and Talk is a division of roles. One person is the talker while the other is the mapper. In time, the mapping and talking roles are shared and the parallel between turning taking in conversation and turn taking in the mapping helps create shared ownership of the content and the process of what is being discussed.

The methods apply equally to talking as a group, or facilitating team building, sharing feelings and ideas, conflict resolution, creative work or reflective practice alone involving self-talk. Map and Talk can track complex interactions as an observer or researcher and one application of Map and Talk to teach yourself can be to track a novel, play or film.

The mapper's role can vary moment to moment: from being an outsider to the conversation listening in with the map; to being more like an interviewer participating in, guiding and shaping a reflective conversation with the map; to using the map to draw out the patterns of interaction in a specific moment, incident or story; or using the map to help discuss the relationships in the immediate process of the conversation. The ability to be looking out from the inside of each other's experience in a heartfelt and mutual way is the test of the helpfulness of the mapping process.

If it is a one-to-one session of Map and Talk, or with a small group of up to eight, then themes and stories to map may emerge spontaneously from the discussion. With a bigger group the moment or incident to map might need more staging following some preparation to decide what to focus on. With work teams doing reflective practice, as illustrated in Kirkland and Marshall 2021, chapter 6 p80, there is a pre mapping phase of gathering topics or incidents to Map and Talk about and then a choice of one or two. There is scope for groups to Map and Talk around a theme such as well-being, decision making or conflict resolution, or consciousness raising and sensitivity training around issues of racism and sexism.

Who is taking part?

If it is one-to-one, then explain how the mapping may help with listening to and shaping discussion. Your aim is to try it together and see if it works for the two of you. The role relationship may well be quite clear. One person is talking and exploring what they want to say and how to say it and the other person is listening actively and compassionately and figuring out how to respond helpfully. There are two people creating a listening relationship and going over past stories to make maps that crisscross with life experiences in the present.

If it is a small group that can gather around paper spread on a table, or even more informally with a young group on the floor, then the aim is to find a focus on one key story or incident. Be a bit insistent on sitting down so you are all sitting around a big sheet of paper (flip chart size) and can all see the map the right way up and reach out and touch it. Small groups can make most progress mapping the discussion of a moment or incident. The power of the mapping arises from enabling the group to see local patterns and draw general parallels.

A third alternative is that a couple or small group (partners at home, or work) are talking of shared feelings and ideas with someone in the role of mapper as an **outside facilitator**. This compassionate outsider role is familiar to a lot of therapeutic, consultancy or advisory work. The Map and Talk process allows the outsider to be a participating observer and get involved enough to feel and empathise with what is going on but to stay detached enough to see another perspective or level of thinking. They may more easily notice parallels between the stories being talked over and the way of talking about them.

If a larger group of more than eight and anything up to twenty or thirty, then there needs to be more structure and clarity of the purpose. The focus needs to be on mapping a moment shared by all that points to patterns in the current work of the team. The experience of mapping several such moments over time with a bigger group, such as a hospital team or a sports team or community association, is to build a culture of conversational awareness as described in Chapter 6. Not everyone needs to take an active part to feel actively involved in the process. Everyone, if they are paying attention, is learning how to use the mapping process and how a reflective and conversationally aware team discussion might feel.

One way of working with this is to break everyone into small groups of seven or eight and appoint one person from each group to convene or chair the meeting and one person to map the topic or incident and a third person to map the process. This structure need supervision and choregraphing but can work well in giving a pathway to linking personal experience with overall elements of the culture of the team and the organisation. It is important in such a context to not be looking for solutions or addressing crises but facilitating a space for shared thinking about the organisation or team as a whole. It can be evaluated pre and post using the Conversational Awareness Measure[29] and checklists such as the Helper's Dance List (www.mapandtalk.com/downloads).

A fourth alternative is the training context where mapping and talk is being learnt by taking turns to try out and gain skills as in the example of Speed Map and Talk on page 111.

Finally, there is the use of an experienced consultative mapper who is mapping for and with an individual or group as part of their professional role such as a psychotherapist or reflective practice facilitator.

Allocate and demonstrate the roles

In learning to use Map and Talk it is best to allocate one person as the mapper. It is more along the lines that the mapper is the helper to the conversation, but the ownership of the conversation belongs to the main speaker or speakers. If there are more than two people a third person can be the process mapper and their role is to map and track how the conversation is going. With a larger group it can help to have two people leading the mapping activity. One may be more in the role of chairperson or facilitator or conversational host and this frees the second person up to focus on the mapping. A trap to avoid in this context is that the mapper becomes invisible only popping up at the end to report on what they have mapped. This may happen sometimes, but the important purpose of the mapping is to visibly track and shape the conversation in consultative and helpful ways as with the example of Sally on page 17.

The mapper needs to be clear that they are mapping a conversation or story and it is not a map of the person or their strengths and faults. It is not an assessment of someone. It is in support of adding layer of discovery and self-reflection and as described on pages 115-119 of hovering and shimmering between different positions.

If a bigger group, it is better to have a white board or flip chart on a stand. There is an example in the section on applications at work on page 17. With a group bigger than twelve it is essential to find a smaller group who will be active speakers and who are the main actors and voices of the story or incident being focused on. The remaining people stay silent for this round of mapping and talking in the bigger group, and they can be given the role of mapping the process of the conversation. They may be listening to what is talked about, but they need to pay attention in this moment also to how it is being discussed. Finally keep an eye on the seating or standing arrangement (so everyone can see the map).

Agree rules about how to talk to each other

Be kind, be interested, take turns, help speak, show compassion and curiosity, make time, respect privacy and keep confidentiality. Model social awareness and sensitivity to differences in power, confidence in and entitlement to speak. Don't let one voice or one style of speaking hog the limelight or control the culture. Affirm house rules about confidentiality, trying to connect and showing good will, taking turns. Allow time to recap and review the map you have made and the mapping process that made it.

The conversational rules for Map and Talk are the same as for any discussion. Show interest and respect for language. Build on each other's words. Pay tribute to moments of finding words that resonate and move you. Agree to keep the boundaries of time and place and role. Aim to be considerate and attentive and share responsibility for seeking and maintaining the best quality of conversation. Tolerate getting entangled and losing track of where things are going. Negotiate where to begin the discussion and give time to reflect at the end. Give time to talking about how the conversation is going as much as what it is about. Seek to work side by side and be mindful that how we are talking with each other is an echo of the conversation going on within ourselves. Acknowledge moments of intrusive awareness of the wider context: the thinness of walls; the limits to how emotional we can be; the sense of judgement about what we are saying from the surrounding society, politics or local culture. Help each other find words that are resonant enough and strong and free enough to help. Date maps when you make them and include the initials or ID of the group, individual and context. Check what to do with them at the end of the conversation. They belong to speaker(s) and mapper. Acknowledge disagreement about what to do with the map. If its work is done it can always be confidentially disposed of.

Learn to listen together with the map

Mapping as we talk is an engrossing and shared activity. It is not talk and then map but talk with the map as the reference and guide. The map is there to aid the process of listening. Talking and listening are intertwined, one cannot work without the other. It is a joint activity. It is an invitation to listen together in a process of shared reflection. It is an active three-way process wherein both speaker and listener pay attention and see what they are saying through the medium of the map. We can tell in the most subtle and hardly perceptible ways when someone is not listening to us. Mapping with pen and paper of any kind can be a signal of the serious intent to listen. It gives a sense of honouring the conversation and shared responsibility and answerability. It is a sign of intending to hold the conversation. Listening depends on memory and unless we have a very good ear for language, we quickly lose the local colour and meaning of what someone is saying. It can greatly help to map and track the significant words and phrases such that they become part of the shared memory and scaffolding of the conversation.

Map and Talk can be introduced as making 'listening' maps. 'If I just put words down to keep track of the conversation it will help us see where we are going.' You are not making a map of the person speaking, but of the conversation which you are having, and the stories being shared. Every time a conversation is assisted by pen and paper it makes the process of listening more visible, more accountable, more democratic and tangible. The implicit patterns and structures shaping the conversation are drawn out by the explicit mapping on paper.

When listening with a map, the aim is to track the conversation and not to dictate it. There are times when the mapping is going on without any overt reference to it by the mapper but both the person or persons speaking can see the words going down on paper without being remarked upon. Even so they can have a quietly containing function for the conversation and allow the flow to continue.

The map may be an external source of reference to review and change the conversation. In a group someone wanting to speak or hoping to go against what they see as an unhelpful flow to the conversation can use the words on the white board or flip chart to make an interruption. Such a three-way relationship between individual or group, conversation and map can make interpersonal differences and conflicting ideas more manageable and easier to negotiate without it becoming too personal.

Love of paper

Don't overlook the power of large sheets of paper. Paper is such a brilliant invention. It is available, portable, unobtrusive (notice if it does become intrusive) and versatile. Paper is such a cheap and familiar technology we don't remark on our relationship with it. Before mapping and talking, even if only talking with yourself, reconnect with paper as a tool. Feel its texture. Try writing a short spontaneous letter to it. Dear Paper, you have always been part of my life and now I am going to use paper for making word maps of conversations.

Paper or white board has several uses in map and talk. It is a space between us. A space for externalising. It is a projective space for our conversations. It is an extension to short-term working memory by helping hold in mind over time. It can organise, contain, hold, sort, and be a sounding board.

Having an A4 or A3 sized sketch book to hand is a great statement of intent to practice mapping and talking. I always have a sketch book or folded up sheets of A3 paper with me. A smaller sketch book can travel with you and be the record of brief moments of figuring a pattern to something by talking it through with yourself or others. Or doodling on paper to see if there is any pattern to different words, ideas and feelings that on are on your mind. Getting them out on paper can help turn rumination into a more tangible and visible conversation with yourself. Here follows a list of actions that can help build familiarity and confidence with map and talk.

The margin and the frame

Once mapping and talking is underway, we draw a margin line down one side of the sheet of paper so that there is a small area for background notes and ideas for maps of other topics or stories to map. The margin line does several things. It creates a space for memory joggers and background information. It gets you putting pen to paper, and it signifies that the main part of the paper is going to be the more worked out map of a moment or story. If the person offers to give a little background or context to what they are talking about then you have room inside the margin to put notes.

If you are working one-to-one and sitting side by side make sure you are on the right side of the person if you are right-handed, or the reverse if you are left-handed. This is because you want to make a shared open space of the paper between you. If you are right-handed you are going to put the margin line on the right side, so all the blank space is between you and your mapping partner.

Gathering a picture sharing the landscape

The shape and focus of a conversation varies in many ways. Some start with a focus and a clear rhythm and open up, lose momentum and then pick up steam. Others lack focus at the beginning and roam here and there. Slowly or suddenly a key incident or story emerges and the focus goes to that.

Conversational mapping has to follow this freedom of speech to roam. It might be that the process of mapping is nothing more than putting down key words spread out on paper or on the white board. The mapper is not looking for a pattern but creating space a on paper between words for a possible pattern to emerge.

Recap with the map

Recapping is an active, multi-layered and collaborative form of listening that is only possible with a map. It involves going around the map to check for shared understanding of what is being discussed. Every so often the mapper walks his or her finger and pen around the map, showing their understanding, checking for connection and agreement and reviewing progress. It is an active and containing form of listening using the map as a scaffolding for retelling, rethinking and revoicing or rewording things. It is using the emerging map as a listening aid. It allows the mapper to share, test and negotiate understanding and check if the discussion is going in the right direction. Recapping brings immediacy and is an open invitation to have second thoughts, hold different views and share mixed feelings. New words may be found, or new connections made. If the mapping is only as good as the conversation it sustains it might more precisely be said that the mapping is only as good as the recapping that flows from it.

Recapping is mirroring or echoing and hopefully enhancing the listening and reflective process that is going on all the time. It is a moment of seeing, saying and touching through circling, highlighting, underlining or crossing out words. The mapper is using the ideas of hovering, shimmering and constructively dithering. Where words resonate, we are inviting moments of integration between the brain's mapping networks where new thinking, new narrative, and new shapes to the map can emerge. It is not a race for closure but a process of working at understanding while nurturing a new conversational relationship of holding, exploring and recovering new feelings and meanings. Recapping pays attention to new connections and feelings and is a process of conversational discovery. In this way recapping becomes part of a reflective and developmental approach to the conversation. It can help see where a pattern or story is developing and open it up further.

The activity of recapping builds our skills and our capacity to be relationally aware and reflective. This ability, which is initially assisted by mapping, becomes part of a conversational style and generates a more open-minded way of talking and a negotiator's stance to the conversation rather than an opinionated or avoidant approach. The Map and Talk work is a joint effort and its visibly messy and unfinished feel can be jointly owned and thereby reduce the pressure and anxiety on the mapper to produce the goods.

Recapping can bring attention to the relationships involved in the process of talking. If just one person is talking it can help them keep in mind distinct roles, they are playing or different parts of themselves. If a group, the same applies but also the different group roles and interpersonal positions can be expressed or touched upon with the map.

Recapping is when one or more patterns and links between different positions may more clearly come into focus. Though also the blank spaces on the map are also part of the recapping. They may point to things not said or thoughts not had.

Recapping may also be a moment to check notes in the margin and to wonder if there is another story spinning off from the one currently and actively being considered. With experience the mapper may habitually make two maps, one which focuses on the story or content of the conversation, and one which focuses on the process of the conversation.

Choosing when to recap is every mapper's dilemma. Do we wait until it can come naturally with a pause? Or do we interrupt the flow of words? Recapping is best 'nodded to' and named for its part in the conversational process when and as it is done: 'Sorry, I might be interrupting but can I check where we are on the map.'

Recapping may be different at different stages in a session of talking with a map.

First phase recap. Words spread out on paper help ask the question: is this what we are saying? Is this where the conversation is going? What are we missing?

Middle phase recap. As a map becomes established the aim is to consolidate the co-creativity, co-ownership and awareness of the conversation. Recapping may lead to detours into other conversations around other stories, pauses for reflection on the conversational relationship and each and all of these may be a prompt for new maps on new pieces of paper or revisions and extensions to the existing map.

Ending phase recap. It may help to do a special recap by audio or video of the shared understanding of the words on the map and the conversation they point back to. The mapper or the talker might start the reflective commentary at the beginning but sharing and taking turns giving voice is important). The recap needs to be clearly addressing the microphone or phone and to be mindful of naming where the recording (especially if it is only audio) is referring to on the map. Care should be taken to not name names or give details that might be a breach of confidentially if heard by chance by someone not involved.

Mapping the process

Mapping can sometimes make it difficult to talk, so keep checking if it is helping or getting in the way. If the mapping is not helping then stop, but also take time to wonder how the conversation was going and what unhelpful part the process of mapping was playing. Reflecting on whether to map or not can help reflect on the management and ownership of the conversation more generally.

In every conversation there are ways of building confidence in working between the surface and the depths or what is visible and hidden. One option when learning to Map and Talk one-to-one is to have a third person quietly mapping the process between mapper and talker. There will be overlap between the two mapping activities but what is striking is the act of listening to and mapping the here and now process which often has a different 'music' to it compared to the music of the story being told. For the 'process' mapper, it is hard not to be pulled into the content of the stories. At the end of the mapping of a story and after the main mapper has recapped the story with the map, then the process mapper can share their observations of the interactions between mapper and talker. The process map might have some push and pull of roles and responses as detailed in Figure 5.1, though as with any of the depictions of maps in this book, it is not remotely so tidy. Such feedback often brings new insight into the main map and content and of the discussion. Those who have experienced this three-way mapping exercise have found it a very useful way of listening the process as well as the content of a conversation. Working in threes like this can be a great way of building confidence by repeating the exercise and rotating roles so everyone gets a go at each role.

If only two people, another way of mapping the relationship between us is to use two pieces of paper, one for the story emerging from the conversation and one for the process.

As confidence and skill develops there will be moments where shimmering and hovering will bring recognition that the way we are talking is already on the map of what we are talking about. One or two common examples highlight this. If I am telling you about an experience where I was very anxious and uncertain and felt under a lot of pressure, the way I am telling it and the way you are mapping it may also be anxious and uncertain with a hidden pressure to get it right or meet the demands of some invisible hand. Or if I am telling you about making light of some of the setbacks in my life and - when you show compassion - I then make light of your concern, then the maps of what we are talking about and how we are talking are resonating with each other. It is an opportunity to see the map as a mediator that can build confidence in talking about the here and now relationship between us whilst also tracking what we are talking about.

Chain of responses in the process of tracking how a conversation is going between two other people

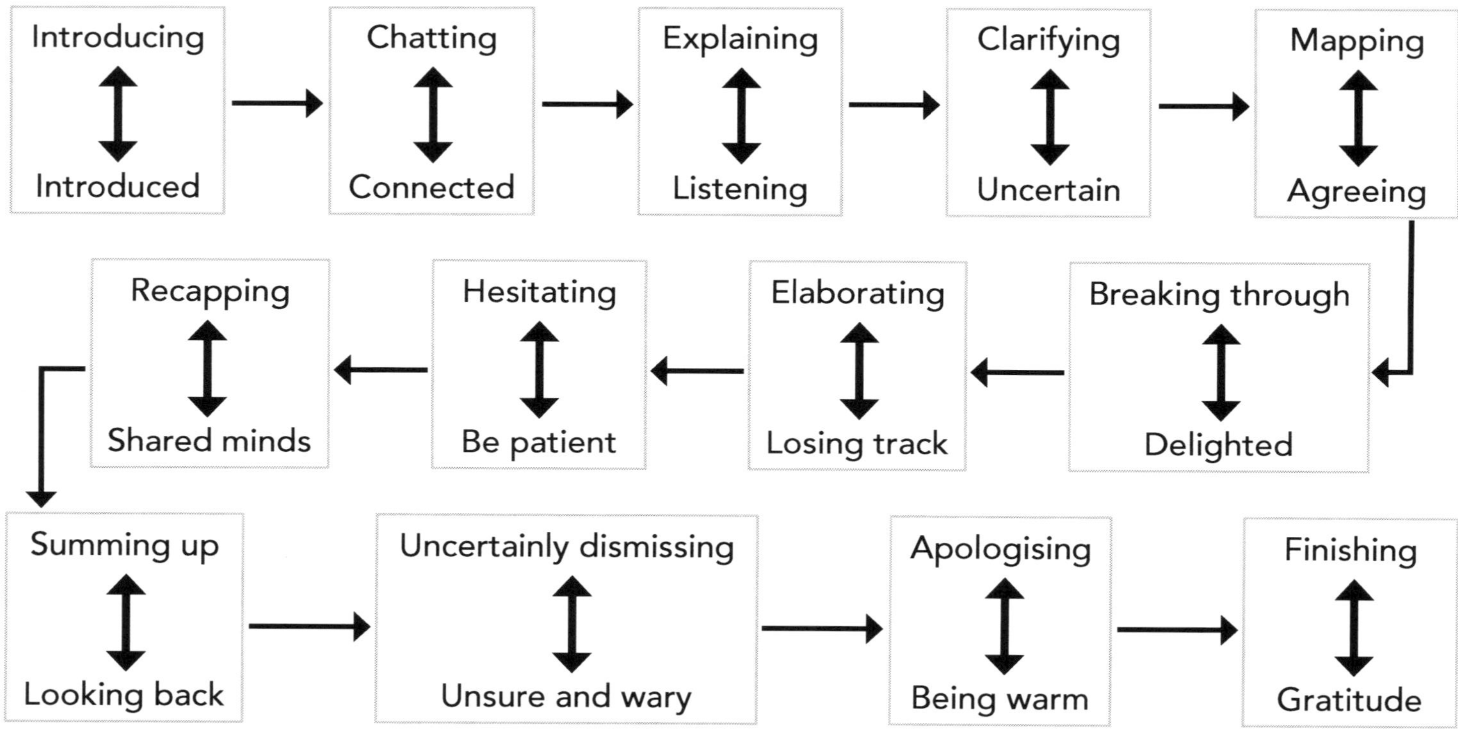

Figure 5.1

Mapping moments of shared awareness

Regardless of what we are talking about we had better also talk about how the conversation is going. Lots of factors can make a difficult conversation more difficult. Noise from outside, lack of time or privacy, a conflict of personalities, doubts about what to share or what the benefits of talking may be.

So, what is the mapper listening out for and how is the process of putting words on paper going to help the listening and the flow of the conversation? Won't it get in the way? Will it make the conversation feel contrived? There are moments where the triangle between what is being said or about to be said and what is on paper or about to go on paper brings the conversation into a mutual here and now awareness. These are moments of tangible, visible listening from the inside of each other's experience. It is a moment of shared subjectivity. Having a feel for these moments is as important as getting the map made. Indeed, just saying 'is this a mapping moment?' may help the reflective side of the conversation be recognised.

Make it ordinary and special moments will come

Be modest about how you think the mapping might help. If it helps the conversation along it is a success. If it helps the conversation stay open to different feelings and ways of thinking it is a success. If it feels like mapping has oiled the wheels rather than get in the way, it is a success. There is no need for trumpets and prizes. The mapping process is not the story. The story of the conversation is the main story. It won't matter if the map is forgotten or is left behind once it has done its job.

Don't look for stars, certificates or badges in doing Map and Talk. Each time is a fresh beginning and depends on the mapping partnership. If you gain confidence in using Map and Talk don't fall into set ways of doing.

Recording and ending

A key to conversational awareness is taking account of what was discussed and how it was discussed using Map and Talk to help record and remember it. A final recap with the map is a basic way of recognising and honoring the ending of a conversation. It may lead to some reflection on the process and some mapping of that may be both brief and beneficial. In the two-dimensional grid of Figure 5.2, the vertical axis marks a line between more keeping a map as a record of what was discussed to more trusting to our memory and letting the conversation go. Asking whether it is helpful to keep the map or trust the memory of it can help the reflective process. What are people taking away or what can be done to remember the map and return to its theme the next time if part of an ongoing conversation? The horizontal axis is from discussing and managing the ending on the left and ignoring it or overlooking it on the right. The latter can happen 'more-often-than-not' because time has run out with a group and the meeting is breaking up. The top left quadrant might be judged as the ideal, in which a record is kept, its purpose and value and content is discussed, and it helps contain and manage the ending of the session. The bottom right quadrant is the one to avoid, in which the discussion is trusted to memory and the ending is overlooked and ignored. This is too casual and won't build trust the next time that group or individual enters a Map and Talk conversation. The bottom left quadrant is one that might bring interesting reflections on the contribution of Map and Talk to the session. Perhaps the map did its work, and the many lessons will be taken and remembered. The top right quadrant is a more common institutional and bureaucratic outcome. A record is kept, the map becomes part of an archive, but the ending is not negotiated. Where does that leave the people who took part? There is something problematic about the power dynamics in this outcome and the choices and implications for ownership and record keeping of the work done is important.

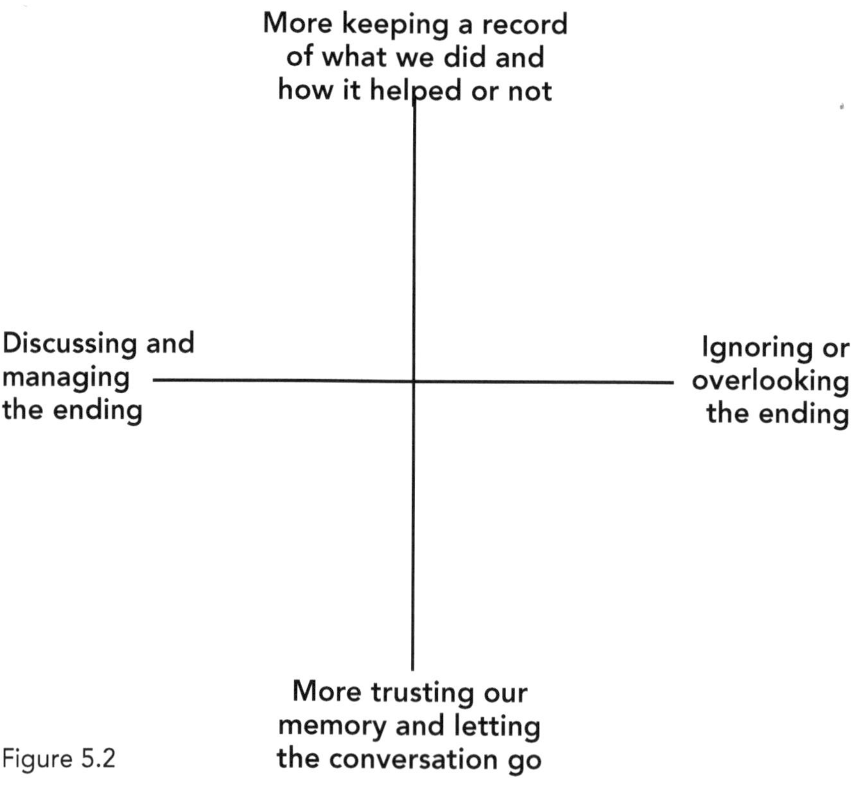

Figure 5.2

Personal reflective mapping guidesheet

Once a day, take some time to sit down with pen and paper and have some private conversational thinking time for yourself about work and life in general. Mapping takes time to become skilled. Just like learning to play the piano or learning to drive, it requires some practice. While mapping with friends and colleagues is one obvious way of practicing, mapping alone can be a resource for self-reflection and our 'inner' conversations. It might not work every time, or for everyone. Try it. Here are some pointers to what to do.

1. Sit down with a pen and paper.
2. What's been going on? Reflect on the day and the times and places involved. Make a list at the side of the paper of some of the events. Choose one that interests you and give it a provisional name or title across the top of the page.
3. You are aiming to make a sketch of words like in Figure 5.3. Start where it starts in your memory. This may be with someone **doing** something or you doing something. Try and capture it with a key verb (a doing word) in the active present tense.
4. Then think about what you, or others, were **feeling** because of that action. Write the feeling words at the bottom of the box as in the diagram. You might work with the feelings from your own perspective or from others involved. Ultimately you are hoping the mapping process will help you hover and shimmer in and out of different perspectives. This is one **'doing and feeling'** hub or hot spot on your reflective map and others may be added later that contrast with or connect with it.
5. Where it says 'Intending' write what comes to mind about the **intention** behind what was being done. At the same time fill in the words for how you were **managing or coping** with the feeling (at the bottom of the box).
6. Finally, what did you do as a way of coping and managing the situation? You might spell this out in terms of looking back at what you wanted or needed and how you evaluated your way of coping. Did it increase the core feelings, or distract from them, or make you 'join the dance' and be at the **Doing** end of the role relationship between doing and feeling?

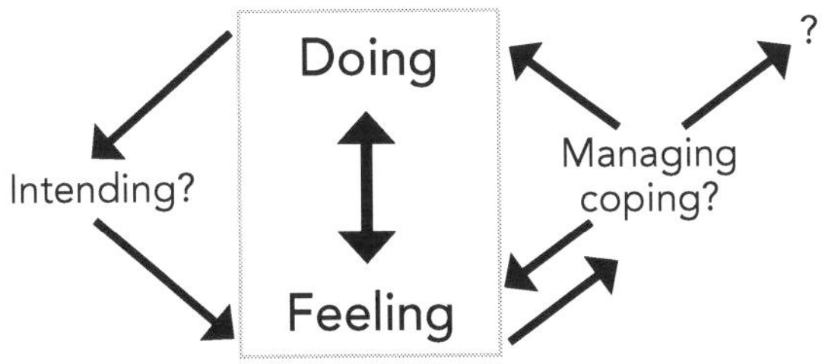

Figure 5.3

7. Keep in mind that the words on paper are showing the links but are like pieces of a jigsaw puzzle, waiting for you to free associate with the words on paper and uncover further links to add as steps towards some narrative coherence for the time being. Think about the people involved by adding pronouns 'me', 'you', 'them' to locate the possible interpersonal source and direction of the actions and feelings.
8. Go back over the words you have and talk it through with yourself in search of qualifying words (adverbs, images) that give context and colour to what you already have.
9. Make it messy, cross things out (you can make a tidier version if you wish at the end as a way of having a final reflection).
10. Remember it is the reflective process and it is your inner conversation that matters not the neatness or the brilliance of the map.
11. As you reflect and recap, change the tense of verbs from passive to active or past to present to loosen the feelings involved.
12. It is okay to feel confused – sorting them out on paper is the assistant to sorting them out in your head. With this reflective mapping we are untying knots of memory where the feelings, actions and ways of coping are tied up and entangled with each other. For example: **doing** = trying to a get job finished; **feeling** = under pressure, stressed; coping or **managing and coping** = finding distractions to take my mind off the pressure.
13. Use the hopes and fears template to see you move from one feeling to another. The template starts at box 1 and the challenge or task we are facing and the feeling it gives us and what we hope for and strive for (box 2) and what we fear and try to avoid feeling (box 3). In our hoped-for place there is always a longing for a dream place that is idealised (helpfully – because it inspires us, or harmfully – because we stretch and fall for something beyond our reach) and in contrast a nightmare place that we would do anything to avoid experiencing (shame, destruction). Box 4 is our 'safe and relieved bystander but limiting place', where escape from hopes and fears comes at the price of perhaps being stuck and not involved.
14. As you reflect with the map, listen out for feelings and gestures of good and bad evaluation through self-praise or self-criticism. Or reactions of frustration, detachment or engagement and excitement. Flag them up where they occur on the map as you talk your way around it.
15. Stop the journey round the map at points of connection and insight. The mapping process is helping you develop relational thinking. Your approach is conversational with yourself; the event being remembered; and the words on paper. You may have insights after a few seconds or minutes of mapping. You are not completing a task but enabling moments of open dialogue with yourself and your world.

A template map for navigating our hopes and fears as we talk or reflect

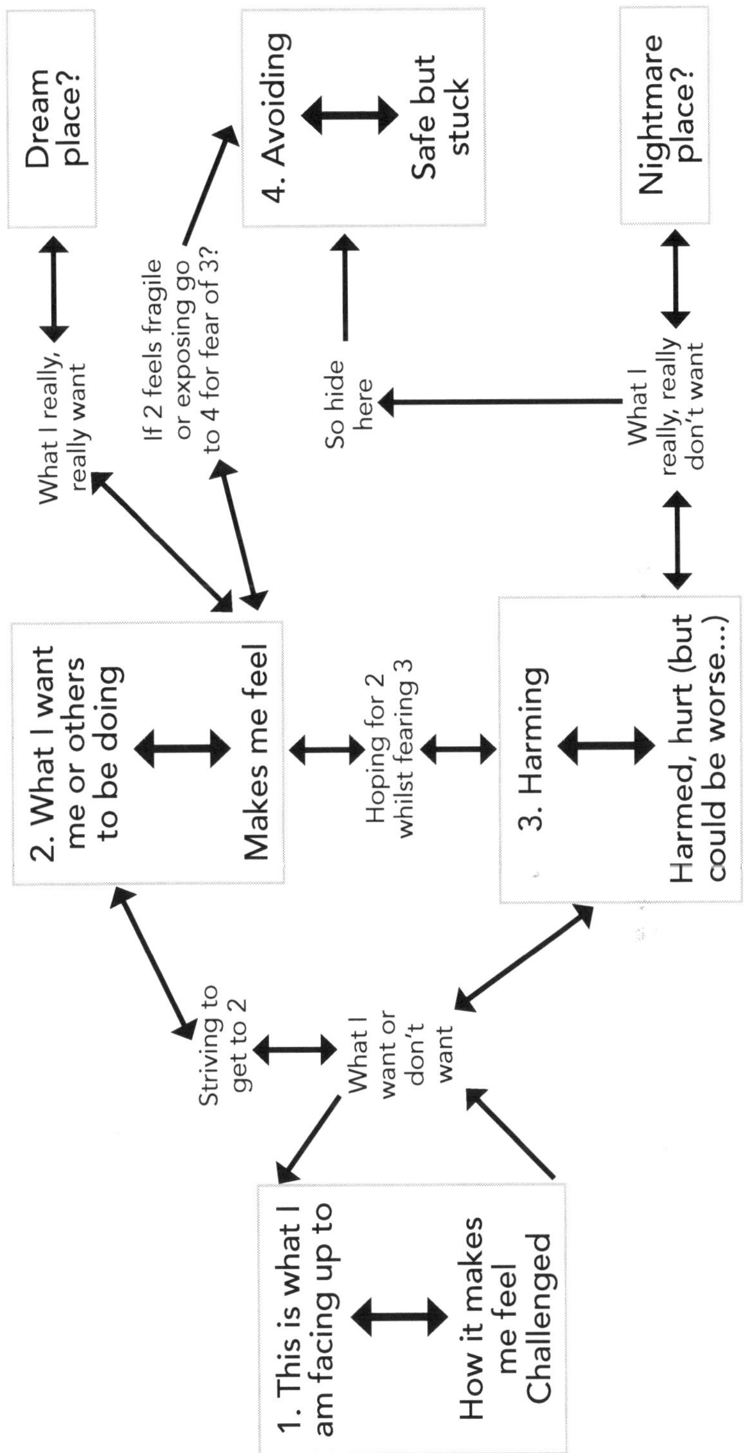

Figure 5.4

16. Don't judge the quality of the map but the quality of the dialogue with yourself. You can stop mapping as soon as your thoughts and feelings are flowing. You are extending your working memory with the words and the map on paper. It may be easier to follow your memories and feelings as they arise. You may make a connection that otherwise would not occur.
17. Before you finish with one sketch go around it again with your pen or finger and see if any new connections come up. Circle words that matter, add arrows where you see links.
18. In a single mapping practice session, you may just do one map of one event or several maps of several events. You can save the maps (date them if you do) or destroy them.
19. At the end, reflect on what you have learnt from the process. Write a note/short letter to the map for yourself. Try not to look too much for conclusions or solutions though they may appear. It is more about extending an open, compassionate and curious conversation with yourself.
20. Remember you are just a beginner, and you always want to stay a beginner ready to learn afresh each time. Or a map of one event may be the outline or template for other experiences. Don't worry about mapper anxiety, that is normal. Perhaps it is the anxiety of taking our thoughts, feelings and reflections seriously.
21. The test of these few minutes of mapping is: did it help you reflect? Did you see another point of view or tolerate mixed feelings? Do the links between doing, feeling and coping in this compassionate and curious process of self-reflection link to other memories? The mapping process may help work out the steps to the interaction and what is coming from you and what came from others.
22. Finally, be kind to yourself and talk to yourself in a conversational way with the map. Don't go where you don't want to go and seek help from others if something troublesome touches you. These guidelines are part of learning to map in reflective and open ways with yourself and others. They are not a manual for self-care, treatment or self-improvement. They may help, just as thinking things over may help, but each of us has to test out the possibilities of self-reflection with a map and judge its merits for ourselves.

Try having a deliberately good talk

In the same spirit as the preceding guidelines, try having 'a deliberately good conversation' with someone you trust and get on with. Prepare for it by choosing a time and a place. Use big sheets of paper and pens to keep track of the talk by mapping out the key words and drawing out the patterns of interaction in the conversation and the stories that are shared. Once you get into the flow it should offer layers of conversational awareness that help work out what the ingredients of a deliberately good talk are. Hopefully as you talk you will forget the deliberate aspect of the good talk and be talking mutually and spontaneously. However, keep an eye on the deliberate and aspirational aspect of the talk just as you would if deliberately trying to cook a good meal. Reflect on it with the map as you go. What were the ingredients that helped it be a deliberately good conversation? What led it to faltering or going wrong? What did you do when it hit a sticky patch? Did you forget yourselves at times as you were absorbed in the conversation?

Practice in small groups

We only learn anything if we practice and mostly, we only learn in practice with others. A great way to gain confidence is to practice with small groups of four or five around a table with a big sheet of paper that all can see, touch and add to. Choose a moment or event you all have some interest in and knowledge about. A safe starting point is to map a discussion about a celebrity you all have some knowledge of or a political incident or fairy tale character, for example Cinderella. One person volunteers to take the pen initially and start mapping. It is important to begin mapping a moment such as Cinderella working away and build the story outward from there. Another person could be quietly making a map of the conversation as it develops and share this at points during the discussion as described on page 101 in this chapter.

The map is a scaffolding for the conversation in the spirit of figuring it out together. This quality of openness means that the process of the conversation will be talked about as much as the content. In this context an ally is not someone who agrees with your view, or the view emerging on the map, but the person who can hover and shimmer between different feelings and ideas and bring another perspective.

Developing skill in mapping comes from watching and copying each other. Gaining confidence in mapping comes from practising until a point is reached where putting words down is an automatic extension of the process of listening. We are listening and developing a shared understanding with and through the normal rhythms of a conversation such as body language, eye contact, queries and interruptions, with the map as a shared memory space. Don't make a big deal of it or be controlled by the idea that there is a right way of doing it. Let the rhythm of talking and mapping come naturally. When mapping is embedded in the conversation it is akin to the pauses for breath we do as we talk and the punctuation we use in writing.

Make friends with mapper anxiety

It was the great contribution of Lev Vygotsky, a Russian psychologist in the 1920s and 30s, to point out that we internalise the relationship as well as the skill when we learn something with someone. The parent who was overanxious in their behaviour when teaching their child to use a hammer to bang in nails teaches the child to use the hammer with anxiety.

In developing a reflective practice approach based on Map and Talk with teams we soon came up with the idea of mapper anxiety. This is the anxiety the person in the main role of making the map feels about getting it right or wrong or ending up with a mess or not getting going with words on paper in the first place and there is so much worrying about what words to put down they don't give their full attention to listening and get lost. The description of mapper anxiety in the chapter on Steps to Reflective Mapping (Potter in Marshall and Kirkland 2021) is as follows:

'Just as there are first time nerves when learning to ski or play the guitar or be a parent, there is what we have dubbed mapper anxiety. This anxiety may be more than an anxiety about being a good mapper or getting the map right. It may also be a signal anxiety between those taking part that something important or troublesome may be touched upon. The mapper needs to befriend and tolerate his or her anxiety because it may be the key to being able to hover and shimmer with the uncertain process of working with feelings in the moment or feelings that are being transferred onto the activity of mapping. If the anxiety can be tolerated and such traps as perfectionism, doing the mapping for the person, or putting the mapping off or dismissing it as a conversational aid can be avoided then anxiety can be an acceptable and integrated part of the process of reflective discovery.'[30]

The important point is to let the mapping help us do the listening. The mapper is not digging for some hidden truth or showing brilliant interpretive or therapeutic skills. They are tracking the essentials of the conversation. The interpretations and discoveries of new meaning will come from recapping the conversation with the map and getting to the heart of whatever story or stories are emerging from the conversation.

One source of shame is that what we write down, if it is not polished and perfected, it will be criticised, echoing the shame we might have anticipated or felt as children in school for not being neat or tidy enough with pen and paper.

All our conversations can make us anxious whether we are mapping or not. It is hard to sustain goodwill and we can be unsure. We get snappy, or we are sarcastic. This is not because we lacking in analytic ability or the capacity to be articulate or an absence of the gift of the gab.

The worst conversations can be so fluent they are pat; the best conversations are sometimes painfully uncertain and searching. Sometimes caring for others is attending or waiting for something to become clear. Simone Weil[31] makes the point that we are often waiting when we are listening. Mapping can help us tolerate this process of waiting. Some silences in our conversations can be mystifying and impossible to decipher in the moment, and persecutory for either party. The potential of the map is to track where we were before the silence and where we might go back or forward as a step to making sense of the silence and returning to it.

Speed Map and Talk

Speed Map and Talk (originally known as speed supervision) has been used as the backbone of two-day introductions to CAT methods for would be therapists, experienced clinicians, in patient teams in mental health, nurse specialists in cancer care, counsellors and psychologists from different professional settings and ways of working, people in different countries working as specialist teams or learning to be CAT psychotherapists. Now, many years on, it has changed the way I do therapy, teach and supervise people. For me, and for others, it has endorsed the central importance of joint activity, co-construction of meaning, the co-emotional, embodied experience of minds working together using, words, hands and gestures and the tools of pen and paper. It involves a tolerance of not knowing together where the exploration may take us but trusting in the spontaneity of the joint activity of mapping as a companion to the talking.

Speed mapping with changing partners is a lively way of developing skills in Map and Talk. It involves a group of people meeting regularly and working in pairs and swapping roles of the one doing the mapping and the one doing the talking. The talker takes his or her map done in the first ten-minute session to a new mapper and goes over the story again. After another ten minutes and with a more extended map the talker goes back to the first person they mapped with and spends ten minutes sharing and comparing what they are discovering. There is value in the map as a product of the session but there is more important attention to be given to the process of consulting with and being listened to by two contrasting people. The group convenes in between rounds and at the end to share lessons and experiences and the exercise is repeated with a reversal of roles. It needs an hour and half with eight to sixteen people and a facilitator and timekeeper. One variation of speed Map and Talk is to have a third person in the partnership who is mapping the process of the Map and Talk session and feeds that back to the Map and Talk pair at the end. A detailed description of how to do speed talking can be downloaded from www.mapandtalk.com/downloads. It is a useful guide to conducting a variety of sessions of learning to map and talk.

Conclusion

This book is written from the perspective of the person or persons mapping a conversation with each other or for others or for themselves. The more it is a joint activity the better. The mapping then mirrors the side-by-side quality of the conversation. We may take turns or be mapping for a group. If there are intense or troublesome relationship difficulties, mapping needs to be in the hands of a third party who is trusted by all and neutral. And before any mapping can help, the agreement to talk compassionately, curiously and openly needs to be affirmed by all who are taking part.

Map and Talk has grown out of individual and group therapy practice, out of teaching and supervising reflective practice in teams and consulting with groups. Workshops are available either online or face-to-face. It can be tried on a peer group basis or with an invited trainer to work with an in-house team or community group. The details of short courses are available at www.mapandtalk.com/bookings. For links to an evaluation measure for Map and Talk and for a pre and post Conversational Awareness Measure go to the research page at www.mapandtalk.com

Chapter 6: Conversational awareness

Introduction

The methods of talking with a map point to conversational awareness as a leading benefit. This will now be explored in more detail. This chapter is in two parts. The first part lays out the details of a conversational awareness grid or matrix of sixteen elements. These make a framework for developing an imaginative engagement with the multiple directions, lines and qualities of our conversations especially when assisted by the work of Map and Talk. The grid creates a visual reminder of the variety of processes making up a conversation. It invites a compositional or orchestral awareness that links how we are talking with what we are talking about moment to moment.

The second part of the chapter details more general qualities of conversational awareness. These are forever playing into and against each other as we move the focus of our talk from past to present and future, towards and away from attention on ourselves and more or less openness to others. Or as we make links between a big picture perspective and small details, set order against chaos, or move suddenly from the outsider and observer position to the insider and emotional engaged perspective. These can be mapped out along contrasting lines of intensity (such as hot-cold, loud-quiet) to create a linear space on paper of more or less intense engagement, emotion or activity. These mini, two-by-two grids can be used as conversational trackers alongside the work of talking with a map.

Part one

Four directions and qualities of conversational awareness create a grid of sixteen elements.

- Four directions: within, between, around and beyond us.
- Four qualities: hovering, shimmering, participating and authoring.

The grid sets out four directions in columns: between us interpersonally; within us internally; around us locally and socially; and beyond us in more universal, elusive and transcendent ways. Cutting across these columns are four qualities of talking: with 'hovering' referring to lines of thinking; 'shimmering' referring to lines of feeling; 'participating' indicating lines of action and 'authoring' meaning lines of authority, agency, responsibility and power.

The conversational awareness grid has been derived from analysing the textual variety of many Map and Talk sessions with individuals and teams resulting in an interactive and evaluative measure of conversational and relational awareness (CARA).[32]

Our conversational sensitivity, expressiveness and versatility is an extraordinary and central aspect of being human and the dictatorial and subversive or disorganising threats to it down the ages are still very active in present times.

The grid seeks to signal a versatility of dialogue: in different directions; along different lines; with different qualities that help us step away from historically formed or politically motivated ideologies and our personal attachments to them. Awareness of the layers and dimensions of conversational sensitivity, control, connection and expression pointed to by the grid is something that can be helped by talking with a map. It seeks to help us see how to meet each other in dialogue through more open conversations.

Have a look at the grid and consider how each of these sixteen items stand apart from and in relation to each other. They need each other. They co-opt and colonise each other. They defy each other. They add colour or shade to each other and stand in for each other. They blend or bleed into each other, but they also speak of something distinctive that calls out to us and we can call upon when we are in conversation.

Like the colours from a palette of paints, the ingredients in a kitchen, or the instruments in an orchestra they are open to endless variations in composition. Conversations need composing, orchestrating and conducting or, in a more everyday analogy, they need cooking.

The co-creative process of conversational awareness with its multi-sensory, co-embodied, multimedia experience can be encountered and sustained by talking with a map.

The purpose of the grid is not to offer formulas or a paint by numbers/fast-food recipe approach to composing a discussion, but to signpost an openness of perspective that says we can talk more widely and openly for longer and more freely than our routines and customs tend to allow. Its function is to increase sensitivity to, and agency with, the rich mix of elements that make up any conversation. Don't over think or over analyse them, they are like dialogue buttons to a broad and open perspective and a thousand untold stories.

Four directions of conversation

How we talk is a deeply relational, mutual, co-creative activity which is simultaneously pushing and pulling, co-operating and conflicting in four directions. The conversation is between self and others, within self, and with the social context around us as well as a sense of something beyond these three dimensions. These are considered now in more detail.

A sixteen item awareness grid combining qualities and directions of conversation that can arise when talking with a map		Four directions of talk			
		Between us	Within me	Around us	Beyond us
Four qualities of talk	**Hovering** Links and gaps, in or out, pro and con, picture and detail	*Ideas*	*Thoughts*	*Theories*	*Myths*
	Shimmering Hot and cold, here and there, open or closed, sweet or sour	*Feelings*	*Emotions*	*Drama*	*Presence*
	Participating Doing and being, making and sharing, now and then, with or for	*Roles*	*Creativity*	*Politics*	*Congregate*
	Authoring Owning and disowning, acting and answering, for and against, self and others	*Authority*	*Conscience*	*Values*	*Humanity*

Go down the columns first one by one. In each box use the trigger words as a dialogue button to look sideways at the prevailing quality such as hovering, shimmering, participating and authoring. Look at the grid as if we are painters of conversations and this is your palette.

Start with the first column of how a talk is going **'between us'**. This is the interpersonal and immediate face-to-face connection of ideas, feelings, roles leading to or presenting the opportunity for the exercise of authority together. It is an interpersonal meeting between two or more people willing and seeking to recognise and answer to each other not just in role or around a task or topic but in a fully human person-to-person way. Between us we hover over contrasting and conflicting ideas. We notice and name each other's feelings and live, well or badly, with the emotionality of the conversation between us as we take turns, act, and give or take control and authority.

Now go down the second column **'within me'** and see how at the same as what is going on between us is happening in a parallel but different way within us. I am aware of my thoughts and emotions, and I have more or less agency and creativity to find the words, give voice and take or share, or hand over the lead in the conversation. I do all this with varying experiences of conscience and answerability. Within me is a conversation which is mostly addressing the world within myself with thoughts, emotions, and a creative or thwarted capacity for action guided by conscience. It is an inner world of impulses, partitions and different roles and sides to self. It is a dialogue or reflection and meditation between a multi-sensory 'I' and various sides of me with different claims of authority on the world around. When talking together it can be hard to hear the inner voice and one important role of talking with a map is to be inside and between ourselves at the same time in compassionate and curious ways.

Next go down the third column titled **'around us'** and wonder about the accepted theories about me and you and the world around us, with its dramas created by the push and pull of forces in society and culture. Around us is a conversation with common, diverse and conflicting ways of thinking through theories and ideologies about the world. It is a source of drama, politics and values. As described in chapter 12, we may be so inured in it and attached to it that we live it as if it is the sum of the interpersonal world between us. It is a process of positioning and being positioned within hierarchy with or without status and an orchestration of roles, times and places domestically, ideologically, ethnically, historically, locally and globally.

Finally think your way down the fourth column of the world **'beyond us'** and the myths that carry thinking down the ages and can have an emotional presence in our interactions in ways that are not so easy to articulate. Spiritual conversations of many kinds that guide us can be ones we reach for while knowing their role is to be beyond everyday talk. Beyond us is where, for most of human history, our thinking, our conversation and beliefs were formed and shared in part through myths. We meet it through congregation with art and religious activities in a thousand different ways. It is also where we partly meet the voices and conversations with people who were and are important in our lives and identities but are no longer with us or available. Our conversations with them may have a real, immediate and inner reality and yet feel ethereal and as if talking beyond the other dimensions and directions of relating. What is beyond us is important to our conversations because it has a presence precisely because it is ineffable and not something just to chat about. Its presence in talking with a map may leave space for something at the core of humanity which points to conversations that have moments of transcending ordinary or normal experience.

Map and Talk tracks the lines and directions of conversation

The four directions of relating conversationally might be judged to be four different conversations taking place simultaneously. Am I talking to myself, are we talking to each other? Are we talking to the world? Are we talking of the unknown? It is the unique quality of human language that it is open and flexible and, with simultaneity and spontaneity can do more than one thing at once across dimensions of time and place[33]. The four directions can be at odds and exclude each other or be richly orchestrated and integrated, or any number of variations in between. For example, our discussion might be excessively focused on introspection, and it might seem that the actual tone is self-addressive, solipsistic and I am holding forth for my own benefit. In contrast, some of our conversations are exclusively interpersonal and all about meeting each other's gaze and relating person-to-person. The exchange is so interpersonally focused that we ignore the world around us and neglect our own inner cautions. Inner experience is walled off as is the attention to who is doing what to whom and how are they responding. Or we are addressing neither our inner worlds nor each other but speak to the world around or beyond us in a detached and disengaged way.

Different lines of conversation

All conversations are going simultaneously along several different lines. The emphasis may shift between lines. As headlined in the grid above they are hovering, shimmering, participating and authoring. These are now described in more detail as four horizontal layers with each resulting item in the grid summarised.

Hovering

Hovering is the cognitive capacity to hold in mind more than one point of view, to make sense of the views of others and to zoom in and out between perspective and detail. When we are hovering, we are noticing and negotiating our thoughts and sharing them as they become ideas between us and working to the theories of our culture and society which they imply, work with, or draw upon and the wider, more universally imagined myths.

- **Ideas between us.** A capacity to negotiate and navigate each other's views, recognise moments of understanding and difference and create space and perspective for more than one story, strategy, or truth. It is an openness and a willingness to be in a novel and co-creative relationship. Seeing links between past, present, and future ideas, and the interplay of ideas within, between and around us.
- **Thoughts within us.** A capacity for relational thinking and the ability to tolerate contrasting thoughts, see different angles and sort them in different priorities in different contexts. Being able to independently hold in one's own mind the push and pull, and orchestration of different ideas, beliefs, ideologies and narratives with compassion and curiosity.
- **Theories around us.** Curiosity about values, systems and societies. The conversational resources, traditions and ability to keep making sense of

the complex world around us in the context of diverse lives, cultures, and systems of social power. Ability to discern ideology and propaganda from thought and theory and see self and others in and out of roles in society.

- **Myths beyond us.** A sense of human ideals, dreams and nightmares. A capacity to hold and carry the deep stories and the diverse grand narratives and heritages of all groups in society by allowing them to have a presence and a power even if they are hard to describe and reconcile.

Shimmering

Shimmering is the sensitivity to and potential to express and regulate the intensely engaged (hot) or cool and detached (cold), on or off, sweet and sour, open or closed ambivalence towards emotions and feelings between, within, around and beyond us. It is literally the changing play of light (feeling) and colour (emotion) on the shape shifting surface of conversation.

- **Feelings between us.** A feeling for each other's feelings. The capacity to share involvement and interact appropriately with each other's feelings without being swayed into one state of mind for long, unless it is jointly chosen, named and negotiated. A sensitivity to the push and pull of emotions within and between us, with the ability to ask whether my feelings are our feelings and vice versa.
- **Emotions within me.** A search for honesty and authenticity. A capacity to accept, assert and value the power and truth of emotions within us while tolerating, ambivalence and the simultaneous presence of contrasting and conflicting feelings with changing intensity and direction. A capacity to work with our own feelings with culture and society with courage, compassion and curiosity for what is felt to be fair and not fair.
- **Drama around us.** An ability to participate in and observe the theatre of emotions and feelings within and between our groups, in and out of roles, communities and societies. A capacity to name and negotiate patterns of prejudice within and between work groups. A tolerance for times of confusion of changing roles. A capacity to tolerate the absence of drama and not seek thrills or stir trouble. An awareness of malice and societal danger through the suppression or manipulation of feelings and the emotions beneath them.
- **Presence beyond me.** Awe and joy, sadness and pain in the moment. A sense of shimmering between active hope for great things and compassion for and a willingness to tolerate disenchantment, hurt and failure for self and others. A sense of something greater through art and spirituality in everyday life that reaches beyond the local and to something ineffable. A conversational ecology with nature and all life in the world and beyond it.

Participating

Participating is action now and then, past, present and future and it is done with intention and attention out of choice or by accident as outsiders or insiders.

- **Roles between us.** Management of self in relation to roles status and tasks. Taking part in a role with self-control and expression. The ability to choose and act, to do things with a mix of self-restraint and expression in a way that orchestrates the parts, the roles and the whole sense of self as a person. Knowing when and when not to hide or protect self behind a role by living with a divided sense of self and managing by appearances for the sake of a specific task or context.
- **Creativity within me.** The capacity to set out to do, to make, or co-create, and work at, and seek apprenticeship and guidance and take pride in the process and result of producing something. Delighting in seeing something singularly or jointly achieved and mutually owned and attributed.
- **Politics around us.** Consenting to ways of leading and organising and to ways of being led and organised. Knowing how to participate in and out of role, formally or informally. Active involvement in a democracy of ideas and feelings in co-operation with others and systems in society. A culture of mutual aid in helping each other contribute and act. The courage for self and others not to bullied, silenced or disenfranchised.
- **Congregate beyond us.** A communal sense of needing to gather together to be human. Searching for meaning and looking beyond ourselves for something that flows through us, precedes us and endures beyond us and is larger than us. A capacity to share and trust in a common set of values that transcend and embrace life experiences regardless of context of time and place.

Authoring

Authoring is owning, acting and choosing with agency and narrative. It is being responsible and answerable. Authoring is a process of internal, interpersonal and social accountability for ideas and feelings, roles, activities and ways of organising. It is being answerable to the process and the content of the conversation.

- **Authority between us.** We can give authority to a conversation by our commitment to take it seriously, to respect each other's views and honestly negotiate. We help each other weigh our thoughts and feelings not because of our opinions but with reference to theories and beliefs in the wider world. We share authority through our roles, politics and values.
- **Conscience within me.** A capacity to draw on conversation for self-reflection and second thoughts to be in a position to take or share

responsibility by owning it within me. A sense of duty that is open to respond to context and be mediated by all aspects of inner life.

- **Values around us.** Seeking and sharing a common sense of emotional and social democracy as a form of governance and politics. Owning how we are accountable to ourselves, to each other, to society, to a sense of humanity beyond us. The call and response of these values – which are sometimes complementary, other times conflicting and competing and cannot easily be reconciled.
- **Humanity beyond us.** A capacity to be modest or humble and accept that no one can claim the reins of power and governance and ride it as their own. Our long and varied human story cannot be contained by or reduced to one great narrative, one empire or system of politics or faith. Our future destinies cannot be foretold by a current ideology, religion or will to power. Our duty to the larger multitude of human narratives beyond us is to be in dialogue and seek conversational awareness.

Use the sixteen items of the awareness grid to think of a specific conversation and explore your awareness of how it went and could have gone by putting your own words into the boxes, circling the ones that stand out and drawing lines and arrows to sort them and associate them in new ways. There are examples of this for two teenagers on a first date on page 209 in Chapter 11 and in relation to contemporary narcissism in politics in Chapter 12 on page 229.

Some elements of the grid will resonate and have more weight than others. Thinking about one element and its direction and intensity may trigger relational thinking or emotional links to others. Hold this use in mind as you go through part two of this chapter and the other parts of the book. Don't think of the grid as a done-and-dusted scientific formula but more a chalk board of notions to be mapped out in the 'human relations laboratory' of conversation where they are marked up, rubbed out, or rewritten in the process of talking and relating.

As with talking with a map, working with the grid invites a spontaneous semi-performative quality of speaking out loud with feeling and imagination and thereby finding words that connect with and enhance each other by their coincidental proximity in time and place. This can be poetic-by-chance (even and especially at more difficult and painful times) when words stand beside each other (without syntax or context), and they invite relational curiosity and offer fertile ground and unexpected connections and meanings.

A good conversation can be a fragile achievement and mutual awareness of how to hold and maintain it can be easily lost. Through part two of this chapter, keep in mind the leading purpose of talking with a map is to develop an orchestral or compositional awareness of the ingredients of the grid such that we can help each other conduct our discussions more effectively in more wholehearted ways.

Part two: general qualities of conversational awareness

In contrast to the relational word maps of Chapters 2-5 (often using the ideas of reciprocal roles from Cognitive Analytic Therapy) most of the following qualities are explored in terms of one or two grid lines or intensity scales such as from hot and engaged feelings to cool and detached ones. The words for these scales are always ones from the conversation being tracked with pen and paper. They point to the richness and simplicity of drawing a line on a piece of paper in a conversation so as to place ourselves between two extremes. These can work well when introduced as 'more or less' lines and can be used as conversational trackers which help open up reflection on the discussion and help develop awareness and shared agency over the process of talking together. For example, the two lines in figure 6.1 might be an aid to take stock of how we are feeling about the sharing and managing of our emotions in the conversation. The horizontal line might be where we note feelings shared or emotions held in more or less intense ways. The vertical line and the four quadrants then created can explore how much we sense we

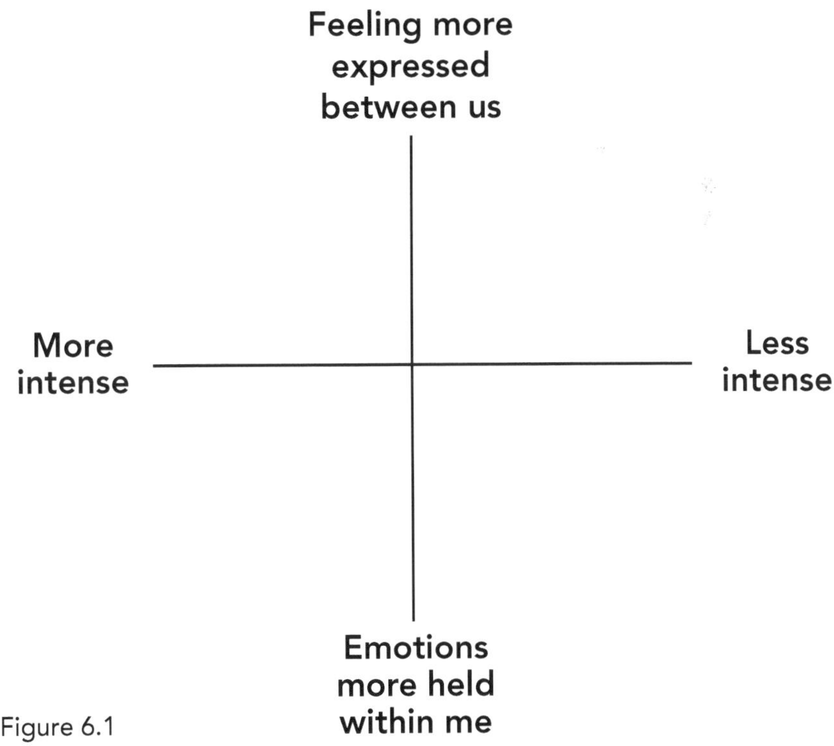

Figure 6.1

are expressing those feelings between us or holding them more within us. We can mark where we are now and where we would like to be. Emotions that might have been too intense or risky to share may be more easily named and negotiated with this laying out of feeling words on paper.

Another example could be in a discussion someone might say they are frustrated. Put a line with 'more frustrated' at one end and 'less frustrated' at the other. Ask the person or the group where they are on the line just now and mark it for themselves and then mark where they would like to be and where they would not want to be. The discussion that follows is what can we do to help each of us move a little to where we want to be, or help each other, or help ourselves not being pulled or pushed to where we don't want to be.

Navigator's awareness: notice, name and negotiate

In any conversation we are in a continuous, multi-directional, multi-sensory process of noticing. Our attention goes here and there. We are making a mental map of the conversation: the people, the words, the context. When we notice something make the conversational choice to name it. By name it, I mean we find words for it and vocalise them. We can notice something and not name it for many reasons. We may not know the words, not be fully conscious of its resonances, or fear calling it out because of some aspect of the conversation.

Mapping as we talk aims to help us live in the spaces between what we notice and how we name it, or not. Words spread out on paper create openings and gaps that we don't usually stop to experience in the rush, excitement and anxiety of our talking. As in the adjoining Figure 6.2 the visual gap on paper between the act of noticing and the moment of something being noticed invites us to consider what choices we make of words to name our thoughts and feelings. The link between noticing and naming invites us to negotiate with ourselves, with each other, the written words and the patterns they are making or might make.

The movement back and forth between noticing, naming and negotiating is multisensory, cognitive and emotional. It is engaging several parts of our brains. We notice with our bodies, with our eyes and ears and other senses. I notice I am hungry, or I notice I am talking too much. I notice you are upset. Naming what we notice is hovering and shimmering around the sixteen elements of the awareness grid.

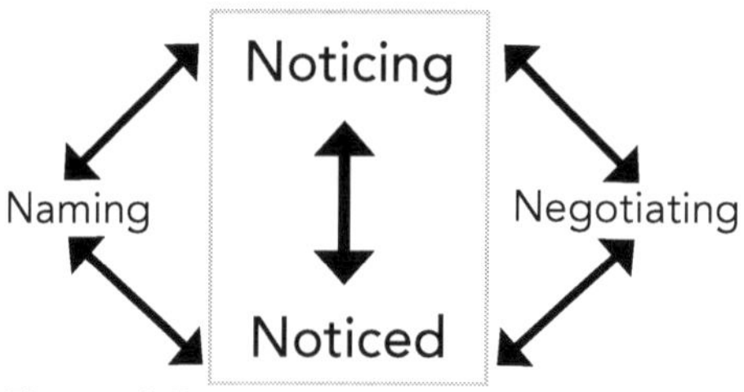

Figure 6.2

Mapping it helps us hover and shimmer and invites us to participate and share authority in speaking.

The naming process of finding words and finding how to voice what we want to say is a negotiation between the elements of the awareness grid and especially what is within me and between us. The other person or persons in the conversation is/are reaching out to share in the naming moments. Perhaps they feel they know what we are going to say. We have to be attentive not to rush or bypass these moments of shared negotiation by going with easy turns of phrase and readymade exchanges. In the flow of naming comes moments of remembering, restorying and new emotional and cognitive connections.

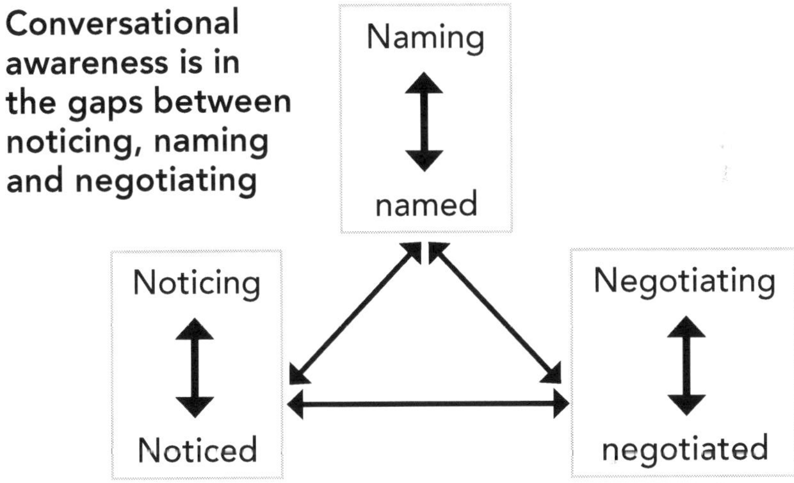

Figure 6.3

We need one or more other people as helpers to be our conversational assistant in noticing, naming and negotiating. The triangular figure 6.3 shows the three-way relationship between what we notice in conversation, how we name it (or not) and give it words - either to ourselves through inner speech or to others through shared speech. We negotiate back and forward through the process of talking and listening together. The negotiation can change the naming and the noticing. Indeed, conversational awareness comes from allowing this process of revision and rediscovery.

This is where mapping can come into its own. We can only navigate our thinking around what we notice. We can only negotiate with each other using what we name. We use the mapping process to help notice links and patterns, but we also need to be open to what we do not notice, or we name but don't negotiate. Throughout this book there is a concern to choose when to navigate away from or towards difficult feelings, hidden roles, or challenging stories.

In Figure 6.4 the contribution of Map and Talk to navigating and negotiating conversational awareness is summarised by a map that might be used with people learning to talk with a map. In blank form it can be copied and filled in with the words that come to mind in that specific situation and context.

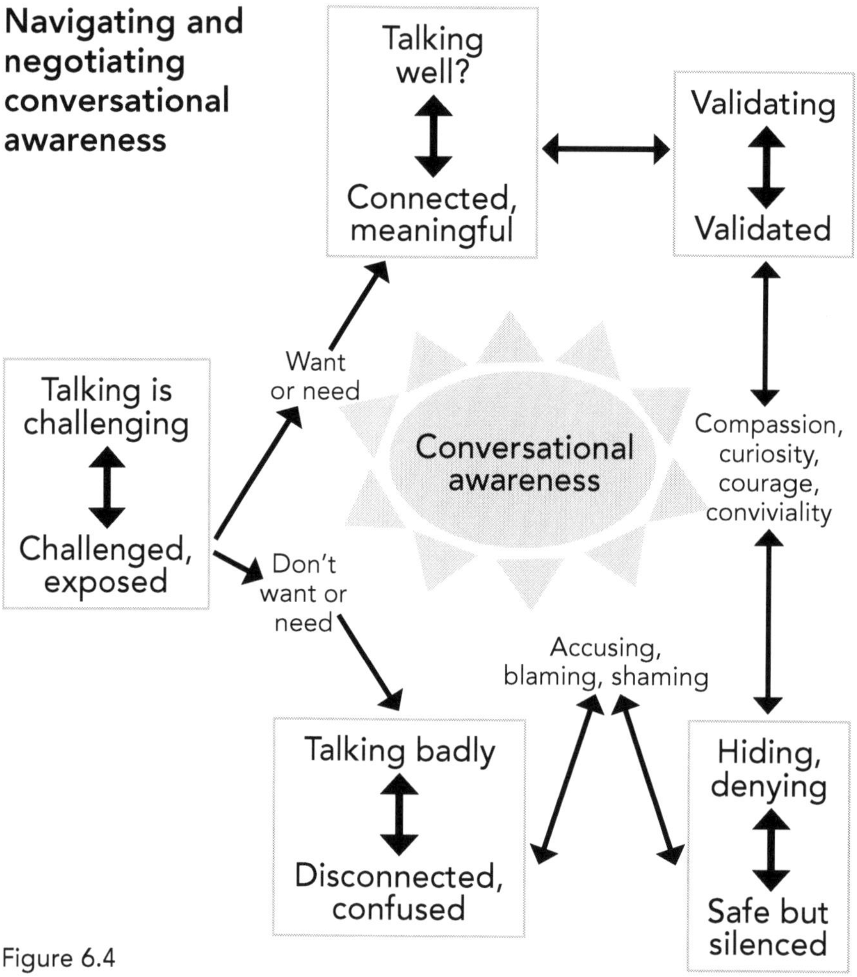

Figure 6.4

When we talk, we are exposed and challenged (for better or worse) and our needs might simply be divided into what we want and don't want (see left centre of the map). We want the talking to go well, in the sense that it brings and shares a sense of connection and meaning and feeling among us of talking well and being connected. It is important to acknowledge, either implicitly or explicitly, that this is affirmed and valued: either indirectly by a wish to talk again – or to talk further in this way – or directly by reviewing how we have talked well. We may forget to affirm the conversation because our attention is so focused on what we are talking about that we omit to notice and name *how* we are talking. Our awareness should extend to compassion, curiosity, courage and conviviality (the four Cs) in pursuit of a good conversation. If that is too much, we may notice how we go to the bottom right corner on the map in Figure 6.4 and find ourselves hiding and denying to gain safety, but at the price of part of or all of us being silenced by playing safe. We need our conversational awareness to extend to this pattern and to keep in mind what we don't want which is for the talking to go badly and us to feel disconnected, hurt and confused. As will be further developed in Chapter 9, this can lead to being divided within ourselves or against each other, creating a conversational poverty. Blaming and shaming patterns of relating take charge of the conversation. An example of developing conversational awareness through the micro detail of noticing, naming and negotiating is in Chapter 10.

Holding a conversation

In our everyday speech we talk of holding a conversation. It acknowledges that something distinctive is being given attention and shape. Like holding a baby, holding a job or holding a party. How we hold the conversation will set the tone for how it begins.

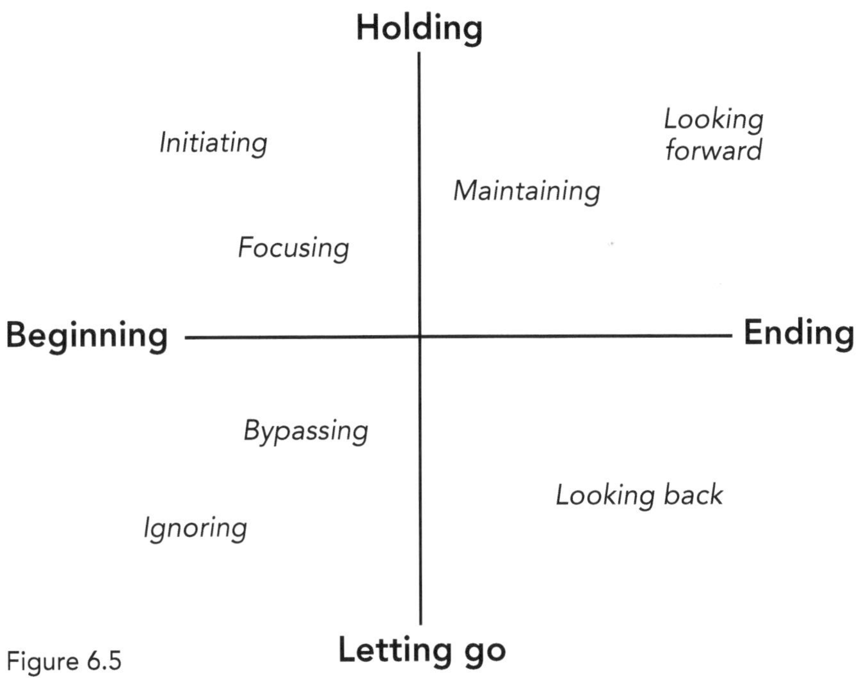

Figure 6.5

Mapping can help hold and steady the hand of listening – sometimes literally but certainly metaphorically. The grid in Figure 6.5 can be useful to track progress in a conversation. The top left with a mix of holding and focusing and initiating at the beginning may also need to be alert to the bottom left of bypassing and ignoring topics or dynamics. Do we notice them or let go of them? In the bottom right there may be elements at the end of a discussion in which letting go is an important part of looking back and leaving behind. Or the top right on holding the ending of the conversation well is looking forward and drawing lessons from what was discussed.

Wholehearted awareness

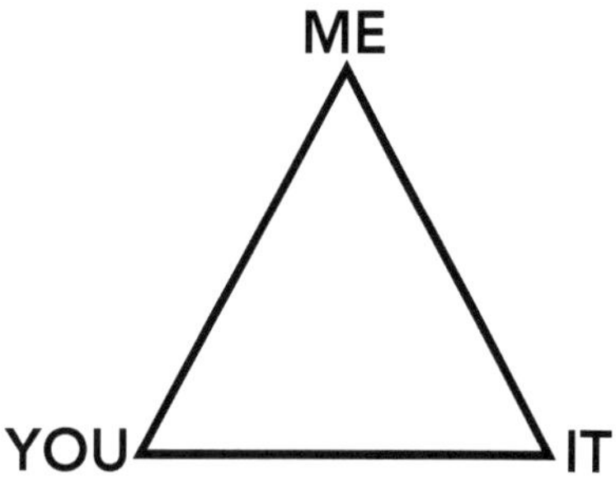

Figure 6.6

The ideas in this book come in large part from psychotherapy. One of the gifts of therapy is being there in a wholehearted way. Martin Buber, whose legacy of ideas played an important part in post-World War II thinking, with his book introducing the three-way relationship between I and Thou and It.[34] Many have taken up his existential and humanistic thinking. For example, the Russian philosopher Mikael Bakhtin was influenced in his more dialogic approach. Carl Rogers, the generator of an enduring person-centred approach to therapy and education spent time with Buber to learn with and share perspectives.

Buber drew an important distinction between relating authentically as 'I and thou' (the term thou is the more intimate sense of 'you' found in French, German and other languages). He contrasted it with a less involved relationship between 'I and it'. His point, among many, was that we are in trouble when we relate to people on the 'I to it' basis rather than the 'I with thou' basis. He drew on his own experience. He recounted that a young man had come to see him and clearly wanted to talk and seek his guidance. He said he did not have time and the young man went away. Some days later Buber heard the young man had taken his own life. Buber recalls being distraught that he did not give the time or have the mindset to respond in a fully human way to the possible call for help from this young man. His subsequent promise to himself and his philosophy was to be genuinely present in his interactions with people.

For Karen Horney, writing in the 1940s, the process of a therapeutic conversation needed to be what she aptly called 'wholehearted' if it is to heal. Carl Rogers picked up on this theme with his emphasis on congruence. Robert Hobson working in the UK wrote a vivid account of his work, citing Buber's I-thou philosophy. His book on a conversational approach to psychotherapy is called *Forms of Feeling*.[35] His work has been a continuing influence on the tone of this book. Hobson first and defining theme is described as:

'I conceive of psychotherapy as a process of learning, and learning how to learn, within a personal conversation. The central feature of this relationship is the mutual creation or discovery of a feeling-language – a language of the heart.' (p15)

Mapping as we talk can help us discover and sustain such a feeling language. Hobson goes on to note that this feeling language does not just come through talking but from moments of emergence held by a conversation. I take him to be saying we don't know what words will mean to us until we share them in an open and compassionate relationship and conversation. It is easier to do this with words between us on paper as compassionate witness to the conversation.

Turn giving and taking

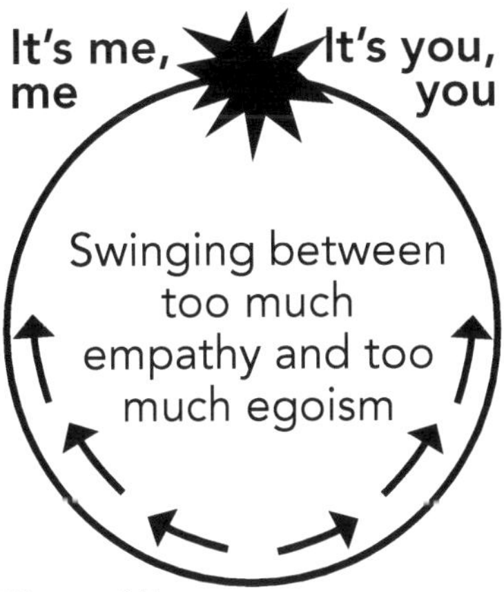

Figure 6.7

Our earliest infant development which is carried over to our time as toddlers and children is the ability to take turns, to ask for turns fairly and to notice the need in others for turns. Turn taking depends on a conversational empathy for each other. Empathy is capacity to be in the other person's shoes. It involves imagining, projecting, and identifying with the other person's experience. It is a delicate balancing of empathy for others with empathy for self. Think of it in terms of the empathy horseshoe as in the adjoining diagram (Figure 6.7). At one extreme it can be so much about you that I forget my own needs. At the other extreme you can be entirely focused in a narcissistic way on yourself and have no time for, or sense of, me, other than some token recognition. The point of the horseshoe is to have a sense of the swing between you giving the attention to another, and you turning the attention and the limelight on yourself. Any conversation and relationship will move back and forth and if it is stuck at 'six o'clock' on the pendulum nothing is going to happen to the conversation or the relationship. Far worse is if between us you are stuck at the top of one end of the pendulum, metaphorically at minutes before twelve, jumping up and down and demanding all the attention and I am stuck at five-past-twelve quietly leaning in saying, 'yes, what can I do to keep it all about you?' Movement is needed for conversational empathy to be a shared experience but too much movement is toxic to conversational awareness.

Side-by-side

Our best conversations are conducted side-by-side: long walks, driving in a car, working on something jointly, sitting up in bed. There is room to turn and regard each other and to look together at what is in front of and between us. Lines from Seamus Heaney's poem Album capture it well. *About a love that's proved by steady gazing, Not at each other but in the same direction.*[36]

The poet Paul Muldoon writing about his conversations with Paul McCartney gives a rich indication of the conversational creativity, awareness and openness that McCartney found in his childhood, then later in his collaboration with John Lennon and with the various kinds of music and media. Speaking of McCartney:

'...he acknowledges that the interplay of Lennon and McCartney was "nothing short of miraculous", describing how they "wrote with two guitars". "The joy of that was that I was left-handed, and he was right-handed, so I was looking in a mirror and he was looking in a mirror".'[37]

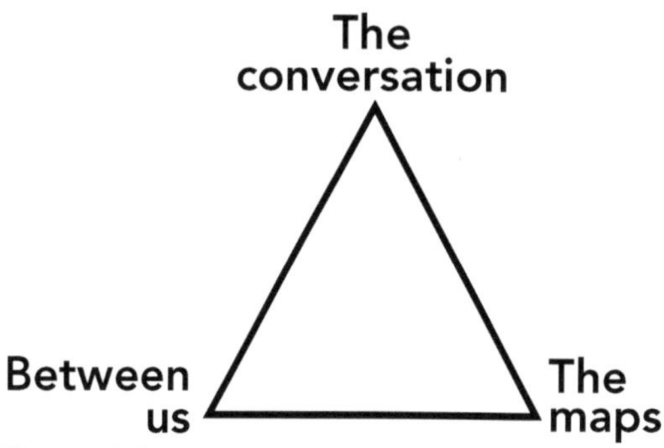

Figure 6.8

This side-by-side feeling is a key quality of a good conversation and of map and talk. It is important to sit side-by-side, ideally at a table with the paper between you. It needs the chairs to be slightly turned towards us, so it is easy to move from facing each other and looking at the map. With a group, the side-by-side feeling comes from gathering within touching distance of a big piece of paper and pens laid out on a table. With a bigger group it needs us to stand around a white board or flip chart. When working online a second camera (set up as a rostrum camera) can track paper mapping for the whole group while also keeping visual contact of faces on the first camera. Working side-by-side creates an external and an internal triangle of action, thought and feeling. As in Figure 6.8 there is the conversation with its own momentum and language, there is the relationship between us, the conversation and the mapping process. This creates space and takes the load off just the conversation or just the relationship as the sole source of meaning. If we can work side by side interpersonally or as a group, we can more easily internalise a side-by-side relationship with the different parts of our inner dialogue with ourselves.

Challenging and supporting

The ideal conversation from the point of view of awareness is mostly in the upper left quadrant in this grid which is widely used in counselling and coaching and for which I can find no historic reference. I have been using it for many decades and I suspect it came from group relations training workshops in the early 1970s.

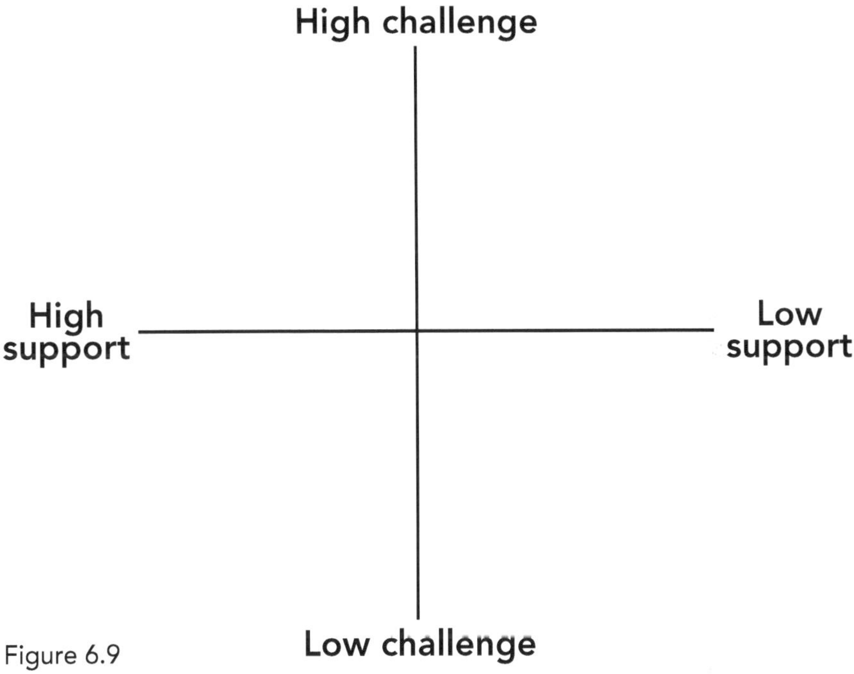

Figure 6.9

To be able to talk in ways that are both appropriately challenging and supportive is likely to lead to a feeling of safety and openness. High challenge and high support is the conversational relationship that individuals and teams look for but perhaps also have mixed feelings about. The anxieties need naming to avoid slipping into the other quadrants. High challenge with low support will lead to mistrust and too much anxiety or self-blame and withdrawal. Low support and low challenge are a recipe for an empty conversation without risk or support. High support as in the bottom left quadrant combined with low challenge may feel safe for all parties to the conversation but nothing is likely to be happen or be memorable.

Risk or safety

Some conversations are difficult because they have so many layers and threads to them. Others are difficult because the trust, openness or goodwill is not there. Others because the topics are controversial or risky. We need the tools of mapping as we talk to edge along the line below from making it riskier to making it safer according to the context.

We need to edge up the line and face up to complications by noticing them, finding ways of talking about them and negotiating what can be done. It may be that we are honest about the limits of the conversation, and in the process we may be deliberately and openly avoiding the complications but not denying them, or pretending it is simple. It suits the darker forces in our society to make us fearful of talking despite now having the education, the resources and time to talk openly if we cared to. Mapping as we talk can give us confidence to stay with the more personal or controversial topics.

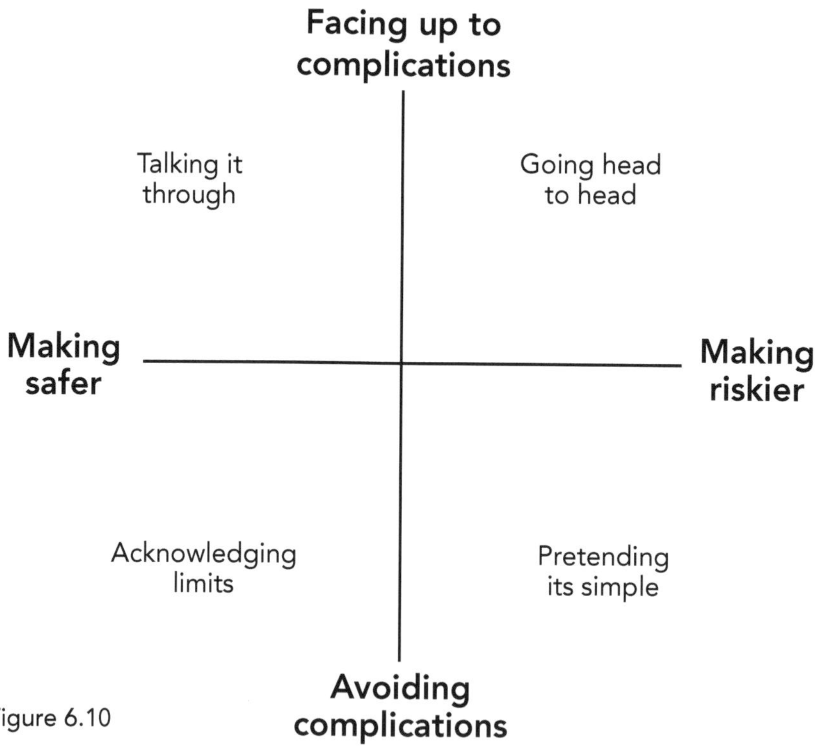

Figure 6.10

Every conversation has its risky moments when upsetting feelings might be triggered or opinions and positions become non-negotiable. Having compassion and curiosity for such risky moments, spotting them building and not being hijacked by them in ways that threaten the fabric of the conversation are important. One golden rule is to talk about how we are in our relationship in this risky moment. One way of using this grid as with the other grid is to ask a work team or colleague to reflect on the recent run of conversations and mark where they/we feel we are and where we would like to be.

More hot and intense, more cool and distant

Some conversations, and the relationships that accompany them, are too 'hot' emotionally to handle. Others are too detached and 'cool' to connect with. We shimmer in and out of a zone of conversational comfort and awareness. One simple way of tracking the changing emotional intensity of a discussion is to draw a line with hotter and more intense at one end and cooler and more distant at the other. In advance of talking about something it can be worthwhile predicting how heated or cool the discussion might be by marking the points along the line as to what you would feel if it were that hot and how you would cool things down. We might then be more able to negotiate how to have the conversation more in the 'Goldilocks' zone of not too hot and not too cold.

The 'Goldilocks' zone of 'just about right'

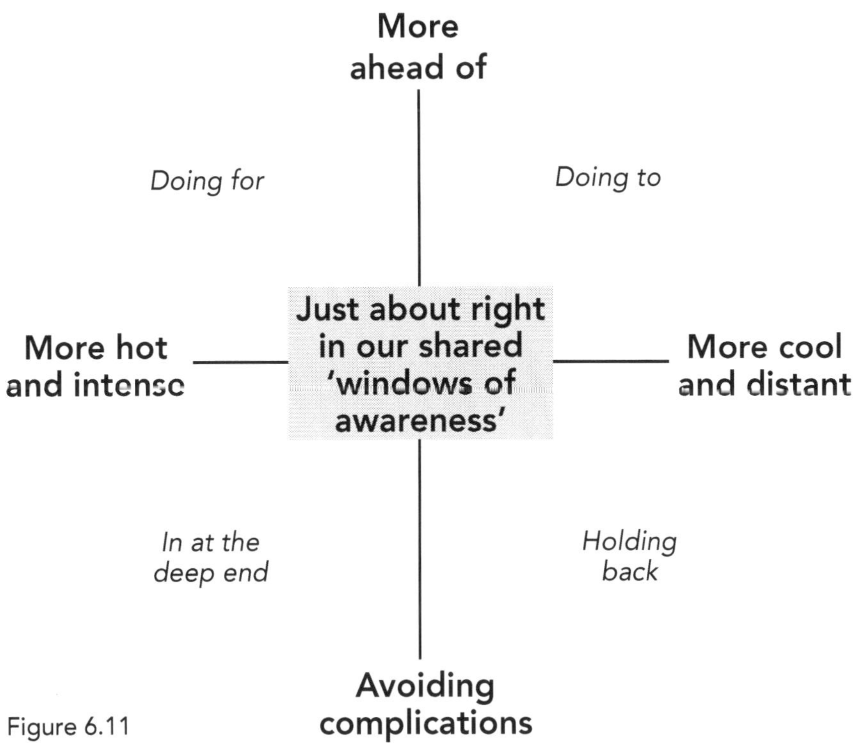

Figure 6.11

It might help to set the horizontal line (Figure 6.11) against a vertical one with 'too far ahead' or fast for the person speaking or listening and 'too behind' or slow at the bottom. A conversation that is both cool and ahead of the person talking may be verbally impressive but leaves no room for relating. It might feel like the conversation is something we are 'doing to' each other. One that is heated but behind and slow may need escaping from because we feel in at the deep end. If it is too far ahead, fast and too hot, it may generate fleeting emotions but no space to root them or make sense of them. The conversation may feel like the hovering and shimmering is being done for the other person or the group by the one, or ones, taking the lead. A discussion that is behind the pace and slow and cool may have room for ideas and feelings but not sustain our attention unless mediated by some other activity such as walking or playing chess. We may find ourselves holding back. Awareness of the push and pull of these two scales can help us sense how to move the conversation in one direction or another as its pace and temperature changes.

Here and there, then and now

Nothing captures the texture of an open and aware conversation more than the simple juxtaposition of *here and there* in place, and *now and then* in time. A single line between now and then can help explore changing images of self or social attitudes over time. Mark along the time line what someone or a group felt about themselves at one time, then another time and then now. Talking about the past (or the future 'then and when') tends to link to an attitude or experience not in time but in place. Do you remember when? Yes, where were we?

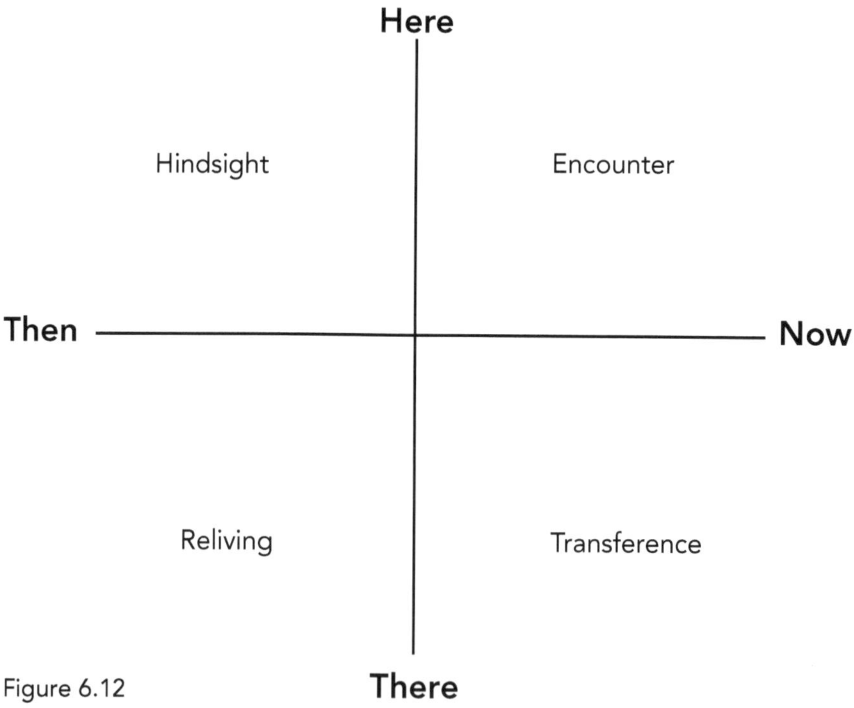

Figure 6.12

The vertical line in the Figure 6.12 between 'here' and 'there' adds a dimension to 'then and now'. In the top right quadrant when the focus of the conversation is on 'here and now' it is about us in the moment. It points to a meeting or encounter between us, or among us. When the focus of the conversation is on 'here' and 'then' the question of hindsight (or foresight) takes centre stage of the conversation. From where we are now, how do we see ourselves looking backward or forward to then?

Hindsight, as the cliché goes, is a wonderful thing in conversation. We can spend much time on it. The risk might be that we go to the bottom quadrant of then and there and gain a new connection but risk getting lost in nostalgia or overwhelmed by reliving an experience. Conversations work by carrying an awareness of the movement around this two dimensional grid and being open to the bottom right quadrant where time and place are both 'now' and 'there' and patterns of relating in the past 'there' and 'then' are rekindled in the present moments of discussion.

Towards and away meets sweet and sour

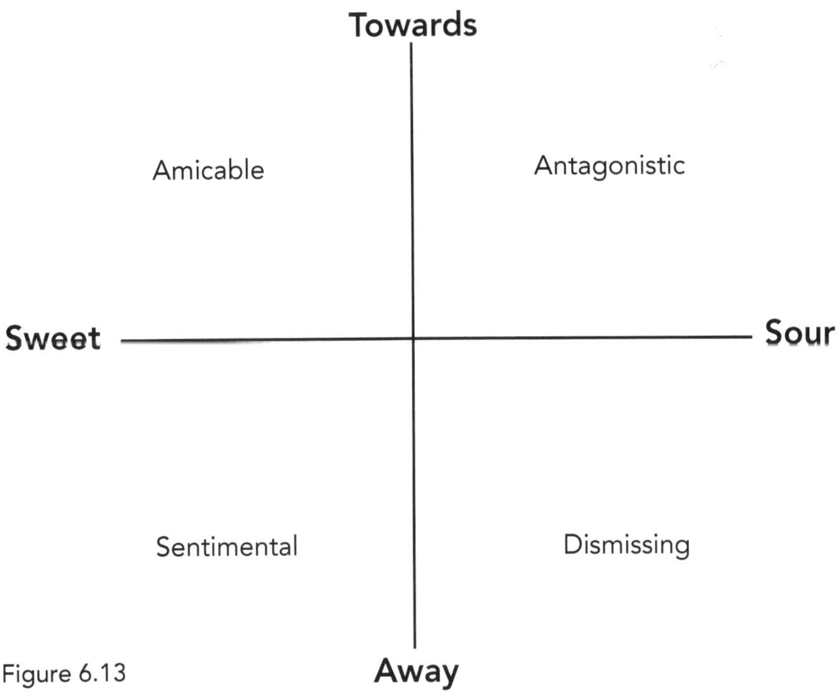

Figure 6.13

Every conversation has moments of deepening contact as we move towards each other with our ideas and feelings. As Karen Horney (greatly neglected and pioneering relational psychoanalyst with a feminist perspective and a legacy of ideas that are still relevant) richly pointed out we can move towards each other warmly or antagonistically.[38] Mapping can help us see the movements in the conversational relationship, marking out how we negotiate choices and recover balance. There may be times when feelings and ideas push us into disagreeing and contradicting each other. We may maintain an air of warmth or sweetness between us in the talking we are doing while being more distant and away from each other. It might feel fake or sentimental or nostalgic. In the top right-hand corner, we may be close and engaged but the dominant tone of the conversation or the relationship is antagonistic. It might feel like we are up against something, and it works to feel more like we are up against someone or ourselves. Or vice versa. We may protect ourselves, the relationship or the conversation by being distant and talking about ideas and feelings at arm's length.

Other words can easily substitute for the words in grid depicted by Figure 6.13 but the idea of mapping out where we are and where we would hope or fear to be can build shared understanding and a conversational bond. It may, for example, reveal that we opt for being sentimental and superficial in our discussions to keep away from strong amicable or hostile feelings for each other and alternatively disguise this by being antagonistic. For the classic conversational version of this see the relationship between Elizabeth Bennett and Mr Darcy in *Pride and Prejudice* which explored in this book in Chapter 11 on page 217.

More open to ideas or feelings

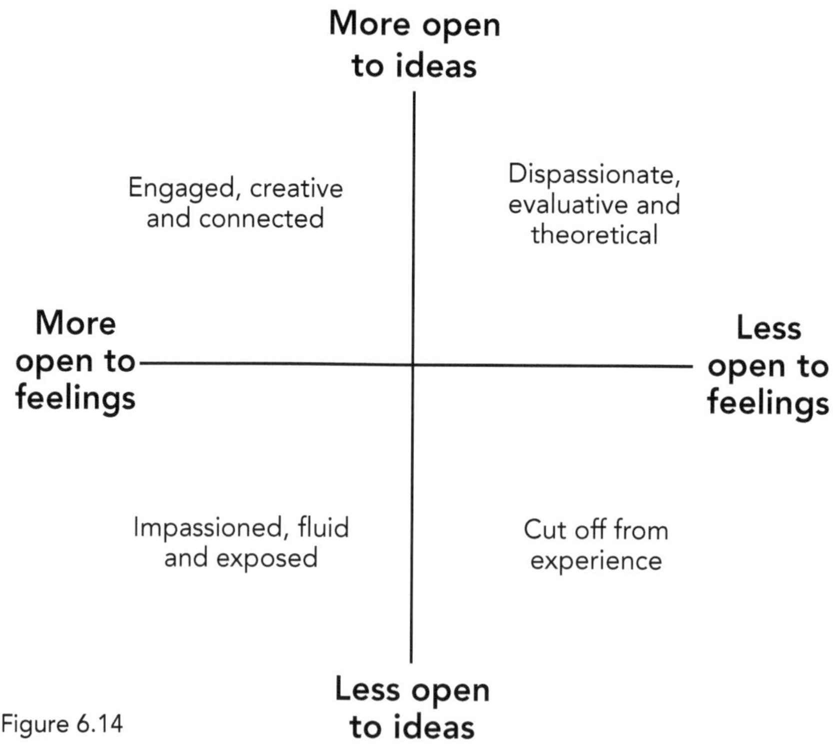

Figure 6.14

The key lines of the conversational awareness grid are between the more hovering style of relational thinking within and between us and the more shimmering style of responding to emotions and feelings. One conversational ideal might be an openness to ideas and feelings as in the top left quadrant in Figure 6.14 where we are both engaged in sharing our ideas about our feelings and our feelings about our ideas. The bottom left corner wherein we are open to feelings but not ideas might be exciting and teasing or impassioned but more cause for anxiety and loss of the thinking self to an emotional self. The bottom right corner is a conversational atmosphere that is cut off from experience because feelings and ideas do not speak to, or of each other. The top right quadrant is one that is highly valued, but the ideas may not thrive or develop in discussion or evaluation because the feelings that can nurture them are closed off.

Transactional awareness

Much of our talk is transactional and the conversational quality is felt to be unnecessary, purposefully limited or suppressed. The horizontal line (Figure 6.15) from more transactional talk to more conversational is a useful check to seeing where you are in talking and where you would prefer to be. Some

Different qualities of talk

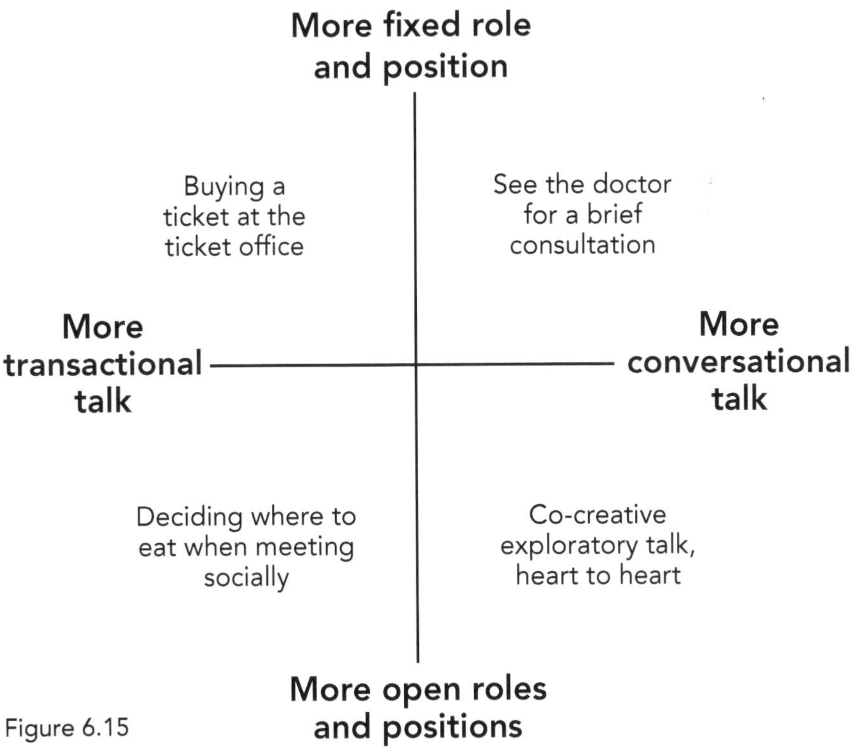

Figure 6.15

more transactional talk is conducted through fixed roles and other talk from more open roles and positions. Transactional awareness can help us see and attune to the kind of conversation or talk we are in and adjust or accept accordingly. We can all think of exchanges at a shop, in a café, on a train that were assumed to be transactional but became conversational for a time. If you're having a talk that would be better done in a more conversational way, for example between partners or parents and children, then the use of the grid might help notice, name and negotiate small moves from the top left quadrant to the bottom right one.

Between me and you and us and them

As the process of conversational mapping develops there is scope to see which patterns and roles focused on me and which on you. This is detailed in Chapter 3 where the same simple depiction of a reciprocal role relationship can point internally (self to role in self) or interpersonally (role to role and person to person) or socially around us to roles in society and its institutions.

Many of our life stories are about attachment and belonging or not. Am I part of this group? Are we all of the same mind? What can and cannot be said? Are some stories sacred to the group and others taboo? Are you included? How do people join the group? Are some of us insiders by nature and others of us

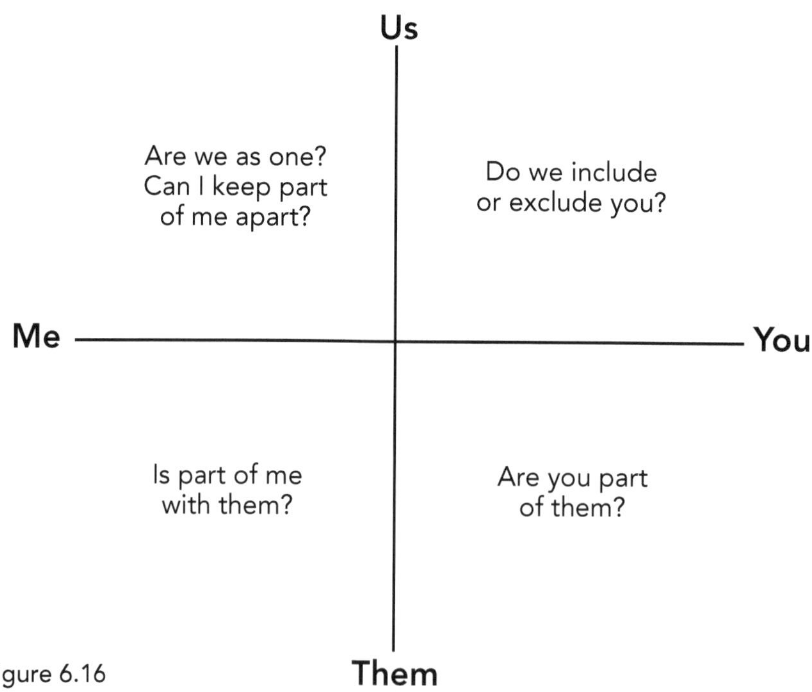

Figure 6.16

outsiders? If they exclude you, do I go along with it for fear of them excluding me too? Can I belong to more than one group or use a group for an important need but not really feel signed up to their way of doing things?

What is a good group in a transitional and globalized world? Can a group and its affiliation be local and global at the same time? Do groups get carried away by their beliefs and turn them into ideologies and invest themselves or their leaders with narcissistic features that create a myth of entitlement, righteousness and of being the good group by destiny? This last question is one of the themes in Chapter 12.

The us and them, me and you grid (Figure 6.16) is a simplified way of thinking how Map and Talk can help us notice, name and negotiate our sensitivity to these social dynamics that are so deeply woven in us. We live in a pluralistic world which is to say we belong and become attached to more than one identity. We present ourselves as one to our groups but carry with us a baggage of identities and allegiances. The activity of talking with a map and developing conversational awareness helps us present ourselves as one person with a unified sense of self, and live within a plurality of sides to ourselves, whether they be social identities, roles or elements of our personality. The relational psychoanalyst Philip Bromberg describes the challenge well: 'Health is the ability to stand in the spaces between realities without losing any of them. This is what I believe self-acceptance means and what creativity is all about. The capacity to feel like one *(unified)* self, whilst being many.'[39]

It is very easy for conversations about us in the world to become divisive. They become binary, splitting into either/or, right/wrong, us/them conversations. There are many economic, political and historical forces driving this. It is as if the need for a clear story and a clear allegiance gets entangled and we cling to ideas which become fixed and part of our identity and belonging. Especially vulnerable to splitting are ideas held at a distance without interpersonal mediation such as some differences of social identity, ethnicity, class and culture or lifestyle. The idea of 'us' gets set against the idea of 'them' and it is hard for me to relate to you as you. Whenever we do relate as persons, prejudice disappears. At any one moment of relating as a group about one of your identities see if Figure 6.16 can help map out the pressure and the freedom to be part of a group or be among groups without losing our diverse sense of self.

Connected or isolated, exposed or protected

In the adjoining conversational axis, our conversations move minute by minute back and forth along the horizontal line from feeling more connected to feeling more isolated. If the line was extended there could be a point where we are either too connected or too isolated. The vertical line captures the movement in any conversation between feeling exposed or protected.

A healthy and open conversation will move around the grid as describe in each of the boxes of text in the four quadrants. To search for meaning in a conversation we need to take risks to share and tolerate our moments of confusion and vulnerability. But we also need to know we can be protected without being abandoned and isolated. Some of our conversations can be too cosy and mutually protecting of each other. The sweet spot for conversational and relational awareness is the top left quadrant where we are out in the open with each other, but we hardly expect to be there all the time.

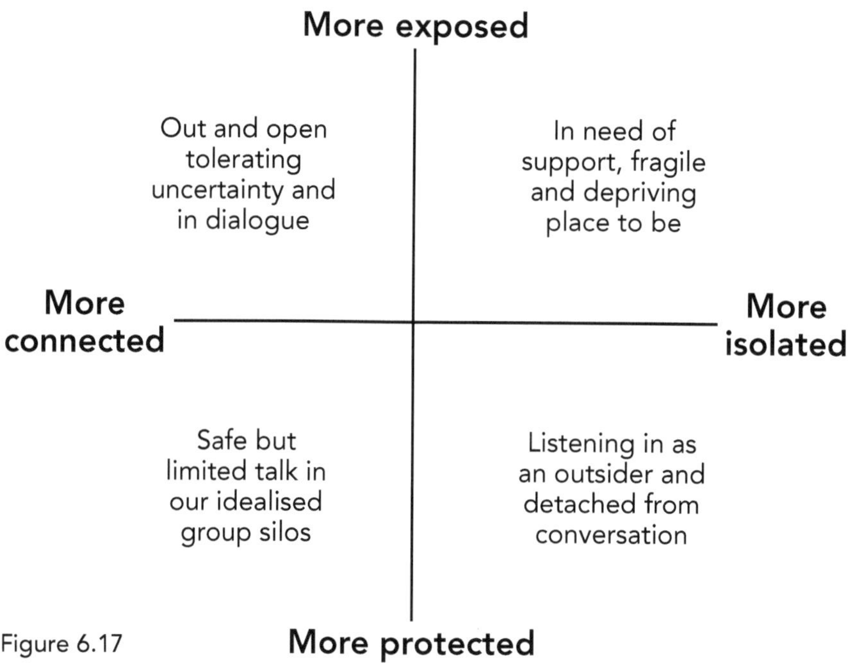

Figure 6.17

Talking with or against each other

To conclude this long string of ways drawing out conversations along contrasting lines it might help to offer the most general one of all. Mapping as we talk can help us see when 'talking with' slips across to 'talking at or against'. Use the grid as a template to check from time to time where the conversation is going. Conversations that frequently go head-to-head and become antagonistic may be sparky and entertaining for some, but they are likely to be shaming and silencing for others. 'Talking against' each other may feel normal in some parts of life but it is akin to verbal bullying. Nothing suits dominant or controlling parties more than to set a tone and a style of conversation that is antagonistic, verbally bullying and carries under currents of superiority, derision and contempt.

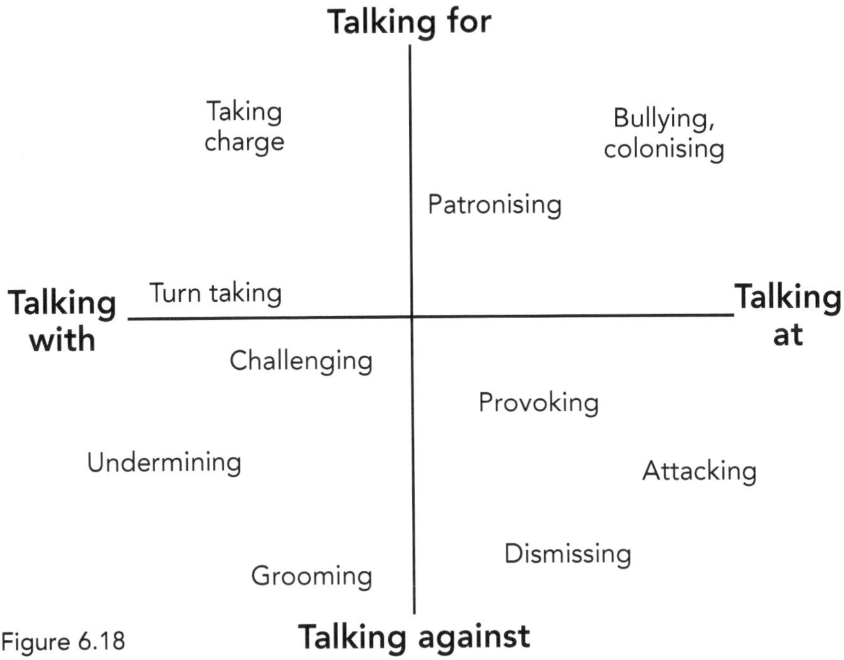

Figure 6.18

'Talking for' someone is tempting when there are silences and uncertainties, or the power structures of a culture have set up fixed roles and status positions where someone always speaks for someone because that right has been taken or ceded. In some situations, I may prefer that someone speaks for me, but I need to give informed consent to that choice. There is an array of professions from lawyers to pundits, lobbyists and politicians who talk for us. We need to be sure they have the mandate and speak honestly and transparently and honour their accountability to us in principle and practice.

In response to being 'talked at' the listener can become passive, and the conversation is mainly going one way. When we are talking at people interpersonally, we are not likely to be talking with ourselves internally. It can trigger childhood memories of being talked at and talked down to. We might feel we are being told off and shamed in some way. The social and institutional structures of sexism and racism, of class privilege and educational advantage can be expressed personally as talking at people. Finding the conversational qualities for moving away from talking at each other and towards talking with each other is a one reason for this book and the work it describes.

Is consciousness no more than conversational awareness?

Perhaps consciousness[40] itself is no more and no less than a conversational companion to the complex and unfathomable daily orchestrations of our brains, our bodies, our social ecosystems, and our individual and collective life stories. Every time we prepare to speak, make gestures or find shared words we are raising the question of our consciousness and reaching in and among these orchestrations with as much relational awareness, compassion and dignity as we can muster. It is tempting to see conversational awareness and self-consciousness as the same thing. They draw upon the same qualities and have the same variations in intensity, direction and orchestration. It is a question best left to the philosophers and neuroscientists, but Chapter 8 offers an imaginative turn around the subject and cites some authors that have influenced the thinking and practice of talking with a map.

The talkability tests

How we are doing as we talk, whether in more transactional or conversational ways, is something we are constantly evaluating, judging and reacting to informally. The methods and ideas in this book support bringing the monitoring, judging process compassionately into the conversation. The ever-present call is to spend as much time talking about how as talking about what. This chapter concludes with reference to two measures designed to evaluate talking with a map and conversational awareness. One measures qualities of conversational and relational awareness. The other measures the benefit of mapping to the quality of the conversation. The conversational and relational awareness measure (CARA) offers a reading of individual and collective awareness scores in all the dimensions of talking highlighted by the grid at the beginning of this chapter. The emphasis on contextual variation (home, work, school, past and present) in how we talk and relate to each other is an important corrective to the dominant tendency to measure individual personality and individual competencies independent of context. The measure of talking with a map assesses the benefits or otherwise of a single or series of sessions of mapping and talking. To link to current online copies or contribute to routine evaluation and research go to www.mapandtalk.com

Conclusion

Map and Talk helps us stop and reflect on how our conversations are going and make links between how we relate and how we discuss. It builds awareness of appropriate sensitivity, connection, expressiveness and control in our conversations. It helps hold in mind the rich and changing mix of ingredients to a conversation highlighted by the awareness grid in part one of this chapter and the changing dimensions of relating interpersonally and contextually as laid out by the two-dimensional grids in part two of this chapter. A process of conversational tracking alongside the talking with the map helps switch between content and process. It helps combine attention on the how, what and why of the conversation and the relationships involved. It helps us hold in mind the different directions a conversation can simultaneously be going, and the different lines and layers of connection and expression involved. If we can find the sweet spots of awareness more often and navigate and learn from the hot spots, if we can mark out and discuss where we want to be and fear being, it can act as an informal guide and support to the conversation. It helps us be in dialogue with words and language, with relationships, with the emotionality and clarity of our voices and all the contexts to the discussion. It helps bring out the rich human potential in any conversation to be more versatile, more open, more negotiable and more able to help us navigate our ways in the world.

Chapter 7: Writing, mapping and voicing words

> *'Every word gives off the scent of a profession, a genre, a current, a party, a particular work, a particular man, a generation, an era, a day, and an hour. Every word smells of the context and contexts in which it has lived its intense social life.'*[41]
>
> Mikhail Bakhtin: The Dialogical Principle

This chapter invites you to try writing short letters to the words and patterns you have mapped conversationally together with another person. The writing is for reading and giving voice to ideas and feelings. The chapter introduces a brief, focused and spontaneous form of writing that is here called discovery writing. It could be called journaling or reflective writing, but the emphasis is on discovering words in a moment or a flow of understanding through prose writing in ways similar to the process of mapping and recapping while talking. It draws upon the use of therapeutic writing in models such as cognitive analytic therapy and from creative and therapeutic writing more widely.[42]

The chapter first describes discovery writing as an activity that can accompany talking with a map. Secondly it looks in more detail at the gap between the words in our heads and the words on paper as our conversations and stories develop their voices. Thirdly it directly explores the contribution of our voices to the experience of recapping and talking our way around a map or in reading out bits of discovery writing.

Discovery with writing

Discovery writing is addressive to someone, something or a time and place. Like in letter writing it is personal, handwritten, freestyle and conversational. Unlike letter writing the recipient and the addressee are not the same. The recipient of the letter is either the immediate conversational partner (or partners), or me the writer. The addressee is the person, idea, the thing, or time and place to which or to whom the writing is addressed. This tension between 'speaking of' and 'voicing with' creates a space between what and who we are addressing. It invites new connections and relational awareness.

Discovery writing has the voice and subsequent reading out in mind. It is writing to help open out the conversation with myself and others. It externalises thoughts and feelings onto paper and onto a space where we can work with them and see them in their fluent or disjointed form. It is writing to be read back to yourself and out loud to others to feel how the words composed in a private, inner, conversation change when voiced and heard. It is a promise to go back over, stop and reflect and revoice and reword.

It is the prose writing equivalent of Map and Talk and a supplement to it. It is like a silent, more indirect form of the recapping from the map described in earlier chapters. Writing quickly and freely is not some fast route to the truth but a way of opening a space for further reflections, second thoughts and constructive dithering. The writing may be addressed to the whole map or one small, appealing or troublesome aspect of the map. One person wrote the following letter to their map of the moment.

> *'Dear blank space,*
>
> *I see you there. You might think I am coming to get you and fill you with words, but I want to accept you. You can be the unknown, unmarked part of me. You can be alright as you are, and I can leave you alone.'*

Try writing a letter to something or someone for a few minutes. You are not going to send it, but you are going to sit with it and let it have a voice. You are writing to discover your intentions or needs and own or disown the words which come from the pen. Write with pen and paper and don't worry about spelling. Write tidily enough that you can read it out loud afterwards.

Write for yourself: no one else is going to hear it or read it out unless you want the experience of sharing your writing with someone, you trust them and you want their response. Choosing who or what you are writing to is important. It is part of the discovery process to identify a target of address. It might be a thing, a person and idea or a moment in time or a place. You are writing to discover your relationships with it and with whatever is associated with it. For example, supposing I feel I eat too much, and I want to exercise more control. Do I write a letter to food or to the idea of eating too much? Do I write to the food that is most difficult for me to resist? I need a phrase that captures an open target of address that will bring other things into view. Something like:

> *'Dear fridge door,*
>
> *When I open you and peer in, I am hoping to see cheese and pies! And? And the warm embrace of my mother. I remember when I opened you and the fridge was empty, I wondered who is going to look after me and what stops me looking after myself...'*

In other words, I am writing to a moment, to a context with an intention to freewheel and see what connotations and connections come from the spontaneous process of writing. Did I know I was looking for the containing presence of my mother in the fridge? Not until I wrote it. Do I know what it means? Not until I read it and see what the words written in the spirit of an inner conversation are transformed with my voice behind them and meet the mixed feelings (shimmering) and memories (hovering) and further associations that are carried by the shared experience of voicing.

How will I respond to what I have written when I read it over or read it out? That too is a process of discovery. I may dismiss it as random nonsense or I may think afresh about food and comfort in childhood or what food means when I am grazing between meals. I have one memory just in writing this now and it is that my mum loved giving us small treats of cake or biscuits as reward for efforts and jobs done. I can remember the process of promised treats more than I can remember the treats or the jobs done. The phrase stays with me now: 'We are doing well. We deserve a reward.' As will be indicated later, writing can very usefully develop a quality of having a conversational correspondence. The main focus or addressee of my writing (the fridge door, my mum, food) could write back to me with me as both author and recipient).

Discovery writing is free style and should not be burdened by too many expectations. You are not writing to tell or confess the truth or find a far-reaching meaning. You are writing to enter into your inner world of words for feelings and ideas. The opening sentence in discovery writing anchors who or what you are addressing at the start, but you might be helped by having a contrasting position in sight as well. Signing off the process of writing in the form of a letter may point to a change in authorship. Do I sign my letter off to the fridge and food as me or do I include my mum? Has an 'I' become a 'we'?

If you do have difficulty getting going with discovery writing then start with something familiar, ordinary, acceptable and immediate. Or try this exercise of writing to the steps along an imaginary line between two contrasting positions. For example, supposing I am feeling low and overwhelmed by the things I have got to do or want to do. I might start writing, 'Dear helpless now....' To help write more freely I would 'put helpless now' at one end of a horizontal line (as in the preceding chapter) and imagine the opposite. As I write to the feeling helpless end, I would think about what writing might say to help or hinder me moving along a bit to the more empowering and agentic end.

These are the elements of discovery through writing. It makes a difference to do this writing and reading out in the context of talking with a map and in the spirit of developing conversational awareness. In so doing we are writing to the bedrock of how conversational language became our uniquely human superpower half a million years ago as evoked in the next chapter (8) through Cora and the 'mother of tongues'. Words or rather the utterances we direct at people and things around us were arrows (pointers and markers), which with syntax become relational and social forms of shared thinking. Words have 'legs on' and become transferable giving one meaning here and another meaning there. But they are transferable and generalizable as symbols only because they began with an immediate local context in time and place. Each word is a carrier of little stories and maps (its etymology) but ready to lend itself to other uses in the context of the moment. The olive grove where Socrates held his conversation classes which gave voice to the Western philosophical narrative was reputedly owned by a farmer by the name of Academius. Little did he know he would give his name to all kinds of colleges and campuses and a certain style of relating. This footnote of history may now be, shall we say, academic, but it is surprising how many words have legs on, and move here and there until their origins are lost.

In talking with a map and in discovery writing we are taking words as arrows – whether in written, spoken or mapped form. Whatever a word or phrase is carrying as content, its other meaning is in the process to which it is pointing and linking from or to. When we ask in conversation or in reflection: what do you mean? We are also asking where are you? Or where are we going with this? As infants our earliest vocalisations and utterances are like finger movements. Words point us somewhere. They point, they locate, they invite attention. They (we) are looking for meaning by making links to maps in our brains. We are navigating our paths and positions as we negotiate meaning. Words call out for a response. They team up with other words to make sentences and thread sentences together which are then gathered into paragraphs of writing, or passages of speech and networks of maps and map-making skills in our brains.

Do we have control and agency over this? Do we hover and shimmer and step in and out of participation in things as authors? We might settle for saying that it is a co-creative process. We may say that we chose our words but at the same time words take on a life of their own. Put two words together and they will change each other's meaning. Dog-walk or dog-tired take us in different directions. Forget about Freudian slips of the tongue and think more about the vitality, mischief and exuberance of words. For Mikael Bakhtin words are dialogic. We need writing and mapping and talking to trust our words to surprise us as we speak to and of them.

The act of writing creates a triangle between the word on paper, the thought or feeling in the moment and the reflective sense of self. Opening a multi-sensory space between pen and hands, voice and ears, eyes and paper, self and others engages all aspects of our brain. What am I saying? Why do I want to say it? How shall I say it? How will it be received and understood? What will the response be and what response do I want, or hope for or fear?

Writing demands the three Cs of compassion, courage, curiosity: compassion for self and the world; courage to trust self and others and get alongside difficult feelings and ideas and challenge them; curiosity about how it all works and is orchestrated. Curiosity is a shared quality, and we need to look for the companionship that allows us to be in the middle of different points of views and not right or wrong. We won't ever write with a spirit of discovery without awareness of the cultural context, and for this we may need the third C of courage to trust ourselves to take a risk and reach out with words. Courage might be judged to be something that comes from within but equally it is something that needs mutual encouragement. Companionship with 'my' self might be added as a fourth C. A conversation with myself is a friendship with 'my' self. In the sense that I am not talking at myself or giving myself a talking to. At the same time companionship is a quality we achieve and validate interpersonally and hope to find solidarity in the culture around us. Some cultures dictate the terms of companionship and others celebrate the freedom and diversity to be companions in whatever ways and with whatever language we chose.

Writing to the whole map in the manner of a 'Dear Map' letter is one option. Alternatively, try writing a paragraph or short letter to one part of the map that resonates or calls for further scrutiny. Or write a short spontaneous letter, no more than a paragraph or two in length, to each of the places on the map.

Where a pattern is beginning to be mapped, tracked and written out it can help to connect in a more heartfelt way with the memories and experiences triggered by the mapping or writing by identifying a person, time, object or place as the addressee of a spontaneously written letter. For example, if my dad was an ice-cream salesman and never let me eat ice-cream, I could spontaneously write:

> *Dear ice cream,*
>
> *You were always so enticing and desirable, but you were kept from me. There was never any explanation and the bullying and controlling way I was forbidden to have one made me long for you even more. I was always left in the dark as to why eating ice cream might be bad and never learnt to think for myself about it. Now I am obsessed with ice cream, and I cannot think about my dad without thinking about ice-cream. The conversation and the relationship are iced over.*

It would address my dad and my feelings but slightly at a tangent. The processes of projection, imagination and reciprocation are allowed with more room for analogy, metaphor and relational awareness. You could try a version of this by writing to something tangible in your childhood knowing that you are connecting to a significant person through it.

It can be interesting at the end of a conversation to write a spontaneous letter to the side of you that you feel you have shared in the conversation (or some aspect of it) as a way of evaluating and validating the experience. It offers a space to connect from the outside of the conversation while it is still fresh. Such impromptu writing is fishing for hidden connections and patterns.

Imagine saying this at the end of a conversation or at a point where the conversation is stuck: 'let's stop for ten minutes and each write and then read out a short letter to the conversation as it is for us just now.' Once written, the letters are read out in turn. It is likely to bring us into the present, equalise the relationship and help us negotiate how to continue the conversation.

A variation on the ice-cream letter is to write a 'Dear Homeland' letter. These letters speak of childhood home and family indirectly by addressing the locality and its geography. Many of us have left the area where we grew up. For some it no longer exists or cannot be returned to. Even if we have stayed 'at home' the place and time of childhood was very different to how it is now. Try writing for ten minutes to a childhood place that strikes a chord: the walk to school, the local shops, the surrounding hills or the city centre. One person wrote to the river in her town, another to the first house in which they lived. Some people have found it powerful to then write a letter back from the street, or country, or homeland place. A dialogue with places, times and voices across the gaps and divides between past and present, is potentially discovered especially when reading out and voicing as described later in this chapter. What has been written and read out can also be mapped out and talked about more.

In all these examples the addressee of the letter can be the source of a reply. My fridge door could write back to me (*'Dear compulsive opener of fridge doors! Why blame me? It is you that come to me and open me. I am not enticing you. Am I? Why don't you have more will power or find better things to do? Go and look for your inner mother elsewhere'*).

Writing can play an important part in developing conversational awareness and can assist the interaction between mapping and talking. It can be a scaffolding for hovering and shimmering with conflicting and confusing feelings and ideas. Short bursts of spontaneous writing for ten minutes which are addressed to a specific issue, theme or moment can help discover and recover a more open dialogue.

In summary this is what to try and do.

1. Have pen and paper. Create some space and privacy for twenty minutes. You are writing a letter to revitalise your relationship with something specific in time and place that you want to connect with and address. It may be part of you (Dear red wine) or around you (Dear climate crisis) or inside you (Dear angry and grumpy mood) or from others to you (Dear bossy managers).
2. Find an opening phrase for the target of your writing. It is a tag line or something indicative of what you want to address. The quality of who or what you address is important as it needs to be not quite head-to-head and not quite side-by-side. For example, if you were wanting to connect

with your views and feelings about the climate crisis it would be different if you started with, dear climate deniers, or dear oil companies, or dear wild and windy world.

3. You are writing with ears and eyes on words that resonate and trigger further thoughts and feelings: words that make links and bridges, words that carry feelings. Start writing and engage with it as freely as possible. But don't go off on one. You might lose yourself from time to time and find yourself again, but don't forget the observing and orchestrating part of yourself.
4. Write double-spaced so there is room for edits and add-ins later when you recap, read over and revise what you have written. Don't worry about spelling. It needs to be legible for you. You are not writing a novel or a poem. This is just for you and the conversation you want to build with yourself or someone else. There may well be ordinary poetic moments of feeling and connection with words on reflection.
5. As you write you are having a conversation with yourself and your writing. You are writing your way up and down the perspective ladder of seeing the micro and the macro point of view. It is a spontaneous process of reflecting on reflections, so write about the strong or conflicting feelings but comment on their impact as well. Discovery writing involves reflecting spontaneously as you go. Am I saying this? Okay I am saying this but why? And why now?
6. Don't give up when you dry up. Start from another angle or point of view. Read back what you have written and get going again.
7. After ten minutes or so stop. Before you read it back to yourself, just write a few more lines about the process of writing. How did it go? What was helpful or difficult? Give thought to the gap between having written the letter and reading it out. It is mulling over time. Now read through what you have written, and you may add and amend, comment on bits, or connect with some elements of it. Or read it aloud with the person with whom you are in conversation.
8. If you have been mapping a conversation and have been writing to one part of the map or one element of the conversation, then link the writing to the words on the map.

Words make stories and patterns

There is a gap between the finding of words and them being written on paper. A gap that is between the wording and the being worded. It is a gap filled by hovering and shimmering with the voicing of our thoughts and feelings. Once spoken, meanings emerge from the shape and structure of the words on the map (they are 'listening' maps) and there is room in a good story sharing experience to retell and reword it in response to our immediate feelings. In this we can see the relationship between words in the conversation and story, but also more generally see our own and other people's relationships with language and speaking.

Our ambivalence about sorting and finishing our stories is that on the one hand we might reach conversational closure and clarity and on the other we might have to face the end of the conversational relationship. The value of stories developing conversational and relational awareness (Chapter 6) assisted by mapping is that the storying process is not finished. As we see the gaps and links between words, we have more chance to construct alternative words and phrases. We don't just mull over or ruminate for the right words, but we also discover them in the back and forth of conversation. We have to trust the messiness and anxiety of this. Our mental maps and the maps embedded in our words and stories meet with the tentative mapping of words on paper. In Figure 7.1 we start with voicing and sensing the meanings we need to express and find the words that are strong enough to help. The activity of openly and transparently mapping and talking helps us do this, and from it, conversational relationships and stories emerge. As already described the story gets storied. And it is the conversational life of this process with its making of links and touching of gaps that the process of retelling and rewording stories is engaged.

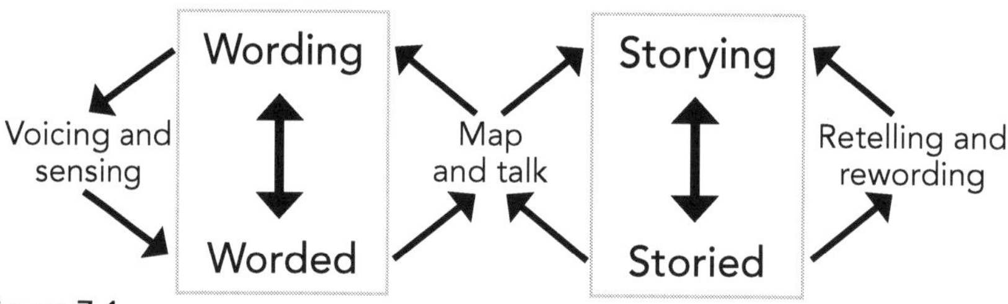

Figure 7.1

Another way of thinking about this is to view conversational awareness as a process of 'unstorying' fixed and closed stories. We bring stories to our conversations and relationships in the hope of a kind and helpful experience of 'unstorying' them. In the process we find that some important element of the experience has never had its story told, or the new telling and the restorying brings out new emotional links and ideas.

Some stories about our lives are partly shared as cover stories. They bypass darker stories or difficult moments in relationships. They serve to protect us or give us familiarity when looking back. But they also serve as a cover for something less easy to relate to, so we avoid it by covering over any links. The activities of talking with a map, then writing and then voicing can help us choose, alone or together, what to approach or knowingly avoid.

Conversations give rise to stories which have their patterns in the form of plots and character. These minor and major life stories are a key part of what we share in conversation. They are like ready-mapped patterns from our memory bank. We apply these 'memorised' maps to other people's stories and to our understanding of the world. They are also woven into the fabric of the culture and societies around us as much as within our identities, personal histories and personalities. They are what position us and structure our sense of self. Their patterns are what we want to be more aware of through mapping writing and talking.

Mapping and writing with and for our voices

Talking with a map and writing to discover meaning have in common an experience of giving voice more mutually and self-consciously. Moments of losing voice, whispering or emotionally choking on our words and feelings of embarrassment or shame at the words that come to mind are of equal importance as the moments of delight and full voice. The work on the voice in this chapter is explored further in a forthcoming book titled *Therapy with a Voice* (to be published 2023) co-written by the author with Lucy Cutler.

Nothing is quicker to making us self-conscious than hearing a recording of our own voice. If we can get over this and develop an ear for the changing vitality and emotionality of our voice, we have another gateway to our emotions, relationships and changing sense of self. The tone the pitch, the resonance and self-perceived authenticity or falseness of the voice changes with the changing words we speak.

There are benefits in reading out what is written. It is a voicing and sharing of the writing. It is an invitation to experience what has been written from a once-removed perspective. Once something is written out it can be a partner in a second level of conversation with yourself. The exposure may be less intensely interpersonal since it is mediated by the text, and we can disown and stand back from the words on paper by saying things that give reflective space such as 'I don't know why I wrote that'. It is a re-reading of the writing that brings a chance to revise and develop it. When recapping with the map the moments of more self-consciously voicing parts of what is laid out on paper may bring new connections which would not have been made without the extra attention to the voice. It is an invitation to engage with all the directions and levels of the conversational awareness grid described in Chapter 6. We hear the voice inside our heads ('listen to yourself!'), the intimate interpersonal voice ('I only speak like this with you') and the public social voice ('ladies and gentlemen, tickets please') and the supplicant or imaginative voice to the unknown ('what's it all about?'). The gaps between how I hear myself and how I am heard can be noticed, named and negotiated and their creative, performative and therapeutic possibilities explored.

Reading out creates a space between what we see written on paper and how it comes across when voiced. How does the voice change in pace or direction of address? Does it tighten or loosen according to the felt or actual response of others? We need an intuitive sense of the 'two-way arrows' behind every voicing as our speech speeds up and slows down, flows and hesitates, rises and falls in and out of dialogue with all that is within and around it. When we tell and re-tell stories of our life experiences, we are potentially giving voice from a different position each time and with a different potential to remember and reconnect with cherished, disavowed or unformulated experiences.[43]

Fluctuating voice awareness is the constant companion to a conversation, the relationships within it and around it, the language being used, and the stories told. Our voices are a hovering and shimmering presence. As we Map and Talk with pen and paper we are mapping and talking with our voices. Moments of voicing from the map are the gateway moments between mind, brain, body and culture. What the voice does with its vocalisations, hesitations and interruptions, is find words that can carry a story, make a connection, turn a broken sentence of memory into a whole paragraph of felt meaning. A word previously voiced without emotion or in a fixed and cliched manner can unexpectedly come alive and resonate.

A mutual willingness to be interested in, kind to and surprised by our voices is helpful. Do I know or trust my voice? Does it give me away? Does it sound like it is performing? Is it nervous, shaky or brash? Is my voice different in different roles? Is there a reciprocation in evidence between our voices? What does my voice elicit? Does my confident voice make yours more anxious? Does my compassionate voice bring tenderness into your voice to yourself? Does my monotonous account of my stories bring out a monotonous tone from you or do you counter it with a more varied and urgent voice? If I recap with an authoritative voice does that stop your doubtful voice coming out? These are the questions that might accompany our willingness to be interested in vocal aspect of conversation.

In summary we hear our voice with our own critical or sympathetic ear. Just as we may join a choir or practice our singing voice so we can find our conversational voice more freely and with more relational authenticity through compassionate practice. If we can replace shame with compassion and curiosity, it can help us listen as we speak to the emotional cadence of our own and other's voices. The voice may touch thoughts and feelings that lie beyond or beneath what is being read out. Shy words may grow in confidence, words too often loudly repeated may look a little ridiculous and be reigned in. The voice is the active ingredient in what was described in Chapter 6 as conversational awareness of shimmering and hovering, participating and authoring.

As show in Figure 7.2 we might give too much attention to the top right corner and the outer and interpersonal focus of the conversation. We need an ear for hearing our inner voice or the words when spoken as also addressed to ourselves. The interpersonal vitality of the process of speaking, recapping with a map or reading out some personal writing is enriched if the voices from within and the voices that are locked in rumination can be also attended to as in the bottom left corner of the grid. It is a partly performative and defensive solution to giving voice to go into the bottom right corner and be talking at the world and not having room for empathy for the listener and their voices and the listener within us.

Writing out-loud mediates the inner voice outer voice dialogue

Figure 7.2

It may seem fanciful to suggest that we are listening to an invisible voice but in all conversations, whether therapeutic or not, there are moments of silence and reflection. There may be moments in reading aloud to say, 'Shall I pause there and shall we see what feelings are in the air?' These may be moments to hesitate or refer to maps of the conversational relationship.

Recapping from the map or reading out a paragraph of reflective writing is an invitation to re-vocalise; to hear familiar life experience in a different voice and to take the opportunity to reword, revisit and restory the story. It engages brain and body in a multi-sensory dialogue to experience what may well be familiar words in a different way and in response to a different context with the map as midwife.

In summary here is what to keep in mind

1. See the maps and letters and other bits of writing as a platform and a space for working with the voice
2. Take time to share and take turns to give voice to patterns provisionally identified on the map or in writing. It can help move towards a more emotionally-focused conversation.
3. Rehearse your voice by reading letters and recapping around a map out loud to yourself. Then ask your conversational partner how the voice sounds and how could you or would they voice it differently.
4. Follow the feelings in your voice, or in you when you hear your voice, or when you hear your words voiced by another person.
5. Take time in the style of 'empty chair work' to seek the reciprocal expression of both ends of a reciprocal role by speaking to, of, and with, the voices embedded in the roles.
6. See the mapping, writing and voicing as an enactment magnet for re-wording, re-voicing, re-authoring.
7. Make it an opportunity to be the observer rather than the participant in our stories.

Returning to conversational awareness

The essential companion to any talk, to all conversation, is the voice. We develop all these qualities and dimensions of conversational awareness through talking, mapping, writing, rewording and re-voicing what we are discussing. Raising awareness of how these interact, both in their moments, and in the general scheme of things, is integrative and empowering for us. In Figure (7.3) the circle of interaction shows how when talking we connect and listen, when mapping we are seeing and wording which leads to storying, recapping and restorying and making links and finding gaps. To these we respond by feeling and voicing and having moments of owning and authoring what we understand. We use the insights that arise to negotiate new understanding which leads to more talking, connecting and listening. The richness and complexity of this interaction through different media and activities is helped by mapping, writing and voicing. It gives us tools to negotiate and navigate our world. It helps develop reflective capacity and feelings for conversational story telling which might be called narrative competence. As discussed in Chapter 4 we can rush to quickly to story our life stories and have them tidy and told. This healthy need for being storied and sorted can be challenged by an equally healthy and contrasting need to hold the story open and tolerate the uncertainty and 'novelty'[44] of an unfinished story with several threads in play. One ever present witness to this struggle to keep the story open or close it down is the changing pitch, conviction and tone of our voices.

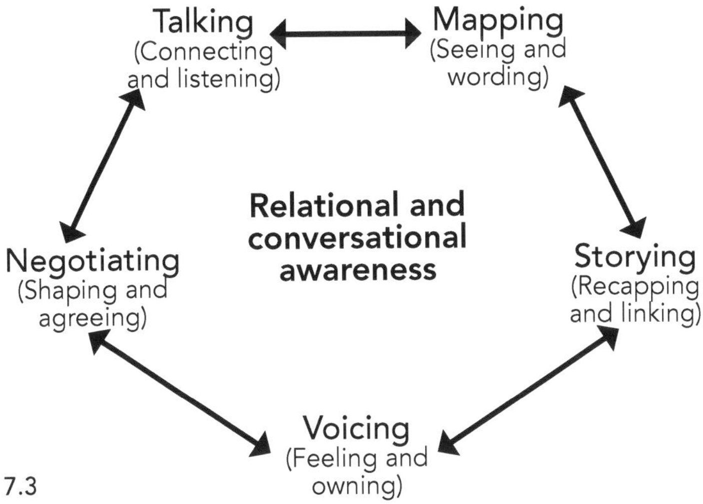

Figure 7.3

Our voices, and the changing ways we vocalise our search for meaning and connection, is central to how we access, recognise, express, and own our feelings and make emotional sense of ourselves. The voice is tremulous with the presence or absence of emotion. We talk in agitated, flat, heartfelt, nervous, loud, hesitant, insistent ways to mention a few of the qualities of voicing.

Chapter 8: Cora, the mother of tongues

Introduction

This chapter is a thought experiment or adventure story rooted in the feeling that, when talking our way through the 21st century – with its rich, and at times bewildering fabric of languages, voices, conversations, libraries and super computers all around us – we are also touching something deep and vital in the very beginnings of language and conversational awareness in the human species. Every infant, in their early years, replays this amazing journey with words and stories with an innate readiness to join a conversation a million years in the making. The more I have talked with a map with individuals in therapy or with teams as a teacher of reflective practice I have wondered at our extraordinary ability to connect quickly with each other through words in the air and on paper between us. It is as if there is a dialogic imagination or relational intelligence that is rekindled by the intimate personal theatre of Map and Talk. It draws on our entry into relationships in early childhood and the growth of language and conversation through those relationships. But it also draws on the slow and multi-sensory, multi-purpose birth story of language and conversation. It is not a story that we will ever know the answer to and fools (like me) rush in where archaeologists refrain from treading.

This chapter draws on four books that are rich in their rethinking of our early origins and of the interplay of language, minds, brains, people and society. One is the *Dawn of Everything* by David Graeber and David Wengrow.[45] The second is *The Dawn of Language: Axes, Lies, Midwifery and How We Came to Talk* by Sverker Johansson.[46] The third book is *A Mind So Rare* by Merlin Donald[47] The fourth is *The Poet's Voice in the Making of Mind* by Russell Meares. Together they offer a multi-disciplinary view. They have freed me from a Eurocentric and colonialist view of the ancient past – as if there was a slow linear development from savage pre-history (noble or base) to our modern times. As Graeber and Wengrow explain so cogently, much of our theorising about the past is to justify some aspect of our present order of things. I hope I have not joined that dance. Sverker Johansson offers a social view of how language developed out of uniquely human needs and relationships such as those around childbirth, midwifery and group living. I have taken an orchestral view of how units of language making combined in larger more versatile conversations and given it a tentative platform through the characters and stories of this chapter. Merlin Donald traces the building blocks of both the evolution of language and mind from mimicry to myth telling and theory building in the progression to the hybrid brains (part in our heads, part in our cultures) of modern times. Russel Meares offers many riches, two of which are mentioned here. One is his concern with how story and conversation play a key part in what is remembered. He writes about culture being 'made of a network of stories, which gives to Homo sapiens an immense evolutionary advantage.'[48] He explores how words, conversation and self are the material of human consciousness and I take from his perspective the added merit of being able to create the analogical space of mapping as a simulation of what we were doing with our early and convivial brains fifty or a hundred thousand years ago. I can only say that writing this chapter has freed my thinking about how mapping, conversation and language lie at the heart of what makes us human and sociable and mutually dependent and co-creative in present times.

There seems to be an integrative and a fragmenting tendency to human language. On the one hand different language communities come together and create a common language all the richer for integrating their separate forms. One the other hand groups separate and divide and create, within a generation or two, their own local dialect, or their own special jargon and ways with words. We only have to look to youth groups and cultures or academic sub-disciplines to see it happening. The impulse to divide is mixed up with an impulse by national elites to disorganise our relationships with the common language and fill it with double speak. The impulse to integrate is mixed up with an impulse to take control and discipline a standard language and terms of communication.

The years of talking with a map with people from different backgrounds and different languages brings me to take the side of a third group. Let's call them the 'Versatilists', who want to be in with both camps: those who value the local language and those who champion the common language. The 'versatilists' are cosmopolitan, multi-lingual by inclination and see all conversation as a form of translation and a shared experience of word finding. They think locally and globally. They hover and shimmer in search of shared meaning between individuals and groups and know we need help talking across our divides and differences if we are not to end up talking in silos or talking such a bland common speech that it has no utility or authority. They know they need help making meaning together, and time talking about how the relationships are going in the conversation. They step back from being always transactional and getting the communication sorted by the cheapest or fastest means possible. They know that conversation is the everyday theatre for keeping human language alive and active. They have often been outsiders.

They are us at our best and (I am going to suggest) they were us at the birth of human conversation. They know that they have to reconcile the inner conversation with themselves with the world around them and especially the people with whom they are most intimately involved. They work for a mix of relational and conversational awareness.

In this chapter I want to play with the hypothesis that our ancient entry into language and conversation was given momentum by early 'versatilists' who saw the need for a double dialogue between the various local ways of talking and some more common ways of talking.

How or when language became conversational we will never directly know, but it is likely that there were times of knitting together several local languages from different realms of activity such as childbirth, hunting, foraging, tool making and navigating. Each had their own vitality and limits. They are not just languages or dialects or forms of speech but in contemporary sociological terms they might be seen as sub-cultural styles arising from and tied to the different kinds of work language evolved to do. I am going to call them tongues. I am interested in how our early ancestors developed conversations out of a confusion and combination of different tongues, and, in the process, words found their symbolic, analogical and metaphorical legs. Some individuals must have had the first gifted conversational and integrative ears for links, gaps and crossovers between words, people and contexts, and been the weavers of words and been mothers of tongues. Imagine Cora as one such person. As homo sapiens spread around the earth, there were Coras in this or that tribe right down to our times. Why was it a woman? Because women were more likely to be the connectors and the relational moderators of all the different subsets of language development.

So, imagine going back in time with these stories of the girl, woman, mother, leader, innocent chatter box, sage person, wordfinder, who we might call 'Cora, mother of all the tongues' and who bore witness to and nurtured that slow time of transition when talking changed from amiable chatter, task management and grooming, to deliberate, constructive and self-conscious conversation. And we humans developed the power to be collectively, and self-consciously interested in ourselves. We developed narrative capacity and greatly enhanced our consciousness and societal complexity.

Cora's story

Cora was a talkative, restless child with a musical voice who cared for the little ones from an early age. She had a great memory. The more she talked the more she gathered words and carried them from one part of her life to another. She used hunting words for nursing and nursing words for hunting. She saw how the boys and girls used flirty words for fighting and fighting words for flirting.

As a youngster, when she was out foraging through the forest with her friends, she was gathering words from the banter as much as the fruit and nuts from the trees. When there was conflict and confusion, people in her community came to her, not to do something but to say something and share her way with words. She became the mother of tongues when conflicts and needs became unspeakable.

Conversation was in its infancy. It was just a background singsong noisy way of messaging each other along with hand movements, facial and bodily gestures. But Cora heard the words differently. She could mimic and spread both phrases and names. Cora could intuitively see the uses of conversation as an aid to our individual and collective narrative capacity. People spoke but syntax was rudimentary and words direct. Cora could sense when visiting strangers had the power of words and were willing to trade conversations. She was hungry for these visits and pushed herself forward to the centre of things to hear and remember every exchange of utterances and every word. She learnt that talking about how to talk was as important as what was talked about. She noted how every so often a different level of consciousness flashed across the communal landscape. A consciousness not of they are talking, or I am talking but we are talking.

Bit by bit through Cora's long life she gathered in the different threads of language by teaching people what and how to say things in the best way. What Cora learnt, with or without realising it, was passed on to the next generation and so on down through time. Different forms and styles of talking rubbed sweet or sour against each other. It was the rubbing of the language that was creating the basis for conversation not the specific words.

The active men and women went hunting, used sign language as much as words and were prisoners of tradition. The women, when pregnant and going on the risky journey of giving birth, held each other close and talked about feelings and carried the wisdom of birth stories in all their painful and joyful variety from one generation to another. Cora sat in on the tool making, stone chipping 'schools' and broke the silence of mimicry by introducing talking lessons – to add phrases and rhymes to highlight the delicate and complex skills of choosing the stone, then finding the best way of holding, chipping and polishing it.

Cora could mix and join with all sides of the community. She would sing the well-loved stories with the old folk, mediate between the loudest voices, and bring forward the quietist ones. She saw how each of her own children and the infants around her learnt language in different ways. They picked up words like they would pick up twigs and berries and play with them. She coached the children to be word foragers. Though the changing seasons would bring feast or famine there was always a plentiful supply of words when Cora was there.

According to Sverker Johansson, we do not know when this was. We cannot dig up Cora's voice. It could easily be at various times in different parts of the world.

It might have been gained and then lost over thousands of years. It could be three hundred thousand years ago or a million years ago. We may never know but we do know that with conversation humans found the superpower that freed them to navigate and negotiate in bigger numbers, leading to exponential development of skills and resources. Perhaps over a million years the elements of a conversational language were being orchestrated together in a virtuous cycle of adaptation and evolution with bigger brains generating smarter group relationships, bigger groups and better nutrition, more adaptive childcare and learning, more varied tools and versatile culture to the point where language requires intention, vocabularies and grammar.[49] We got smarter by combining different lines and directions of language and developed conversational awareness which became the fertile breeding ground for consciousness itself and the hybrid brain and culture so richly described by Merlin Donald.

Perhaps Cora realised that to be a mother (or a parent or a teacher or a good citizen) we must be a mother of all the tongues around us: a mother who can teach and speak within and across several languages and ways of communication. She understood that conversation is a form of translation and negotiating meaning and not just the passing back and forth of time-honoured grunts and whistles however endearing and varied. Cora did not just talk with words in a transactional way but talked about words in a conversational way. In mixing with the neighbouring and passing communities she not only learnt a bigger vocabulary but a different relationship with language.

Imagine Cora in her youth as one of the youngsters, running through a newly discovered patch of the forest wording and singing back and forth to each other as they forage for fruit, herbs, and mushrooms. The last of the summer sun was shining through the trees and highlighting a plentiful supply of berries (red, yellow, and blue) ripe for picking. This is the time to be gathering for the winter and leaner times. The social organisation between them during these seasonal times of plenty is playful and relaxed and hierarchy is loose. Their sounds, gestures and words are direct and immediately descriptive in the here and now: trees are trees, berries are berries.

There is little space for metaphor, symbol, or analogy: words don't have legs. But Cora hears another level of relating with 'wooing and wowing' romancing and bonding in the air. Their singing and wording is helping them gather a 'memory map' of the forest, each in their own way, but with enough common elements that they would be able to describe to others how to navigate there and find the good berries when they get back to the settlement and talk through the evening. They would use their hands and gestures and placename words (big tree, sudden dip, dark wood) to point out and affirm the directions.

This work is taxing and shifting different components of their brains and making them hungry. More than most, Cora senses it, delights in it and feels as if on the edge of sacred new knowledge as their mapping 'grammar' and vocabulary grows.

Cora sees some poisonous red berries growing prettily and colourfully in among the bushes. She picks a bunch and shouts 'watch out for red berries.' The singing and the romancing stops. Now she has their attention, Cora dangles temptingly one of the red berries to her lips and makes a yucky, disgusted look with her face. Cora puts her hand to her throat and waves the berries in the air. 'Don't red berry me,' she shouts at them. Her companions first sensing danger then relief, chorus back turning her warning into song. They all sing, 'Don't red berry me' and grab their throats and gurgle with yucky sounds as if being poisoned. To 'red berry' is now part verb, part noun but a word with 'legs on': a phrase in search of multiple meanings. Cora ties the red berries to her hair and wipes her hands. She is enjoying herself.

That evening, Siro – one of the restless young men was being sexually provocative without invitation to Nira, who was responding by lowering her head and looking away. She did not want to spoil the collective celebrations of the evening with anger, but she wanted the intrusion to stop. Everyone sensed an upset but were not sure what to do. Cora noticed and had no fear to go and quietly challenge Siro to his face. She took the red berries from her hair and waved them in his face: 'Don't be a red berry'. Everyone heard and saw and nodded. Siro was embarrassed; he had been there foraging earlier in the day and had seen the play with red berries in the woods. He held up his hands in 'sorry and surrender' mode with an anxious look to Cora and apologies to Nira. As he walked away he turned back to Cora saying, 'I red berry myself'. There was shame in his head held down and his shoulders turned inwards. Nira looked up at Cora, as if saying, leave it there and don't let the red berry words spill on to me. They sat and talked quietly to each other. The old women and old men who were watching nodded and acknowledged to each other that in their time this would have led to violence.

After the exchange, Cora needed to go and sit alone and hold her head. She was struggling with the magical power of words that can make a map of one small moment and then be used to map another. It hurt when thinking too much in words. How do words kindle and bring fire to a conversation? Can moments of dangerous or special emotions be negotiated safer and faster with less hurt, with words as the go-betweens.

Cora went and found Siro and gave him blue berries, the sweetest of them all. 'These berries say sorry. They are for you to give to Nira but also for you from me to give to yourself.'

In a long life, Cora had many children and shared many birth stories, each with their own life and death struggle of joy and pain. Each birth story was a shared drama for the women, and the struggle to give birth was a special and sacred time involving everyone. Cora loved the soothing power of words in the language of midwives and the sharing of knowhow from one birth to another. Always someone knew another way of doing things. She could share in passing on stories of how this or that birth was dealt with. She loved the way everyone put their heads together. But she also felt the tone of intimacy of playfulness and seriousness along with the curiosity of children gathered round at a birth. It was as if the conversational seeds of language were being planted with the talk of pregnancy, childbirth and the first months and years of life. This was where language was most useful and sensitive in its role of containing and explaining and helping work out the best way of celebrating survival or accepting loss. There were red berry and blue berry moments.

Sandy, aged two and half years, was climbing along the trunk of a fallen tree and Cora went to hold his hand. 'I can', he said. 'I can what?' asked Cora. Sandy replied, 'I can do it'. 'I can do what?' asked Cora as she again offered to hold his hand which he refused. Eventually Sandy found the words that made a whole sentence and a map of his moments of experience balancing on the log. He said with his words wobbling as much as his body, 'I can walk along the log.' 'How can you walk along the log?' asked Cora. Sandy stopped and thought and then turned to Cora. 'I can walk along the log without help now I am big enough.' Sandy then let Cora hold his hand. Cora smiled. She liked his independence, but she liked even more his willingness to let her help him string out words into syntax and give voice to his struggle for independence and find a sentence that can walk its full length of the experience with the log and bring it home to a conclusion. Learning to talk is learning to map our experience and be in it and outside it with another person. With language comes a convivial and compassionate consciousness from which we can negotiate if given a chance.

It was long the tradition that when they were hunting in the early hours, the men and women worked quietly without singing. They had their sign language as complex as any word language. 'Why would they talk like babies', they said, 'and get emotional and disturb the animals with laughter and tears?' In her younger years Cora went with them and watched them gesturing and signing to each other with their bird whistles and shouting they had learnt from the men and women who are now frail elders. When they sang of the hunting in the evenings, their songs, to Cora's ears sounded somewhat closed and ritualised compared to the improvised songs for foraging and the chat of the young people around childbirth and cooking. It was if they were not reflecting on the events of the day but imposing a fixed story on them. Nothing could be learned that way, thought Cora.

One day she brought some of the fleet-footed younger boys and girls to run between the men with updates on where the animals were. She signalled, 'Let us come back and forth among you like *whisper voices* and you can spread out further with more knowledge in the air between you.' They had success in hunting and that evening they talked about it more openly and had less time for the traditional stories. They used the whisper voices more and more in their hunting and not only did it help them hunt it also gave them more to talk about on the journey home and in the evening.

One time one of the youngsters made up a story of a mammoth being near, lying wounded in a gully, and with excitement they all rushed there only to find a rabbit. The hunters were angry at being tricked by the lie and it troubled Cora that words could be used deliberately to deceive and mislead. Cora called the story the moment they made a 'mammoth out of a rabbit' and they made some rules of language from the story which then became part of the laws of conversation. Whenever something silly happened and people got unnecessarily carried away with feelings, they called it making a mammoth out of a rabbit. In Cora's lifetime it happened so often it just became making a 'mammoth'. Language can lead and language can lie and to Cora it became clear you have to have a conversation which watches each other's faces and gestures as you talk to see the signs of honesty in the words.

One evening, Gravis, who was the most dominant of the hunter men, told Cora with a troubled look that he had a dream the night before of words ghosting around him and birthing voices of women calling him and telling him where the bison were. That day he led the group to where the voices told him the bison would be most easily chased. Gravis worried that he would be laughed at if he shared his dream and was seen as the hunter who was led by women. Cora said that the words in his dream come from women's voices but the words when you take them to the forest live in you and are yours. Words are not just from men or women, from hunting, foraging or birthing but from the wind and the forest and the sun and the stars. Words have roots but they also leave them behind. In this way Cora touched something magic. She daydreamed of great conversations that lasted for hours with words and meanings multiplying as the speaking proceeded. She also had her nightmares when words were chopped up and voices silenced.

Cora loved watching the older men and women chipping away at the stone to make the cutting tools: the hand axe's, needles and knives. The skills of making axes took a long time to learn and it was an art that had the highest status in all the tribal communities. The master stone workers knew how to chip, shape and select a likely piece, and they would deftly create a tool and then get the young apprentices to try.

What puzzled Cora was the silence other than murmurs and catches of breath that accompanied this work of apprenticeship, as if the copying of the master's movements needed all the attention and all the senses. She asked questions, echoed the answers and made a song poem of the main movements and the breakthroughs and setbacks. The apprentices joined in and soon the micro details of the skills had words, and the steps had a syntax. The rhythm of the speech tuned into the rhythm of the work and was transactional and instrumental but also conversational. When the rhythm was broken it was not clear to Cora whether this was a breakthrough or a setback. With her cheeky and curious talkative style, she encouraged each apprentice to say what he or she was thinking and intending and learning as they practised. Not everyone liked to talk whilst working, as if their brains were best suited to silent concentration. Sometimes the silent ones made the best discoveries in technique and the accompanying conversation was thought to be a distraction at first. In time it seemed to help make the apprenticeship more deliberate and more conscious. Feelings of failure and frustration were acknowledged. Moments of triumph and pride were not just cheered but carefully dissected for the skills involved. A lot seemed to centre on hard to define qualities of choosing the right piece and shape of stone and holding it in the right way before chipping. The tone of the conversation mirrored this uncertainty by hovering and shimmering over moments of judgement, choices to reject stones and anxiety about working on the right one. It would take generations before everyone would talk about what they were learning from their mistakes and the old guide who knew all the tricks started talking more; not just showing but explaining. The discards and failures were not just discards to make great mounds for future archaeologists to ponder over but each had made a unique contribution to the building of conversation as the unintended benefit.

Cora disagreed with her sisters. They thought it best to show interest in and mate with quiet men or strong men and, if need be, coax conversation out of them as children come. She mixed with all the men and could see that some took more easily to talking and translating between the sign language and the language of the forest, the language of the snows and the language of tenderness with children. Cora did not know why but she had an intuition, a prejudice, that for her community it would be better to seek babies with or from the men who talk the most. Did she know they will make better fathers, raise more conversational children or in turn make a smarter community? Her sisters replied that the quieter men might be better hunters, might make heroes for their boys without having to talk but Cora shook her head. We cannot have one way of talking for the men and another way of talking for the women. Each will be diminished by the process. She encouraged the women to go hunting to bring their language skills to the men. She encouraged the men to stay close during childbirth to hear and learn the talk of tenderness. It was never going to be always true but over time Cora's community became the one that courted conversational men and the so-named strong and silent men soon learnt to dance and flirt in conversational ways. What Cora noticed was it changed how the men related to each other and she overheard them walking to the hunting grounds in pairs talking of plans, of feelings and private emotions.

One day four visitors had come from over the mountains that were covered in snow all year round. Cora, now an older woman, was the one to reach out to them: an older man and a woman and two younger ones. They also had with them a most unusual friend in a tame dog. Cora struggled and persisted to make sense of their language and their stories. They talked for days and discovered common words and sounds. They made a map in the sand of the path over the mountain. They marked it with drawings of animals and places of danger on the rocks. The strangers said they had never talked so much or learnt so much so quickly. Cora thought that a visit from strangers is like the finding of the 'meat of several mammoths' at once.

Cora and her community fed the family and let them stay. It was agreed that a small group would go back with the younger ones over the mountain to return the visit. They said the dog would help show the way. The older couple would stay for the winter and learn the language and the ways of Cora's community. A year later, the entire community from over the mountain came down bringing their own unique wealth of techniques, tools and knowledge from tribes farther away. But they came because they wanted to learn from Cora. They wanted to take their language and conversation to another level. They felt their community was dying because their words were stuck too tightly to the thing they described. They wanted to meet and take stories from the woman they called the combiner of tongues.

The two communities joined and put their ways and languages together and had red berry and blue berry moments and trouble and discovery, but conversation was their healing place and their way of learning, of caring and teaching, hunting and building, dating and mating and sometimes fighting and performing. The community from over the mountains had domestic animals. They had more varied ways of cooking. The new combined community was greater than the sum of its parts and the work of mediation, integration depended on the work of Cora and her apprentices in weaving words together to develop conversational awareness.

Reflections

I hope this chapter evokes a curiosity about the deep social and psychological structures in our capacity for conversations. The Russian literary theorist and philosopher Mikael Bakhtin[50] talks of the 'unfinalisable' nature of words and the spontaneity of language in its forms and utterances. He talks of the simultaneity of speaking in different directions and voices. In some ways a conversation for him is a carnival waiting to happen. What troubled him was the forces that turn the dialogic, open and playful capacity for language and conversation into an imposed monologue which is out of dialogue not just within and between us but with language itself. This joyful and playful, dialogic and conversational capacity for language can be witnessed in children aged five, six or seven years old. Where it has been lost or is too stilted and controlled it can be loosened and healed with the help of a map. In this chapter it is speculated that somewhere in our deepest human roots we were discovering how to map and remap our worlds through talking with each other in open and conversational ways. We became more relationally intelligent because we became more conversational. Bakhtin's work points to the multi-layered and multi-directional elements captured by the matrix of the conversational awareness grid in this book. The prevailing view of the organisation of society throughout our long evolution is one of patriarchy and a tendency towards binary violence and brutality. There is plenty of evidence for this but there is also evidence of its opposite in a more open, dialogic, non-binary and more conversational and convivial way of relating.

Is the next stage of human society and its evolution going to be conversational and convivial or are we entering an age mediated by machines and indirect communication through texts, screens and voice messages? Will we, as suggested by the Astronomer Royal,[51] migrate to other planets not as humans but as divergent non-biological lifeforms? Will they be conversational and conversationally aware? And will we interact with these life forms? Will we get mail? If this thought is rather exotic, are smaller and lesser things happening that distance us from the immediacy and vitality of language and communication that is conversationally alive and answerable from whole person to whole person? Perhaps the exuberance of conversation, the random twists and turns and then the endless processing and backtracking is beyond even the most advanced machines. Where we have to be careful is to not reduce our verbal transactions to the automatic and machine like. Having Cora looking in over our shoulders can help this.

Do we need to prepare for the loss of our conversational voices and spaces? Do we need to draw on the long conversation that got us where we are now over the past million years? Can a distinctively human lifeform continue with its unique capacity for conversational awareness? Ten thousand homo sapient generations of 'Coras' being mothers to our tongues, carrying our stories, not just our myths and images; but the invisible continuity of conversational awareness must be due some recognition. We are Cora's daughters and sons talking after her fashion at work, at home, besides each other on the buses and the underground and in our meeting rooms and bars. What would the imaginary Cora make of our conversations now? My hunch is that she could talk to us and would recognise the struggle to speak the unspoken or unspeakable. It is not clear whether we human beings are at the beginning or the end of a conversational era. We may need to channel our inner Cora.

Chapter 9: Conversational poverty

This chapter explores the use of a template for mapping unmet conversational needs, untried conversational skills and unspeakable thoughts and feelings which can leave us with a divided sense of self and a poverty of conversation within, between and around us. It suggests conversational poverty as a useful added dimension to understanding the context to our experience of neglect and trauma individually or collectively at different stages of our lives. For example, we may be directly affected by hurt and abuse in childhood which we cannot put into words and when we do find the words it is in a binary and prescriptive form of language (sexism, patriarchy, racism) that colonises and limits our words.

In celebrating the richness of human conversation, it is painful to consider the opposite reality of conversational poverty. It seems more honest and respectful to speak of poverty as a shared social problem rather than an individual psychological deficit. I have in mind cultures and technologies that give rise to a poverty of language and discussion in our early years, in our schooling and our work and personal lives. We have responsibility for our collusion with these cultures and technologies of conversational poverty that foster superficial and broken kinds of talk between us.

Conversational poverty is an affliction, an injustice and an affront to our heritage and qualities as human beings, as evoked in Chapter 8. It is not what we spent a million years evolving for. It is the neglect, violation and invalidation of our innate potential to negotiate and navigate our relationships through language. It is also a poverty in the conversational environment, in the architecture, the street furniture, the transport systems, and general control of cultures of communication.

Merlin Donald richly describes homo sapiens in our modern form as a species with hybrid brains, by which he means the flesh and blood circuitry of our actual brains are inseparable from the cultures, group relations, artefacts and institutions around it. The big brain of society is networked with the little 'big' brain of the individual. In this chapter the point of view is that what meshes them together is conversation and what limits and stunts them mutually is conversational poverty. Binary thinking and binary talk are bad for our brains.

How we talk and what we can talk about is contextual. Eloquence is not some innate and general gift but depends on who is listening; who is calling the shots; what we have been enabled to speak of and what has been made unspeakable.

The poverty in how we talk is not the same as financial poverty or economic injustice -although inequality and lack of access to a dignified quality of life feeds into conversational poverty, but the rich and privileged can suffer as much from conversational poverty through cultural inbreeding, ignorance, entitlement and a shallow lack of empathy for others.

In a necessarily simplified way, the map in Figure 9.1 shows how these aspects of conversational poverty damage our capacity to orchestrate multiple directions and kinds of talk. The boxes on the map are numbered and considered one by one in more detail in the following pages.

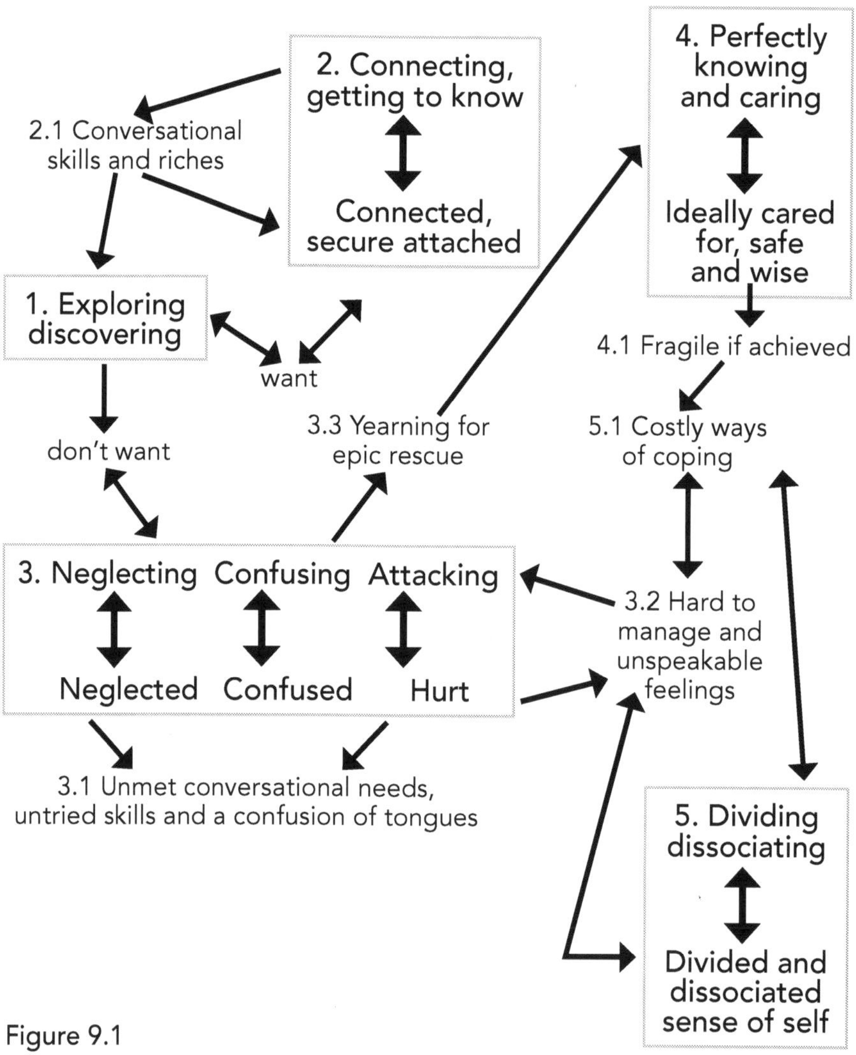

Figure 9.1

Box 1: exploring and discovering

We are born ready and willing to explore and connect and discover the relational space between us for conversation, first through multi-sensory, tactile communication and then through language as well. We are conversational beings wherein the infant is an active partner in what Trevarthen calls convivial relationships.[52] As empathy develops and a capacity to hold each other in mind, we learn turn taking, develop agency and a conversational sense of self. We never lose this lifelong vitality and spontaneity of the infant's will to be human and it never leaves us, but it can be tested and powerfully limited and distorted by the contextual reception it receives, both intimately and socially. It is in one sense such a fragile, necessary and innocent willingness to relate to whatever reciprocation is offered.

Box 2: connecting, getting to know

What we want – especially in our early years but throughout the whole length of life – is the experience of connecting and getting to know each other intimately with a feeling of being secure enough in relationships to explore and develop roles, attach to people, contexts and a world with which we can identify and invest ourselves in. With this big aim in mind, our sense of self is orchestrated, well or badly, stage by stage of development, from the first year of life. Year by year, layer upon layer, we co-create our baby patterns of mutual stimulus and response, like small incremental steps to life's dance enabled or limited by the relational resources available to us.

A parent holds us close. We begin to hold back and, in the process, learn to hold ourselves close. A seven-month-old baby hears a noise and turns to look and see the source of the noise. Hearing and seeing are combined as a small fleeting unit of sensory, orchestral awareness for the first time. A later step is hearing a noise, imagining, then seeing (knowing) what it is and choosing not to turn and look. Making or breaking (leaving a gap) in the link between the senses is held in mind as a building block of self-orchestration and relational awareness. Touch, taste and smell are linked to a co-ordination of our hands, arms and legs and our whole bodies become a first embodied and sensory experience of a sense of self. Fotopoulou[53] sums this up by viewing all the senses as engaged in joint work with increasing orchestration to the point of knowing the boundaries of self, skin and space between inner and outer worlds and bodies.

Conversational awareness grows out of this first relational and sensory awareness. At one year old, the toddler hears then sees a plane in the sky, points and all but says 'airplane'. At two plus years old, the toddler sees a plane and can be prompted to make links from it to memories of a holiday with the help of another. Year-by-year the toddler-then-child grows and develops relational awareness in tandem with moments of conversational awareness. We are making a relationship together becomes we are finding words and talking together. So much depends on the attunement of others. The quality of this attunement depends on the terms and games of language in the child's culture. Will the child be fixed or freed by language, or find their own voice, their own agency and powers of orchestration or not?

2.1: conversational skills and riches

These skills and riches are as described in Chapter 6 in the conversational awareness grid. They are further evoked in chapter eight in the story of Cora, the mother of tongues. Talking with a map is an aid to bringing them out. The way children develop language and a conversational sense of self is extraordinary and can be a joy to behold. The gestural and sensory relationship with words learnt →

early on are implicit in the methods and illustrations of Map and Talk throughout this book. What enables the child to develop language and conversation also helps her or him to develop relationships with themselves, with others and the world around. It is an orchestral or compositional ability.[54] Through a multitude of moments of conversational interaction in our early years we talk ourselves into our participation in the world.

At the same time a particular world talks its way into us. We are given names for what we notice and ways of negotiating how to speak of things. Our conversations and our relationships with the world are fuelled by the same empowering or restricting processes and beset by the same conflicts throughout our lives. Our awareness of how we are talking and what we choose or are allowed to talk about can be a healthy hovering and shimmering in and between ideas and feelings, or it can be critically shaming, self-conscious and inhibiting. Or perhaps more accurately and typically a mixture of both. If we can muster some healthy conversational awareness, it can help us in adapting relationally to the world. The more conversational awareness we can bring to our interactions the more relational awareness of roles, emotions and beliefs we can take in, give out and share.

Box 3: neglecting, confusing, attacking

If the balance of our early childhood conversational experience is in Box 3, we grow up with unmet conversational and relational needs, untried conversational and relational skills and unspoken and unspeakable emotions that hijack and fragment our capacity to relate. It is hard for us to regulate or organise the world around us when we have disorganised resources within us. As indicated in Chapters 2 and 3, we internalise both the 'doing end' and the 'done to end' of the 'reciprocal' roles of neglecting to feeling neglected, attacking and hurting to feeling hurt and attacked. Our awareness may only be of one end of the two-way restrictive relationships. We can be neglecting but have no sense that the neglected feelings are at our own hands. Or we can knowingly be active at both ends of the reciprocal role dance. We can be attacking of ourselves on top of others attacking us and feel attacked by others and by ourselves. Sometimes it is hard not to conclude that the disorganised attachment within self and between self and others is functional for powerful interests. Not so much 'let them eat cake' but 'let them feel chaos'. The political benefits of chaos and the narcissism invested in ruling ideas is explored and mapped in Chapter 12.

3.1: Unmet conversational needs and untried skills

All of us have unmet needs for care, delight, validation or inspiration carried over from childhood. We were loved too little, or too much, or in conflicting ways. The resources and spaces for learning and discovery were there but not enough. The list could be many and varied. Some of us have grown up with extremes of unmet needs – or needs met in ways that were disorganised. Conversationally we needed a relationship that stayed alongside us enough to enable us to build a shared capacity for language and dialogue. Even if we had the unlikely experience of growing up in a perfect environment, we would still have the unmet needs of learning to cope with the disappointment that adulthood cannot be perfect. Some childhood experiences involve tragic, unexpected or horrible neglect, control and disappointment. Another way of talking about unmet needs might be to speak of ill-met needs. The needs may be met in confusing, teasing, conditional, random, or unpredictable ways. With the insecurity of identity and role that follows from this we may cling to, and over associate with, a partial or harmful solution to a need, for fear of having no solution at all. One such example is highlighted by the confusion of voices at the end of this chapter.

Intricately linked to bringing unmet needs to our conversations is the idea of untried skills. We don't know the skills we need or could have in our adult conversations and relationships if we don't see them done with us or around us in our formative years. We don't know how to care or play if no one cares or plays with us. We don't know how to argue or be assertive if no one behaves in that way around us or on our behalf. We don't know how to be vulnerable or tender if no one like us show shows tenderness or vulnerability. We don't know how to talk about feelings and needs if no-one engages in doing that with us. Without these skill-building needs being met we are vulnerable to high-cost ways of coping, limited emotional experience which can have a direct effect on the quality of our life and our capacity for conversation.

3.2: Hard to manage and unspeakable feelings

Feelings that directly hurt but have an apparent cause and remedy are painful but not necessarily destructive or disturbing of our sense of self. Making sense of them gives us a perspective and can lessen their impact. Emotions become hard to manage when they are combined with denial of the hurtful action that is being done to us, invalidation of the pain (it is not meant to hurt) or confusion by the perpetrator being also a seemingly caring or admiring person.

If an attacking and directly hurting or abusing experience is added into this painful early life, we have the immediate hurt but also hard-to-manage feelings of fear, shame and a feeling of madness that comes from not having a coherent narrative. We are then vulnerable to seductive offers of ideal meaning and care as described in box 4 in Figure 9.1. We are so full of yearning for understanding and rescue that we embrace it. When the person or people who are neglecting or hurting us are also unexpectedly but intensely cherishing, seducing and admiring of us, then we are caught in a deeply divisive and confusing space. We make sense of it by clinging to the apparent good stuff whenever we can. Or through substitutions for it such as addictions of one kind or another or most significantly in the investment of salvationist ideas or movements that make unconditional promises.[55]

Confusion is a normal and healthy part of any conversation. We are trying to reach a shared understanding through the process of conversation. The popular expression 'getting it' implies a process of temporary confusion has been worked through and there is an experience getting each other in the sense of understanding, identifying and being with each other. There are other times when confusion seems to be built into the conversation.[56]

Some emotions have an intensity and unpredictability that are hard to manage. They may be triggered in contexts where we are more vulnerable such as public spaces or where our usual emergency coping procedures don't work, or support is not there. They may be hard to manage because they don't fit in with our main stories about ourselves such as being strong or sorted or considerate to others. They may be at odds with our culture, or family history. They may not fit with dominant gender, class and cultural expectations.

Box 4 (and 3.3): yearning for perfect but fragile care

We have a general yearning for care, and while there may be fleeting and teasing moments, it is beyond our sustainable reach because of the weight of our unmet need and the deficit of our untried skills. Our yearning for caring and open dialogue is so coloured by anxiety and confusion that we set great standards and great hopes by it and one set back, or rupture, and we withdraw. The capacity to negotiate our needs is limited within us and around us and we resort to hoping for, and the world resorts to offering us, a magical relationship. We never give up the yearning and searching for a conversational relationship. →

Most societies hold out a place of salvation, a golden time in the past or a future promise of heaven on earth where all is understood, and care is complete. It does two things at once by offering some capacity to tolerate present suffering and poverty with the guarantee of salvation and it distracts from and devalues ordinary efforts at mediation or good enough care. The yearning has healthy roots in a longing for care but is overvalued and becomes dismissive of partial care. Conversations can be hijacked by the narcissistic promises of ideal care as described with reference to talk of political ideas in chapter 12.

This idealised view of relating may lead us to overlook and not take in ordinary good enough care and the yearning for something extraordinary (as in box 4) may be found in dreams, in love addiction or other addictions and in devotion to a cause. There may be moments of fulfillment of the ideal or portrayals and vivid promises of it, but it is transitional or fragile if achieved. An example is the 'brilliant or doomed story' on page 206, and it shows up in varieties of healthy, harmful, entitled and wounded narcissism.[57]

Family and society or cultural narratives can collude with the idealising and devaluing as a way of hiding the everyday suffering. 'Well, everyday life was terrible, but we had great family holidays. Or there is poverty and oppression but our dream 'of a nation restored and society transformed' is held up as the golden promise in some future time. A measure of the value of conversational awareness through Map and Talk is its ability to bring into dialogue this yearning and work with the ideals in more realistic ways without puncturing their importance.

When our life dreams come true, it can feel magical and often the story that led to the achievement is not clear. The dream place can feel hard to sustain without support and can feel fragile as an achievement. We need someone to hold and validate us, to tell us we are not an imposter. To cope, we may attach ourselves to someone who may repeat the neglect or harm whist seductively promising ideal care. We are pulled by them more and more into a divided and fragile sense of self. The search for role security is idealised, magical and addictive.

Box 5: dividing and disorganised dialogue

The restriction and silencing are a process of divide and rule which is so subtle we breathe it in as we learn language. It is our 'forever normal' until we see its face in teenage years and in more public settings. Conversational awareness looks for such moments of realisation and distancing and values them.

The quality of conversational awareness under the sway of a dividing and disorganising dialogue is fixed in one direction of the grid. There is rigid association or dissociation away from feeling because the qualities of shimmering between emotions and tolerating ambivalence is too disturbing. We can deal with the confusion by having clarity in one conversational direction but not others. We may appear very clear in our interpersonal communications, or within our attachment to fixed social identities, but be ignoring of internal voices which feel discordant or threatening of a fragile self-control. One specific high-cost way of coping is to gain control over attacking experiences by becoming the attacker to self or others.

The mixture of rigid patterns of coping, narrow ways of dealing with others and dissociation from unbearable emotions leads to gaps in self-knowledge. This links to Box 5 on the diagram, the splitting and dissociation which solidifies these gaps and may show up as several partially dissociated roles, social identities and self-states. The divided sense of self finds some affirmation in a divisive society as described in Chapter 12. →

We become attached to the limited and divisive attachment solutions and identities available to us. We may become tightly attached and fear a loss of self if losing the apparent identity solution. These limited – and gap filling – methods of survival continue into adulthood but may also have become painfully adaptive. We may build a strong but narrow sense of achievement. Or we invest greatly in an identity of being the warrior, or the rescuer, which gives us esteem and reward. In this way gaps in self-knowledge may be well-hidden by the development of childhood and adolescent identity which is a 'cover' identity that only gives us a partial sense of being wholly in the world. Mapping these patterns out as described in Chapters 2-5 offers a unique way of seeing these divisive patterns in action and their simultaneous effects within, between and around us.

There is a historical context to these forces of division and dissociation. In Chapter 8 we looked back with to an imaginary and fertile joining and blending of languages. What has distinguished much of the politics and dominant form of the last three thousand years is some form of palace culture and society. Kings and queens and hierarchy and patriarchy. Most recently this took the form of the schizoid structure of masculinity and racism to justify slavery and colonialism or various forms of dictatorship and fascism. There were counter narratives of enlightenment and rational humanity which supported anti-slavery and enfranchisement for working class men and belatedly women. It is no psychological comfort to see that the divided, hollowed out and binary sense of self can be at home with these historical forms of exploitative government and be the cause of conversational poverty.

5.1: costly ways of coping with conversational poverty

Hard to manage feelings call out for high-cost (emotionally and socially, inwardly and outwardly) ways of coping. The cost is in the method chosen, such as forms of addiction and distraction, or in the deprivation and neglect maintained, and or in the impact on and cost to others physically, emotionally or financially. One of the rules of language is that speakers assume there are gaps in the meaning they are seeking to jointly create. That words won't cover all angles or convey all meanings. Words cannot go in every direction at the same time. There are gaps in our knowledge of ourselves. Gaps because the feelings and actions that impact on our body and on our memory were never talked through within or between us. The memories are there but without maps and without stories. They are fragments of emotional memory without a story or familiar words. They are disrupters of the self, calling out for a conversation that is helpful enough to bring them to consciousness and integrated into the narratives of our lives.

From a conversational poverty point of view, we might say they are unvalidated experiences and the poverty is a double loss of anxiety about sharing memories and a lack of practice and confidence in the culture of conversation around us.

A confusion of voices

As indicated when talking of the yearning for ideal care in sections 3 and 4 of this chapter, one of the hardest things to make sense of when we are powerless as children or young people is the simultaneous and incoherent mix of love and hurt from an adult figure. The adult figure can be primary carers: parents, siblings or can be a dominant voice in the culture (for example the call to bear arms and give your life for the nation). The child or adolescent brings their innate and innocent yearning to make an emotional attachment and a conversational relationship to this confusing and hurtful but compelling reciprocation. The child feels special, confused and nobody at the same time. It is a teasing and destructive entanglement. In the context of sexual abuse, the 'trauma and confusion of tongues' was described in the 1930s by Sandor Ferenczi (as a favourite son of Freud he threatened to put real abuse and trauma back at the centre of the psychoanalytic model and was excluded from the 'conversation' and silenced by Freud as a result).[58] This current description draws on his pioneering thinking and offers a more open and reparative conversational approach.

The starting point and the end point for this confusion of voices is the mixed message. The person feels praised and cherished and used and exploited by the same person. 'I am groomed as a princess and as special and my body is being violated and exploited' (e.g., child sexual abuse). 'I am being hailed as a hero and my body is being called up to be used as cannon fodder (e.g., military service). In both cases the language turns on saying you count, and you don't count at the same time. Surviving the relational dynamics of this kind of trauma involves denial or dissociation. In the map in Figure 9.3 the challenge for the person (and for anyone entering into a reparative and healing conversation) is to sense that the spoiling and special inner voices are entangled with the hurting and exploiting voices. They are held together by a deeper fear of rejection or abandonment and locked in by denial. There may be a compassionate and caring voice in the past (e.g., a grandma or sibling) which offered a narrative out of the traumatic entanglement, but this may have been drowned out by the denial from more significant voices. The map helps have in mind not just the painful origins of a poverty of talking compassionately or honestly, but helps see the tendency to have different parties to a healing conversation pulled into the different limiting or harmful voices marked on the map. For example, a partner might now be idealised as the spoiling and special one. A surviving sibling or friend as the denying one and a professional helper as the exploiting person. As Ferenczi pointed out it is very easy for those helping and the person seeking help to be pulled apart into these separate and jarring positions. The aim in a healing conversation is to seek a shared understanding of the conversation and the threats to it as mapped out. It might make sense to seek to build a shared partnership in compassionately caring and being curious in the present about the past and seeking a social understanding along with a personal one. The confusion of voices as mapped out in figure 9.3 is a key factor in a number of primary sources of harm and abuse whether child sexual abuse, domestic violence, gang violence or soldiers and populations being used as cannon fodder or heroic sacrifice for an idealised cause. The pioneering work bringing awareness of trauma came from work with veterans from the Vietnam war and workers responding to rape and domestic violence.[59]

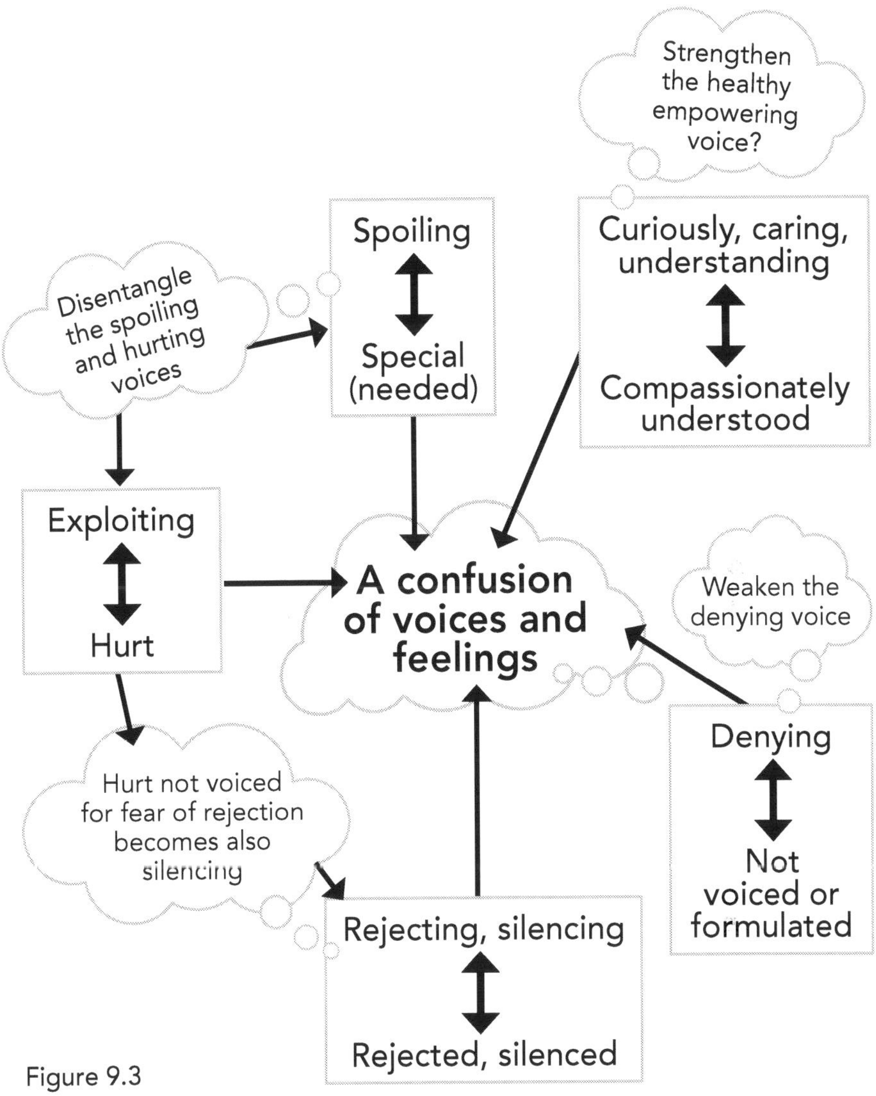

Figure 9.3

The healing conversation is self-consciously and openly aware that it is building a new relationship and a new way of talking. It is one that can soak up and contain the confusion of voices and mixed messages and with the aid of talking with a map can keep seeking to untangle one word or story from another. It is a 'we' conversation in the sense that we are in this healing relationship together as individuals and societies. One person may have the deeper and greater need but one is not doing the conversation for or to the other person.

Ferenczi, in his paper on the confusion of tongues, was aware of the conversational and mutual need to share understanding that is strong enough to bring change.[60]

> *'I may remind you that patients do not react to theatrical phrases, but only to real sincere sympathy. Whether they recognise the truth by the intonation or colour of our voice or by the words we use or in some other way, I cannot tell. In any case, they show a remarkable, almost clairvoyant knowledge about the thoughts and emotions that go on in their analyst's mind. To deceive a patient in this respect seems to be hardly possible and if one tries to do so, it leads only to bad consequences.'*

There are other kinds of horror in our world that have no mixed message and are unspeakable. The horror and cruelty of abuse without any mixed message as in slavery, colonialism and racism is another story. These are systems of evil and destruction of humanity that deny dialogue and silence the voices of resistance or conversation. Personal or interpersonal awareness of answerability for such evil is bypassed or suppressed by a narcissism of political ideas as considered in a limited way in Chapter 12.

A healing conversation

A healing narrative is a process of beginning to weave new patterns of relational awareness across the gaps in self-knowledge and the divided elements of self. If we can develop the awareness to change our conversations to being more open, expressive, sensitive and thoughtful, then changes in our relationships will follow. If we can change our conversations about our personal and communal and social and political lives, we can change our intimate relationships and change our politics.

Somewhere deep in the self comes a memory, a fragment of feeling, a compulsion to react in a certain way without knowing why. Until they can be put into words and mapped, they can feel like words without stories. Sometimes they show up in the spontaneous process of conversational mapping as random words on the paper that, despite recapping and reworking, don't seem connected but do have some emotional weight to them: 'I can say I am angry, but I don't know why because the story is missing.' In the last four or five decades there are many examples of being able to talk about relationships and patterns that previously were silenced or overwhelmed by prejudice and threat. The power to change the conversation through movements against oppression have opened the door to conversational awareness.

Why don't we treat our skills in conversation with the same interest or activism as we might our physical fitness? Is the pub the place we really go for conversational fitness? Or do we drink and fool ourselves and each other into hiding our conversational poverty? It is as if we are so accustomed to our ways of speaking and the qualities of conversations and the kinds of ideas and feelings that get aired and shared that we have no sense of what we are missing. There may be reading groups or writing groups and painting classes, but where is the talking group or talking class? Therapy groups might be offered as the answer, but these are few and far between and time consuming for the professionals or volunteers that run them. An important and under-resourced outlet are all the campaign and support groups in the voluntary sector. They are the keepers of healing conversations.

Every conversation can be healing if it involves small steps in developing untried skills, helps address unmet needs and manage hard-to-manage and unspeakable emotions which, in turn, helps address the divisions and gaps in self-knowledge. It helps to share the load to see that the healing conversation is seeking to heal the splits and breaks between the items in the conversational awareness grid. Talking with a map gives more chance of developing dialogue and confidence in the healing power of conversation by giving voice to a sense of ownership and navigator and negotiator rights over where the discussion is going.

Four stories combine to make a healing conversation

Reducing alienation and distress; encouraging improvements in self-worth and the development of relational awareness arise from the capacity to hold four kinds of conversational story telling open to and apart from each other. These are introduced as:

- the present story (what is happening to us now?)
- and the past story (what has happened to us and what does it mean?)
- the 'understanding' story (how do we make sense and share a perspective?)
- the healing story (what can we do to help, recover and grow?).

We start by telling stories or sharing experiences of the present: 'I am working too hard or have health or financial worries and family trouble.' Out of these stories comes some attempt to understand and see the story in the conversation: 'Is it helping, are we making sense?' At some point the direction of conversation looks backward or outward from the immediate situation. Has it always been like that? Did other people in the past do that to you? Did you once cope differently? Past stories offer new levels to the shared search for understanding.

In shimmering and hovering between past and present then a third story is likely to emerge. It is the story of formulating and understanding that grow out of the links between past and present. This explanatory story, like any historical account of the past to explain the present, is open to many revisions and readings.

When we seek help, we often want a tidy narrative to make sense of distressing and unsettling experiences. The challenge is to get help that is careful and conversational enough to build this third and potentially explanatory story in a collaborative way.

The fourth story is the healing story in the conversation. Mapping can help us see how personal and collective stories of trauma weave together. It can help us see where change is possible or where risk is greatest. It can create space and a level of conversational and relational awareness that helps develop a healing narrative. In the process, we have the space to develop agency, ownership, and authorship over our lives. These four stories can easily be merged and hijacked (one by the other), reducing their diversity of focus to one.

Four stories open to and help apart from each other

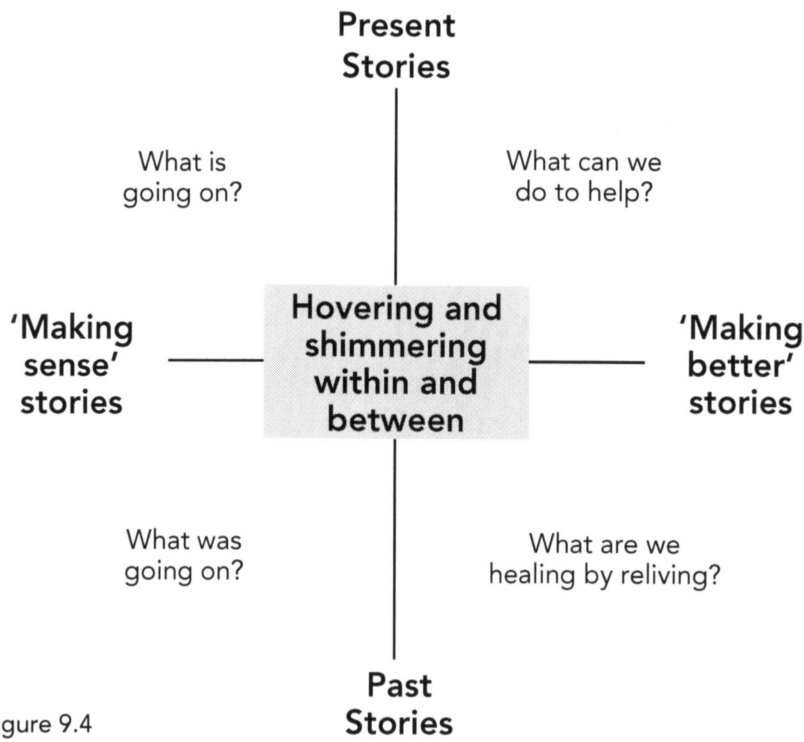

Figure 9.4

Defiant eloquence

Recovering a voice and having a healing conversation may take many forms but one that stands out from working with all sorts of groups and individuals over the years is what I can only describe as defiant eloquence. Out of the hurt comes a voice that can speak and find its way with words. All the mutual aid, acts of solidarity, all the support groups, consciousness raising groups, refuges, halfway houses, campaigning groups, voluntary organisation and the whole welfare system can be a source of defiant eloquence. As can friends, or art and creative activity.

Defiant eloquence is a personal and collective refusal to be silenced, restricted, positioned or gendered in a certain way by external vested interests and against the grain of one's own needs. It involves a time of compassionately sitting side-by-side with the processes of self-silencing that were unknowingly woven into our own language and conversations with the world as we grew up. It involves recognising the conversational poverty within us and putting it back out in the environment where it can more easily be seen and negotiated with others who are able to share answerability for the conversational poverty and find a shared way back into open and sincere human dialogue.

There is the long tradition of defying a restricting language and stepping out of a positioning or gendering. There are many examples in all walks of life of how it takes courage to be defiant and it takes something else to be eloquent. It is best measured as moments of eloquence which come out of a conversation and often as a surprise to speakers and listeners. It has a presence, a clarity of role and authorship and a sense of joining and speaking together in ways that expect to be heard. Map and Talk can help nurture moments of defiant eloquence and give them shape and context.

Conclusion

The tools of mapping help us go back to the relational roles and voices of childhood and add a compassionate observing eye. We are likely to meet strange combinations of roles such as: loving and criticising; idealising and neglecting; cherishing and abusing; exciting and carelessly forgetting. Our need for a mapping process in which we can rehearse and learn how to negotiate our interactions is vital for a healing narrative. Mapping can help us see how personal and collective stories of trauma are linked. It can help us see where change is possible or where risk is greatest.

Chapter 10: Therapeutic conversations with a map

For the author, this book is about the world of conversation outside the therapy room. In one sense, for better or worse, we are all in part our own and each other's therapists, having to self-consciously notice, name and navigate our way into a more extensive conversational awareness in an ever more complex and transitional world. With this in mind I want to give one image of what it might be like to begin the conversation of a therapy relationship in the first session with talking with a map in mind. I want to attend to the details and go to the heart of conversational moments that get stuck or catch on. I want to try and show what talking with a map can do to help nurture an open conversational and therapeutic attitude.

The influential and overlooked pioneering feminist and interpersonal psychoanalyst Karen Horney put wholeheartedness and the barriers to it as the key to the therapy conversation and its curative role. Her focus was on the narcissism, the alienation and anxiety that led to false, antagonistic, submissive or avoidant identity solutions for the person. For Karen Horney, if the therapist is honest about their side of the conversational relationship, then the conversation has a chance to help and heal.[61] What it is doing in her view is addressing the conflicts for the person's sense of self that arise from clashing and limiting ways of coping with anxiety.

This chapter explores moments of conversational awareness as client and therapist begin working together using map and talk and to see if there is a space to be wholehearted together.

Right at the beginning of our first session, Mark tells me has been sent to see someone 'for therapy'. He spits the two-word sentence out. I physically recoil, pressing my body into my chair. It is involuntary. A reciprocation which in part, I imagine, he intended. But then he looks up. It is as if he is apologising for his vehemence: not wanting to offend me or attract too much attention to his defensive feelings. He is shimmering between the dismissing end and the dismissed end of an interaction between us. He is feeling something (dismissed) without awareness of it but what he does to manage and express that feeling (be dismissing) triggers awareness of another feeling (exposed) so what he does is take control of his expression of feelings by turning on himself (dismissively) as highlighted in Figure 10.1. At this early stage I don't share my thinking that this is what we are like as human beings at our most human and vulnerable. We ricochet between conflicting feelings in and out of awareness as our bodies (and the bodies of those around us) turn outward on others and inward on ourselves in search of balance or control.

Figure 10.1

In that shimmering moment of his exposed vulnerability and dismissiveness, I have a feeling for him and his struggle with his conflicting feelings. Alongside empathy is a curiosity. It is something more than empathy: a relational awareness which I hope to bring out in the conversation through the mapping once we get going. I am approaching 'our' interactions with a negotiator's mind that hopes to use Map and Talk to develop a shared capacity to notice and name what we are doing.

What does Mark bring out in me? Does he intend it? Does he have a sense of himself somewhere in and among these shifting feelings? And the same for me. Do I know where my sense of self lies? Will it get entangled with his? Is my capacity to hover between his mind and mine, blocked or limited by my own professional attitude and my habitual style of being a therapist over the years? And what lies beyond the reach of our consciousness as two men caught up in the swirl of masculine identities in the transitional times of the 21st century?

I notice that my body is in a micro-dance with him: it is so fleeting we barely hear the rustle of the movements. I have sympathetically shifted back and forward with him. I already feel warned that I might be taking part in something that he thinks might harm him. I want to be nice to him, want my characteristic niceness between us, but I also feel annoyed and perhaps he would feel safer if I let go of the niceness and share something of the annoyance. I also have a guiding thought, along the lines of Freud's idea of the compulsion to repeat.[62] Something has just been happening between us which is compelling. He has been here before! I have been here before. We will go here again in the hope of making sense of difficult memories and having a healing, clarifying or soothing relationship with them.

My intention with Mark is to create a space where he and I might sketch out a map of words that help us see, on paper, what he and I are doing and saying. In this vein, I am tempted to ask Mark why he has the hostility to therapy, but Mark and I are saved from this big, intrusive, head-to-head question because he carries straight on talking – leaving no room for me to interject.

Mark says of unnamed others in his life 'They are scared I might do something'. Again, I recoil a little into my chair. An observer would not necessarily notice the bodily movement. Though the chair creaked. And perhaps Mark sensed this unconsciously in some co-embodied space we are now sharing. I feel, not so much pushed away – since I have not yet reached forward towards him – but pushed down. We are becoming entangled in each other's feelings without any visible dramatic sign. Paradoxically, it is how we 'have to' be, for the therapeutic work of disentangling (Horney, 1945) or dis-embedding (Safran, 2000) or standing in the spaces (Bromberg, 1998) or re-formulation (Ryle & Kerr, 2020) to occur.[63] We must join the dance to know the dance and step in or out of it conversationally and therapeutically.

Another ill-timed and ill-tuned question forms in my mind along the lines of asking how he wanted to begin this therapy, but of course Mark has already begun. And for the next few minutes there was little room for me to speak. Mark's monologue was full of 'them' words, what they are doing to him, not doing for him, what they say of him, what they make him feel. It portrayed him as the victim of others but as he spoke relentlessly of this, it was me who felt like his conversational victim. The relational patterning of Mark's distress, with which he wanted help, was being created in mirror-form between us. He was pulling me in to experience aspects of the thing he was describing.

Mark is talking at me in the manner of what I call a dog story. A dog story – no offence to dog lovers – is a story that tends to be told complete and contained, all in and of itself. There is no room for symbolism, metaphor, asides, or innuendo. Dog stories are compelling because they are just about the content in a doggishly, dogged way. As a narrative style, they can be comfortingly and safely all about it, there and then and not at all about you or me and here and now. Some of us a lot of the time, all of us some of the time, talk to each other in the style of telling 'dog' stories. As clients, if we go to talk about our pain, our hopes and fears as a series of dog stories, there is no way into another level of meaning. Content and process are firmly segregated. How never meets what. What the story is about doesn't slip into how it is being told. Therapists can also be guilty of reducing a potentially rich therapeutic conversation into a dog story by turning the therapy into an interview with history taking and advice giving. A rigidly or anxiously manualised approach risks the whole therapy becoming a dog story.

The therapist's temptation with dog stories is to wait and see. It is very possible to ask 'dog story questions' but this just takes us further into what the story is about and away from how the story is being shared. The worst thing is to go head-to-head and ask, 'why are you telling me this story?' The client will feel accused, as if they are doing something wrong rather than doing something they need to do to protect themselves.

Something much gentler is needed to draw the process of the story telling out of the content of the story. For me, mapping can do this by repeatedly being the intermediary between content and process and between core emotional patterns and fleeting conscious feelings. It is best to start with the immediate moments in the room to which you are both bearing witness and with the emphasis on the joint responsibility for whatever is happening.

I already have a map in my head of the dance which Mark and I are in, but I cannot find an opportune moment to get it out on paper. Visibly, I settle back in my chair, as if resigned to the dog story role he has given me. Perhaps unconsciously because of my sitting back, he says something that makes me sit up again. Unprompted he has gone up a level and is negotiating with himself and me.

He says in a critical way, 'I don't want to be dwelling on the 'bad stuff'. The dog story telling phase is over and maybe we both had to endure it to establish it as one conversational option between us when needed. There is the beginning of a richness in our awareness of and ownership of the different directions of the conversation, now going within and around us, as it develops between us. There is a feeling (shimmering) and a thinking (hovering) kind of connection between us. In effect suddenly there is conversational therapy in the air between us.

I look at Mark and our eyes acknowledge each other's presence for the first time. I say something which I imagine you the reader will think odd. I say to him 'Thank you' and 'Good'. Like a father to a child who has done something good. Then in the next breath, I apologise to him: 'Oh, that sounded a bit patronising. Sorry. But it is really good what you said'. He watches me like he is the therapist, and I am the client yo-yoing between feelings. As if he knows how to talk about this stuff and I don't. He smiles as if reassured by my admission of lack of skill and guile. Unintentionally in my spontaneity I am modelling an openness to a vulnerability to myself. I don't claim foresight in what might be called an accidental moment of therapeutic competence, but I am aware enough to harvest it. The push and pull of feelings between us is too much to comprehend without something external to aid us. It is time to map and track where we are. I put my hand out for a piece of paper. It is a big blank sheet of white paper from a pile which has been in front and between us on the low table from the beginning. I say, 'It will help me listen if I can put some of the key words on paper'. He watches me shuffling with the paper. I pause and then continue by saying, 'Map them out and see how they all connect up or not'.

Mark says, 'What do you mean?'

I say, 'I don't know yet', which feels slightly stupid. So, I correct myself and say, 'I will see if I can show you'.

The mood between us is uncertain but alive with our involvement in turning the conversation into doing something together. It is open to going in different directions. It is pinballing a little around the 16 items of the conversational awareness grid (Chapter 6) much as the beginning of a healthy conversation might. We are not just talking – we are making something. We are making a conversation and a relationship. The uncertainty of how and why we are going to map words on paper now matches the uncertainty and fluidity of the intersubjective space between us.

Waving the blank piece of paper in my hand as a token of some intent to negotiate our immediate interactions I say to Mark, 'While you have been talking, I have been worrying about how I should respond'. I pause for breath. I continue, 'It feels risky. I want to be helpful but worry I could be harmful. It might help me if we could just put on paper some of what we are struggling with.'

In saying this, I write in the top right-hand corner of the blank sheet of paper 'Mapping – helps me talk' as the first reciprocal relationship. It's a heads up to what I am doing and feeling as a result. As you will see the map which we are about to co-create is not about Mark but about us and the push and pull of feelings and actions between us. It is a micro map of moments and potential movements.

I put a smiley face next to the 'helps me talk' words and smile at him. I have no idea where this comes from. Perhaps I need to show him we are not going to dwell on things. Anyhow Mark smiles in response to this. I say that I would like to put here on paper the 'big thing' you just said about 'Not dwelling on the bad stuff'. I write as I speak to him and write 'Dwelling to dwelt upon' and circle these words, with plenty of space, at the centre of the sheet of paper. And straight away at the bottom of the paper I add, in bold letters the two words 'Bad stuff' (see Figure 10.2).

What have I done? Do I have a secret technique? I have separated out the dwelling as an activity we might be doing together from the feeling of dwelt upon, which might trigger a reciprocation of shutting off or keeping away. I have put the words 'bad stuff' in a separate place. I explain to Mark that it is 'so we can better see how to avoid or approach it in other ways besides dwelling too much or avoiding.' He nods agreement and is beginning to get openly involved.

My intent is to tease out on paper what is entangled between us in this moment. It might turn out to be entangled in his life in general. It is with such notions that therapist can take over the conversation, so I need to be careful and let the map help us scrutinise what meanings we are finding. The mapping as we talk is pulling out the process of 'dwelling' from the content of the 'bad stuff'. I have in mind the push and pull between what we do and feel, and the social and emotional roles involved, as in Chapters 2 and 3. There is Mark's story now around the bad stuff and a therapy and conversational story developing between us.

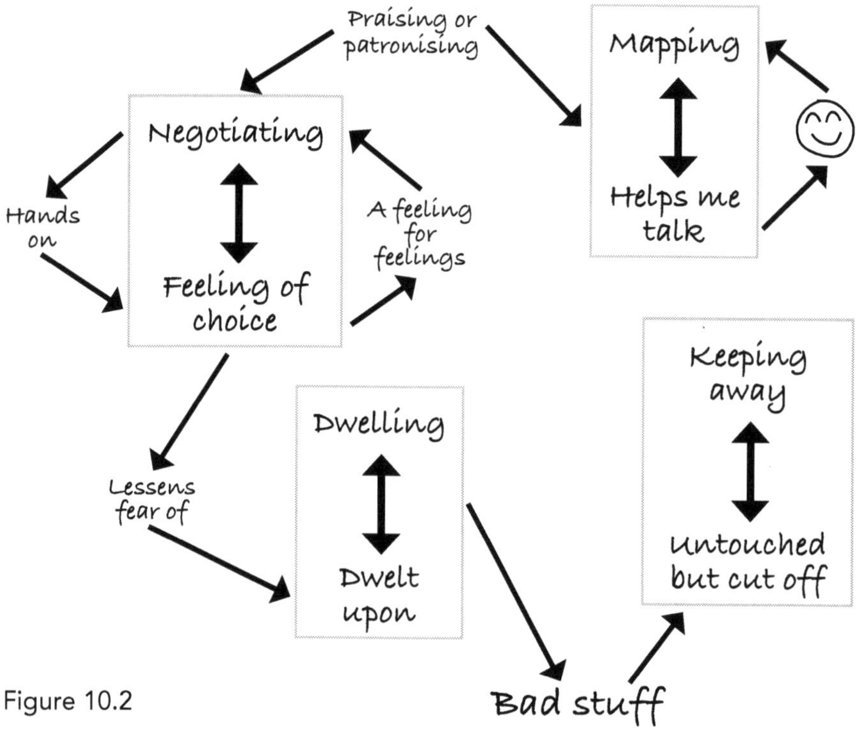

Figure 10.2

These small steps to a shared conversational awareness are developing a feeling for feelings. As we talk about the feelings involved, we also feel the feelings and, aided by the map, we get more safely inside these feelings. Perhaps that sounds pretentious, but I am explaining something along these lines to Mark. We know this is going to involve our emotions shimmering between hot and cool, safe and scary, within us and between us. It is a map about us now and helps us navigate away from dog stories. I started the map with words that showed me struggling to be helpful to him and then put down his strongest word (the bad stuff) in a way that might help us negotiate and feel we have a choice to approach or avoid the bad stuff. Mark joins in and opens up a little more. We are both leaning forwards partly to link to the words on paper but partly because we are engaged with each other.

I recap where we have got to with the map. I say – and put the words down as I say it – that Mark wants to have some choice about what we talk about. 'Choosing and not feeling that you will have to be dwelling on the "bad stuff".' I point at the word 'choosing' and ask him what he would feel if we were genuinely choosing together. He said he thought he would have more control and as he says that word, he leans into the map and towards me as if he is taking more control. It is about to become his map as much as mine and, in my mind, it is an intermediate workspace through which our conversation and our relationship can develop and be called to account.

I underline the word 'negotiating' and ask, 'Is it through negotiating together and not dwelling (my pen circles the word dwelling as I speak) on our own that we co-create a feeling of choice?' As we chew over the added words that have flowed from me recapping, his hand does something which I find moving. It reaches out to the paper on which we are mapping, and he hovers outstretched and then pulls it back. Like an infant reaching for something that connects but not quite. We smile and he looks at his hand and says that he was just thinking.

We are learning to listen together with all our faculties, mind and body. He talks about times at which he has felt a share in a relationship and has been able to negotiate with someone. He thinks and talks of what can get in the way of a shared discussion. We note some of these down on a separate piece of paper. The process of mapping is our assistant and potential mediator. It is a mindful form of mapping and tracking which we negotiate with our voices and our hands.

I say to him as gently as possible, with palms out and upward facing, 'You are figuring something out with your hands moving about the map. I hope it helps you remember and revisit things in ways that doesn't feel like dwelling on the bad stuff.'

He fully puts his hands on the map as if taking ownership of something and says, 'I want choice [left hand hovers over the top of the page] when I think I am getting near this [right hand over the bottom page stuff –the 'bad stuff']. I want to keep away from the 'bad stuff'. My hand movements join his. I add the phrase '*keeping away: not touching*'. Our hands are dancing a bit around the words on the map covering some, emphasising others. I tell Mark that I like the way we are involved, 'With our hands and the map, we may notice when we are stuck on the bad stuff.'

'Hands on,' he says and shimmies his hands sideways and gives me a thumbs up.

Bit by bit, it is becoming our map: neither mine nor his, but a map about us worrying and struggling to manage this situation we are both in. It is not a map of his 'bad stuff'. That is a task for a later part of the therapy when we both have greater confidence in mapping conversationally and therapeutically together. It is a map of the process of helping us negotiate and shape a working partnership or therapeutic alliance. However, we both seem to magically think that the 'bad stuff' is now out there on the paper where it can be touched or bypassed. It is a beginning and a long way from dog stories of the disembodied, soulless gathering of information. It is map of a moment or so of therapy between us; but I imagine, or hope, it will be a map of the way to a deeper engagement with Mark and his troubles.

Reflections

I want to highlight the live process in micro detail of Map and Talk as an aid to a therapeutic conversation that is going simultaneously in the four directions and using the four kinds of conversation depicted by the awareness grid in Chapter 6 of this book. It is simultaneously cognitive, emotional, participative and seeking agency, ownership and authority within and between us. The process is both multi-media (talking, mapping, voicing) and multi-sensory (sight, sound, touch, interoceptive responses). As rather schematically summarised in Figure 10.3, the shared process of noticing key words or 'wording' (1) in the conversation points to noticing by naming what is going on. Such a process shimmers between conscious emotional coping procedures and unconscious emotions. It hovers between different ideas and meanings and seeks to build conversational awareness wherein the negotiation is simultaneously within self, with others and with the world around and beyond.

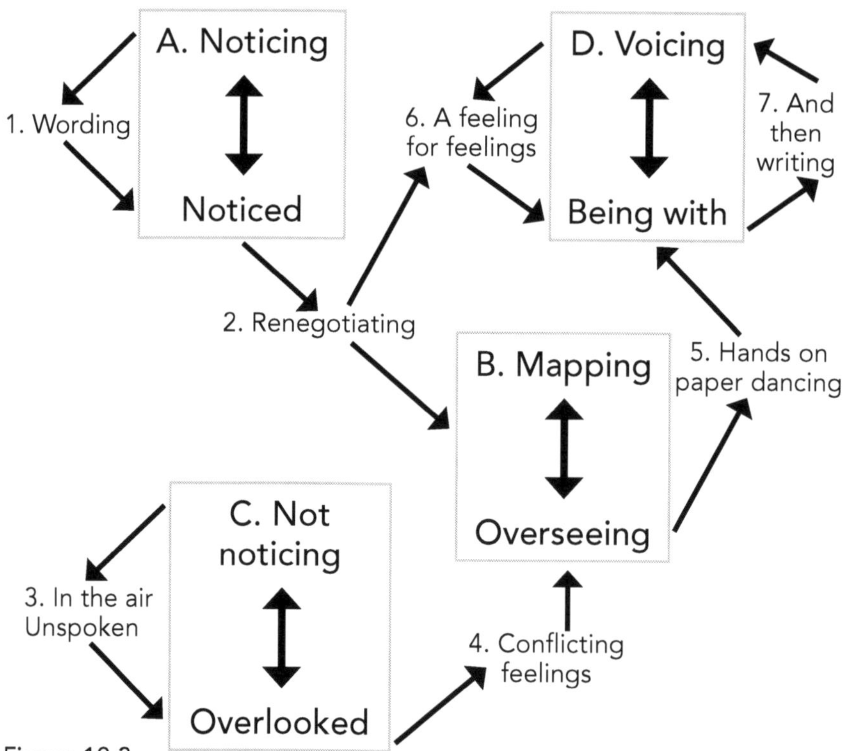

Figure 10.3

Sometimes we don't find the words directly. They find us. It seems to me to be a process of wording and rewording. Each new voicing of a word qualifies and softens or intensifies the previous word and its voicing. In the process we are reciprocating by 'renegotiating' (2) through the activity of mapping and overseeing what is going on. But also, there is an invisible gift to the mapping process which comes from the blank spaces of the map which point to fragments of dissociated, unnoticed feelings bobbing about and calling for attention as unformulated experience. They are often 'in the air unspoken' (3) and can sneak into the conversational and therapeutic relationship as enactment dynamics under the radar of conscious attention.

A responsiveness to signs and signals of 'conflicting feelings' (4) and confusing thoughts on the map is part of the struggle for a more open conversational awareness. The mix of conscious and unconscious interaction has the potential to be connected with and through the movement of hands-on paper dancing (5) which in turn develops a feeling for feelings (6). In sum this creates a world where the complex weave of intersubjectivity, memory and meaning offers the chance of healing through memory reconsolidation[64] while also building a shared experience of conversational awareness.

This chapter has sought to evoke talking with a map as collaborative process of noticing, naming and negotiating as detailed in Chapter 6 and in the other stories and examples in the book. It is a central to conversational awareness in any context but is essential as the mechanism of change in psychotherapy and allied helping and healing relationships. This chapter has focused on the micro awareness of the co-creation of conversation. The therapist uses his professional space and expertise not to be a better conversationalist but to share the mapping process and the relational thinking and openness that can come from it.

Chapter 11: Conversational awareness at work, school, in love or in the arts

Introduction

This chapter has examples showing how talking with a map can help. They are from different areas of life. First are examples of changing the conversation at work. Specific reference is made to using Map and Talk for reflective practice and team building. Second are illustrations of how talking with a map might help us develop conversational awareness at school. Third, there are examples from our personal lives in terms of mapping and developing awareness of how we talk to our bodies and negotiate love and intimacy. Fourth, there is brief consideration of Map and Talk in relation to artistic creativity. The examples highlight the common factor of conversational and relational awareness across all walks of life. How we relate when talking in one context spills over to another context. More examples can be found from the blog on the author's website: www.mapandtalk.com/blog

Developing a conversational and reflective team at work

The following 'Hopes and Fears' template (see also pages 84) can help a team reflect on their working relationships. It is a safe way of reflecting on current processes and patterns without going head-to-head with one issue. If you are the mapper or facilitator to a team discussion, then you are introducing the idea as a way of looking at the social and psychological climate of the team.

Using the template in Figure 11.1 start with box 2 asking what it feels like and who is doing what if things are going well. The reason for starting there with a new group or new conversation is that it puts the good place on the map and makes it easier to look subsequently at what is happening when things are not going well. It can help bond the team and give them a positive experience of mapping together. If the answer is nothing is going well then don't be daunted but ask what would it be like if the team was working well? Or set the bar lower and ask what is it like when things are going okay? You are aiming to have a good or 'okay enough' place on the map as a point of reference for the conversation. It is good psychology and good diplomacy in learning from experience as a group to get some image of the good place the group can get to before looking at the not so good places.

You are putting the action words at the top end of the box and the feeling or reactive words at the bottom end as detailed in Chapter 2. You may ask about the quality of being in this hoped for or okay position. For example, does it feel fragile or normal or unusual? Since those in the group can see the template map you may find the group goes in one or more directions. It may want to recall when it was at point 3 on the map and things were happening that made them a dream team. Or they may – you should encourage this – look at box 1 which is what they routinely do to manage themselves as a team in going about everyday business. With some words on paper and some sense of willing participation you ask what the team would be doing if things were going badly? Again, you are looking for a shared reciprocal relationship between what is being done and the feelings and attitudes it generates. This is using the concept of reciprocal roles and patterns described in Chapter 3 and the push and pull between doing and feeling detailed in Chapter 2.

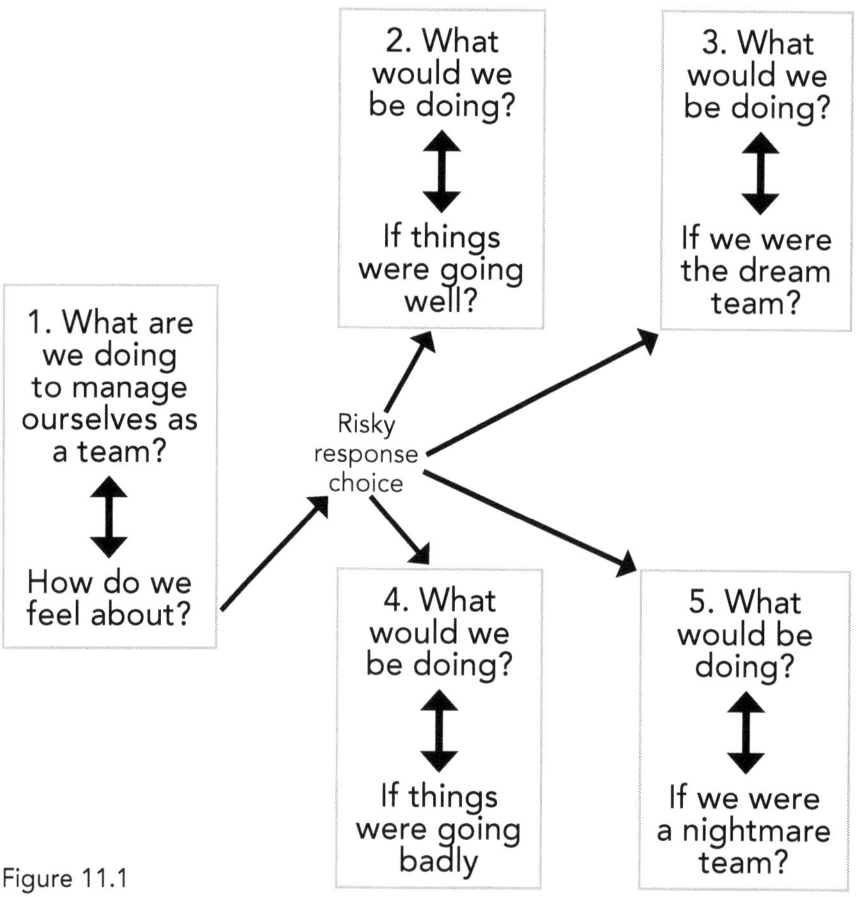

Figure 11.1

The conversation may take on a life of its own at this stage and you are hoping it can go places but anchor itself from time to time around the hubs on the map numbered 1, 2 and 3, 4 and 5. You might then use the map to wonder what the risky moment is when seeking to work well together and get to point 2 on the map. The team can be held back by the fear of going to point 4. The risky response choice is the pivot point on the map because it is from here that we can track the balance of ways to make things work or not. This is the point where shared reflections with the words on the map can help in wondering what is driving the risky moment. From the map it might be possible to explore whether the desired outcome is overvalued or the feared outcome naively dismissed or other mixes of feelings and ideas along these lines.

Once you have words for actions and feeling inside boxes 1, 2 and 4, you are hoping to have enough scaffolding of words on paper to oil the wheels of the discussion and for members of the team to link to specific stories and add more details about how they can switch or yoyo between a hoped-for place and a feared place. The upward and upbeat route is to consider the dynamic between being in box 2 or 3. All teams, like all individuals, have some notion of what being a dream team would be like, if only for the moment. Posing the question while pointing to the word on the map can help think in terms of future expectations. We can say where we would really, really like to be. Or some in the group might be nostalgic about a golden time (real or imagined) for the team which if explored with the map can help everyone have a better sense of its history. Teams can so easily be overly controlled by their own, or the organisation's idealised version of what the work or service provision should be like. There are risks in going for our dreams and missing what might be good enough and crashing and falling down in the process. And equally there are risks in being hijacked by binary thinking that either we will be the dream team or the nightmare team.

It is often easier to discuss the difficult things that are going badly if it is not the only place being talked about precisely because it is not the only place on the map. A team can get stuck in the groove of things going badly for fear of a return to a nightmare time as described in box 5. There may be comparisons with other teams and other organisations where the team has been through a nightmare time of disorganisation.

This simple template is not to be used in a prescriptive way. It is giving permission for the positive and difficult sides of work to be discussed and held in relation to each other. At a later part of reflective team discussion along these lines it is essential to reflect on the experience of talking with the map and how it has helped or hindered the quality of the discussion (for evaluation tools in these respects go to the research page on www.mapandtalk.com). There are many ideas and references in the literature on working to develop reflective practice in work teams in the book by Jenny

Marshall and Jamie Kirkland.[65] The book is written for teams working in forensic and criminal justice settings but many of the ideas are applicable to any workplace.

If we don't know how the organisation talks we don't know how it works

Apparently, the octopus's brain is also in its tentacles.[66] Its intelligence is distributed in its body. The executive team were like the tentacles of an octopus and reached far and wide around the organisation. They prided themselves in knowing what was going on as evidenced by their reach to all branches of the organisation. What they did not realise was that they had a language problem or rather a failure of conversational awareness to see that their executive lingo needed translating into local frontline or coalface lingos. They didn't pick up the somewhat colonial structure where middle managers translated for them and talked in executive terms losing in the process a lot of the meaning and detail of what was being discussed. One of the junior managers called it boss washing a bit like white washing. They like to hear what they want to hear in words that are palatable to them.

The executive had developed their own idioms and jargon which at times of pressure they mistakenly took to be the language of the whole organisation. They only got conversation back in the manner they initiated. There were lots of buzzwords and slogans and summaries of briefing papers, but the possibility was that they were in a conversational bubble with its own language despite their octopus-like capacity and its potential for a kind of distributed and relational intelligence. The challenge is to have the conversational awareness to be multilingual and see the executive team's job is to translate patiently and sensitively from language to another. The chief executive didn't feel in control, but everyone liked to think he was, so he faked it. Over time they faked it with him and developed a way of running the organisation that could only be described as management by appearances.

The one third rule

The following rule was originally developed with teams doing Map and Talk for reflective practice. The rule is a summary of a way of thinking about the source of powerful patterns of relating, that while evident in the moment don't entirely feel that they belong there. It is as if an invisible intruder or ghost is in the room. It is specifically useful in thinking about the push and pull of feelings and roles transferred within and between teams and their members. It is equally relevant to individual conversations when thinking about the social context and the different directions and sources of power. The rule of thumb is that one third of the conversation or the story being told and remembered and re-experienced to some extent is coming from person A, or group A; one third is coming from B; and one third is coming from the context or system around their interaction. Blame, responsibility and agency tends to go binary and get loaded on one of the thirds: it is all the system's fault; or it is down to me; or it is them that are doing it. And of course, it may be all or one of these, but the one third rule is a call for balanced thinking to see how feelings and responsibility are projected, claimed and allocated.

This simple rule challenges us not put all the blame on the system or on the speaker, or on ourselves. Instead, we should try to map out the push and pull of power and influence through social and emotional role casting. It is easy to take blame on ourselves, or project it or push it onto others or the system. It is never evenly distributed in thirds but nor is it ever all loaded on to one person, or one thing.

In the following example a group of frontline managers do well by regularly talking informally to each other and not splitting it into all or nothing and staying with the perspective of the one third rule.

Soaking up, shaking off or choking off

A team of middle managers meet mid-afternoon informally for coffee and mutual support. The meeting is no more than twenty minutes long and by choice has good attendance. They describe their role as to lead from the front and carry the gospel of the day from the higher managerial hierarchy to the coal face. Or not. Their conversations are often about what we called 'soaking up and choking off' the many directives from above or from other parts of the system, some of which were contradictory. They had some discretion as to whether to hold these directives or pass them down to the frontline of the organisation.

At the same time, they were the eyes and ears for managing the teams below them (they didn't like the 'below them' terminology since they came from and identified with these teams and were not paid significantly more but worked out of duty and for the status). They were often on their own using personal judgement as to what to pick up and what to pass on. They were the gatekeepers for most human relations and human resource tasks of keeping teams adequately staffed and moral at reasonable levels. Without them the whole system would be faceless and become disorganised.

Middle managers 'soak and choke' or 'broker and buffer'

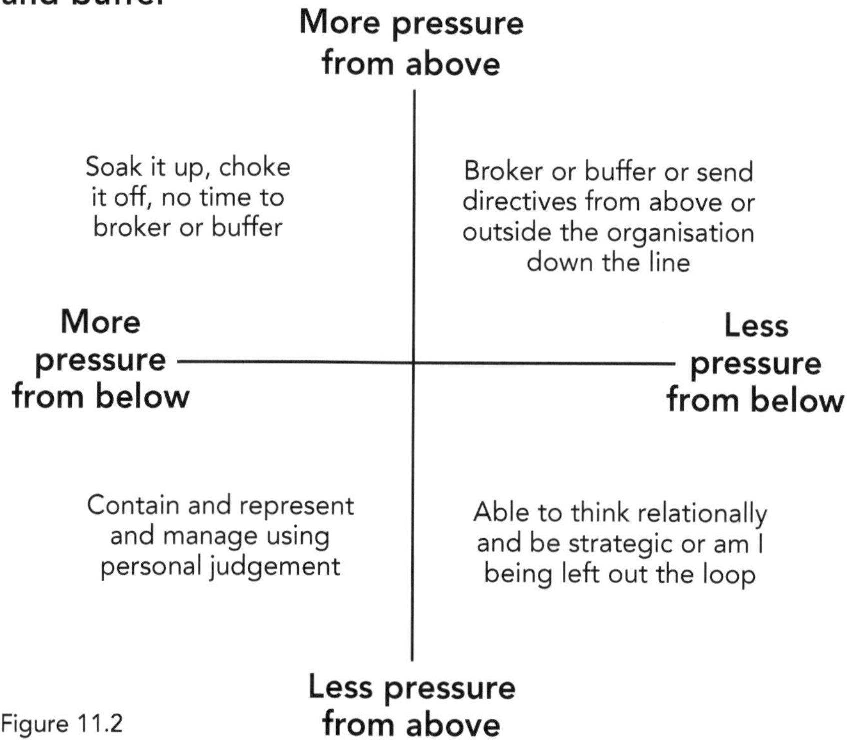

Figure 11.2

In their informal chat their skill and personal judgement was to know when to soak something up and when to shake it off. When to be the broker and when to be the sponge and buffer. They had a two-dimensional grid that helped them map moments of awareness and keep their discussions at a reflective level and not just moaning about the higher ups or banter about colleagues. The horizontal axis of the grid was a line with 'more pressure from below' at one end and 'less pressure from below' at the other end. The vertical axis was between 'more pressure from above' at the top and 'less pressure from above' at the bottom. The top left quadrant showed up as no time to broker or buffer as there was no time process to things and the only option was to soak it up as a managerial sponge or choke it off. The top right was self-defeating because if they went with complying from pressure and initiatives from above and passing them down the line regardless, they were just feeding a rise in pressure from below. They often spent time working out how to discern the best ways of passing on management directives and initiatives.

At certain points of the week and of the day, they felt more in the bottom right quadrant and had two responses: now there is time to reflect and catch up. Or now I am being left out of the loop and why has it gone quiet? The bottom left quadrant was one where they felt best used as managers and had most personal judgement. The trouble was that this was the quadrant that senior managers and executives knew least about or valued!

Can we open the window?

Imagine Lara, newly promoted, is joining a monthly executive meeting for the first time with twenty people around the boardroom table. The room is not quite big enough and, as always, there is a lot of business to get through. The chairwoman moves things affably and swiftly along. There is clear direction of who is to speak to what purpose. Lara sits restlessly in her chair hoping for some ice breaking or banter or at least a chance to be introduced. She senses a mixture of cheerful compliance and polite boredom. There is no conversation, and the talk of the meeting is transactional in style. The secretary is taking notes and is consulted by the chairwoman with a slight turn of the head from time to time about procedure. The room is stuffy, and Lara thinks to herself it would be wise to open a window and let in some air. But no one moves. She puzzles about the enormous and expensive assembly of talent being held idly in this meeting. There must be some hidden story here about a higher purpose which she does not understand.

When how meets what

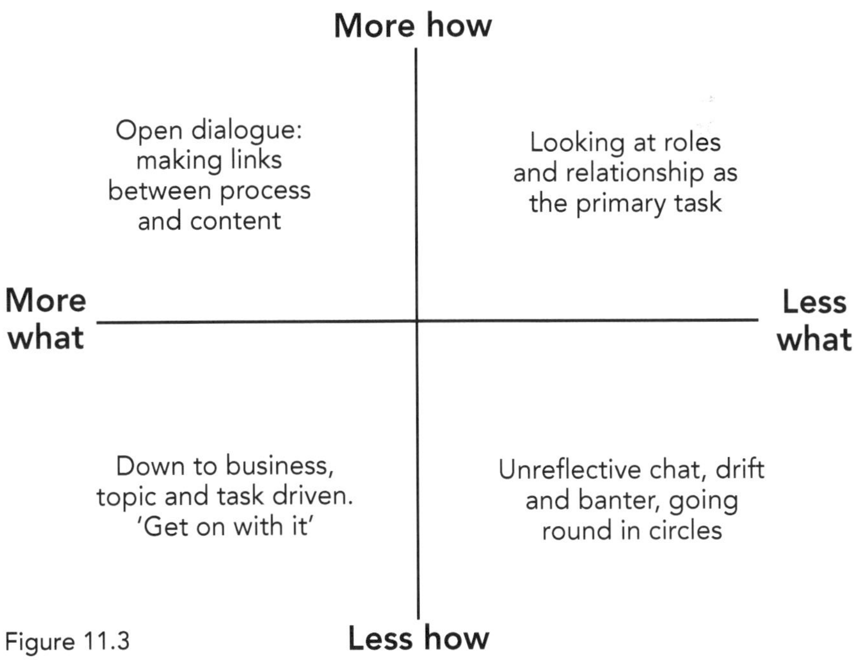

Figure 11.3

At the end the chair asks breezily, 'Any other business?' Lara raises her hand. The chair nods to her. Lara begins to speak and in contrast to everyone else she stands up – like someone taking the floor at an assembly. The tension in the room changes, suddenly instead of boredom there is electricity and interest. Someone straightens his tie, several close their laptops and someone else folds their arms. The secretary puts his pen down as Lara says: 'I am new and have not met anyone and just wondered if in meetings like this you ever have a wild five minutes of talking to each other and reflecting on how things are going like with a white board or something?'

The chairwoman leaned forward, 'What would you want us to do?'

Lara hesitated but thought it best to be honest. 'I would open the window literally and metaphorically because it is stuffy in here and it is as if we are working here together whilst looking in on each other through a glass screen. I would say, naively, that if our business didn't include sharing our curiosity about each other then we won't thrive.' The room was now on edge although someone did open the window. 'I would make it normal to talk about the process between us as much as about the jobs that need doing. Even if things are going well, like they are, I would do that so should the organisation ever need it we are ready to talk about our conflicts and differences without going head-to-head.'

Th chair turns to the secretary for guidance on a response. 'I think you could say duly noted madam.' And she turned to the young Lara and smiled and said, 'Duly noted'.

Jenny's isolation trap

Jenny felt isolated in her new job. Everyone seemed to know their place and there were tight circles of friendships (the 'old guard' she called them) who seemed to know all about each other's lives having worked together for years. Jenny felt not just isolated but excluded. She felt increasingly cut off, hurt and hostile. She half realised that she was hiding her hurt (and her longing to be included) by having disdain for them and their ways. Jenny felt like leaving until a new colleague Wendy joined the team and they got on with each other.

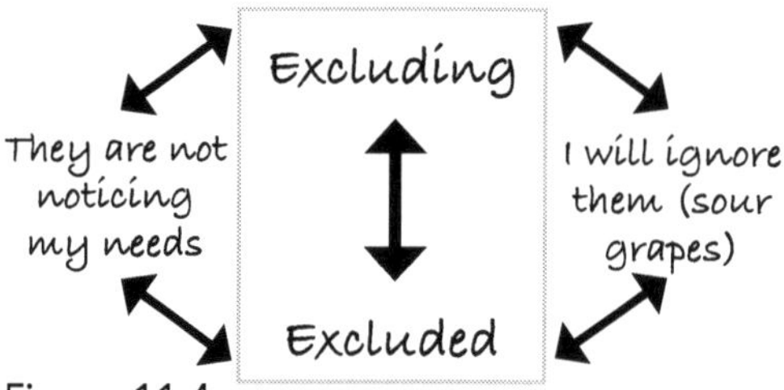

Figure 11.4

Jenny was surprised that Wendy was not so bothered about the 'old guard' as Wendy put it. 'They'll come round eventually and anyway I've got you.' Jenny laughed and softened. One of the leading personalities in the 'old guard' came over and joined the two of them. Wendy broke the ice and in a moment of shared awareness they all discussed who thought who was being off hand and snooty. Their moment of shared reflection was healing and, if it could have been mapped, it would have shown feeling 'excluded' (written at the bottom end of the reciprocal relation between Jenny and the 'old guard'). Jenny felt they 'were not noticing her needs' so she opted to 'ignore them' which took her to the top end of the reciprocal role relationship with her acting to exclude herself from them. The potential for a chance window of contact and conversational awareness between them was shut tight. Wendy came alongside and didn't join the excluding to excluded dance and by chance, or because of some element of non-verbal communication, the invisible standoff could be named and resolved. In our working lives we protectively take positions that are a kind of personal and organisational emotional first aid in the moment but become fixed and limiting if there isn't an open conversational process to come to the rescue.

A conversational school

All schools are conversational. We learn to talk when we learn maths or to read and write. We discuss things and extend our vocabulary and learn a relational awareness through learning the rules of syntax and grammar. We learn also through the invisible or hidden curriculum of the social life and culture of the school.

A conversational school has resources and time in the curriculum for group work, for reflection and mentoring and coaching. It would be as much interested in process of learning as the content. It would have voices and spaces for children who felt isolated or silenced in some way. It would challenge put downs and bullying or inappropriate behaviour. Staff and parents would have an interest in and an ongoing conversation about the learning stories of each individual child and the group dynamics of the school as whole.

All this happens in schools these days and yet alongside is a more transactional and spreadsheet culture of meeting performance criteria. What might get lost because of its nonspecific quality is the process of conversational awareness. How are we helping each other learn both a freedom of expression and a conversational ethics as children and teachers? How do we help each other notice, name and negotiate what is going on within and around us and honour and navigate differences of heritage and values? Do we mostly remember the great moments of conversation with school friends or teachers? Does real learning derive from talking in the spaces between the lines of the curriculum? Is that what the good teacher leader models in conversation with their pupils – a discussion within and between subject areas that develop a relational and conversational intelligence along with gifted learning in specific subjects? Russell Meares cites a fascinating study of children's memories of things seen during a visit to a natural history museum. Apparently, children (aged 4) only remembered what had been also pointed to and spoken of in conversation with their mother. 'If squirrels were spoken about but not monkeys, it was as if there were no monkeys there'[67], Meares goes on to explain. 'Real' in this study is what happened as depicted in conversation. He goes on to explore the kinds of conversation that make things real and memorable and focuses on the importance of memorable educational conversations being ones that are storied in some way.

In the next section an exercise is detailed of remembering the micro-moments of an early learning story at school. It is always surprising, having done this exercise with hundreds of adults, how often what is remembered are the 'hot moments' or 'sweet moments' of conversational awareness. Perhaps the mission statement for a school should not be what did you learn at school today but how well did you learn to talk about it? And how long did that conversation stick in your mind for better or worse? Was it linked to a process of making and sharing stories? How far did it take you into the life-stories of your own?

Teach yourself by mapping a school story

For over twenty years of providing introductory training in Cognitive Analytic Therapy to several thousand trainees we have always introduced participants to an exercise where in pairs each person tells the other a school story that comes to mind from their own experience for ten minutes each. We encourage participants to not chose a big and shocking one but one of those routine moments of validation or shaming, triumph and embarrassment that all of us have in school.

The aims of the exercise are to get experience of mapping and talking side-by-side while also being engaged with real life stories and the responsibility for each other's feelings as conversational awareness with a map develops.

It is always a valuable experience and mostly because it shows how a small story has a pattern to it that is highlighted by the mapping and resonates in the present. It is not just what we learnt at school but how we learnt it and how we gained or lost in emotional and social intelligence through roles and relationships first encountered at school.

Dr Jo Cheffey a clinical psychologist and Cognitive Analytic Therapist shared the following story and letter in response to mapping and talking over a memorable moment in her early school years. Jo recalled feeling nourished and treated as special by her form teacher. The making of the map with Jo started when we were talking through the story as compassionate observers. The conversation and the map developed together, and it was initially as if we were looking back on an old memory. The map tracks the sequence of Jo remembering getting questions right and having her hand up often and being teacher's pet. Then two days in a row she leaned back on her chair and knocked powder paints of the easel behind her and made a mess. She was ashamed by the telling off she got but felt even more that she had 'fallen from grace' and would never be special again. When we started recapping the experience with the pen, tracking round the map a second time, the feelings were activated in a new way as if we were back partly inside the experience and looking forward in time. The phrase (underlined in the map below) 'I will never be special again', which Jo had said minutes earlier, was now restated and Jo repeated it with emotional emphasis which touched us both as if we were children again. The mapping and talking process started in observer mode outside the experience and then went inside it as if reliving it. On reflection and as part of the exercise Jo wrote the following letter along the lines described in Chapter 7 of this book.

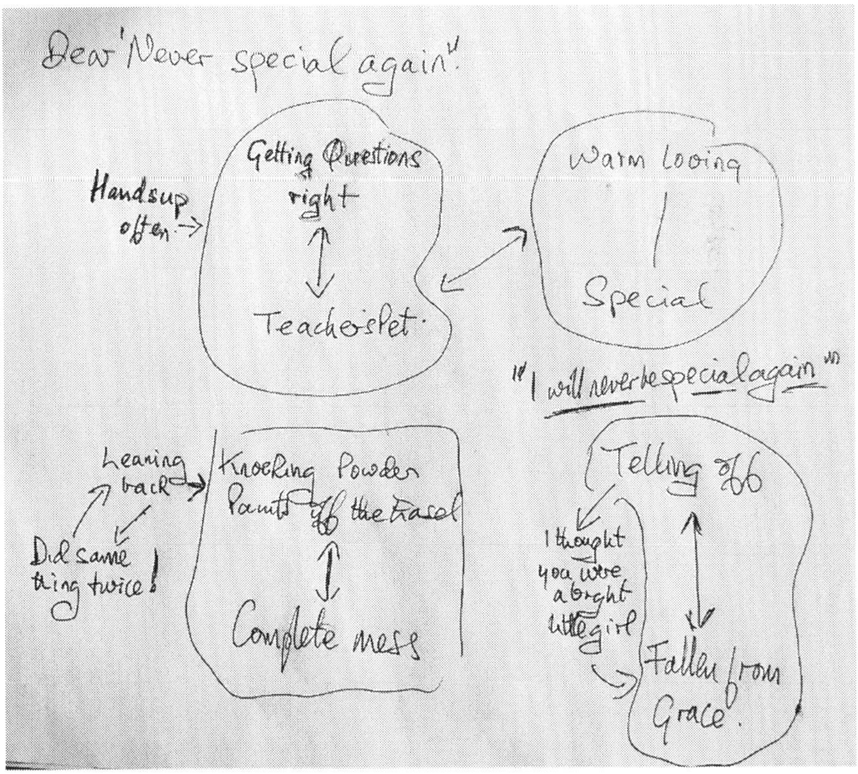

Dear Never be Special Again,

You loved feeling special and bright. You felt seen and valued by the teacher, Mrs A, in the class. This was all shattered with the easel accident and she expressed her disappointment at your silliness ('I thought you were a bright little girl...') and not being sensible enough to avoid the accident for the second time. The paints spilled everywhere and made such a mess. You felt dismissed and hurt, fallen from grace as if you would never be seen as special again in her eyes. You felt like you had ruined something very special, a relationship that no-one else in the class appeared to have with her.

Thinking about this more, you have felt like this on many occasions in your life; a striving to always get things right and be the best you can be. You always hope that your efforts will be seen and recognised. You feel that there have been very few moments where you have felt like the best or the special one; there are always others who occupy that place. The person you tend to disappoint and let down the most is yourself and there is a constant feeling of striving and negative comparison with others which is always with you.

I've been thinking about why this memory came up so easily in the mapping session and I think it is related to how I was left feeling after a difficult conversation with a colleague I was supervising the previous day. There was a feeling on my part about trying to get a delicate conversation about boundaries right and making a mess of it. Yet again that voice in my head was thinking how other people would have managed this better or been more confident in their position and relief that no one was witnessing this. I wonder if these powerful feelings and scripts are related to this early memory?

What does my 'adult self' need to say to the 'never be special again' seven-year-old me? She needs reassurance that mistakes can be rectified, they are not catastrophic and when this happens this is not the end of the relationship. You don't remember whether your special relationship with Mrs A was restored after this incident, but maybe you can allow yourself to put the memory of her wrapping you up in a blanket because you were running temperature and driving you home in her car at a later time, meant that you had not fallen from grace after all.

Have faith and be brave,

Jo

School is a human relations laboratory, and we need more time processing the intended and unintended experiments in developing a sense of self in the formal and informal spaces of our school days. One option is teaching children the tools and ideas of conversational awareness through the methods of map and talk. It is easier to stop and reflect with a map than without one. Even looking back at school years decades later can bring vivid moments or reconnection and insight as present wisdom is linked to old wounds or vice versa.

Achievement counselling

We live in a society where great achievement is so sought after that it can be idealised and take over a young person's life. All their fragile eggs of development and discovery are put in one achievement basket. Those who reach the top academically, in sport, music or the arts or other areas of excellence in life are championed and praised as exemplars.

Higher educational achievement is a central aim of society. It constitutes a huge investment of money, human effort and expectation. On its back ride our collective hopes for the enlightened, open, cosmopolitan, affluent and versatile knowledge economies of the future. Individually, university is experienced as the highway to career resilience and mobility, enhanced income and opportunities and greater understanding and appreciation of society. Individually it can also be experienced as a great personal challenge. There can be a pressure to do something outstanding. Striving and testing of self is an important part of development, but it can be invested with emotional roles that overburden the achievement process and detract from the creativity and delight in achieving. How we manage the pressure to achieve is often left out of the conversation. Here are some example patterns which may help tease out and disentangle a more open conversational relationship with our achievement needs, healthy narcissism and striving whilst also discovering and validating our young selves

Lost youth. All I did in my spare time in my teens was practice the violin. It became part of me, part of my body and I had a love/hate relationship with it. By my early twenties I wondered where my teenage years had gone. It was as if this perfectionist striving around one talent kicks aside other developmental needs which ironically, if I had had time for them might have made me a better violinist because I would have been in dialogue with my relationship with the violin and my body. Once I started experimenting with relationships, finding my sexuality, and learning to relax and be on holiday, I also discovered a different way of playing the violin. I could be an insider and merged with my musical efforts and an outsider who was detached and compassionately able to observe.

Doing it for you. This was the unspoken but powerful conversation which we never had in my childhood years of becoming a competitive swimmer and finally blowing it all out of the water in my late teens. It was such a deep entanglement. You, my dad and I were too close to it to name it and negotiate it. I was doing it for you and my sense of myself was hijacked by that.

Head down. Hard work masks or bypasses disturbance or difficulty. I knew there was things going on with mum and dad and I knew I was feeling weird at times. I just found refuge in putting my head down and studying. I justified the hard work as the road to success but inside me was a private conversation: 'Keep a lid on things, keep focused, lose yourself in work and family troubles will pass or feeling helpless won't feel so useless'. I can talk compassionately to my younger self now and say it was your way of surviving and not bad as such to keep your head down. It was a double win at the time as long as now the template of adolescent survival doesn't become a lifelong saga. The irony of it is that I did do well, and it has helped me find a secure place to live my life, but I have never had a conversation about the cost of keeping my head down and whether still now I avoid conflict for fear of troubled water.

Brilliant or doomed. There are various ways of mapping this pattern out depending on the conversation. One way is to start at 1 on the map in Figure 11.5 and the desire to be brilliant at something and therefore special and superior. It is a place that traps us because we are bound to meet a setback or find a fault and then fear or face exposure and be at the receiving end of criticising and contemptuous voices (either for real or in our imagination and real enough within) which make us feel inadequate and worthless as shown at the bottom of box 2. From this state of mind, we resolve to show up (or show the contemptuous part of ourselves) and

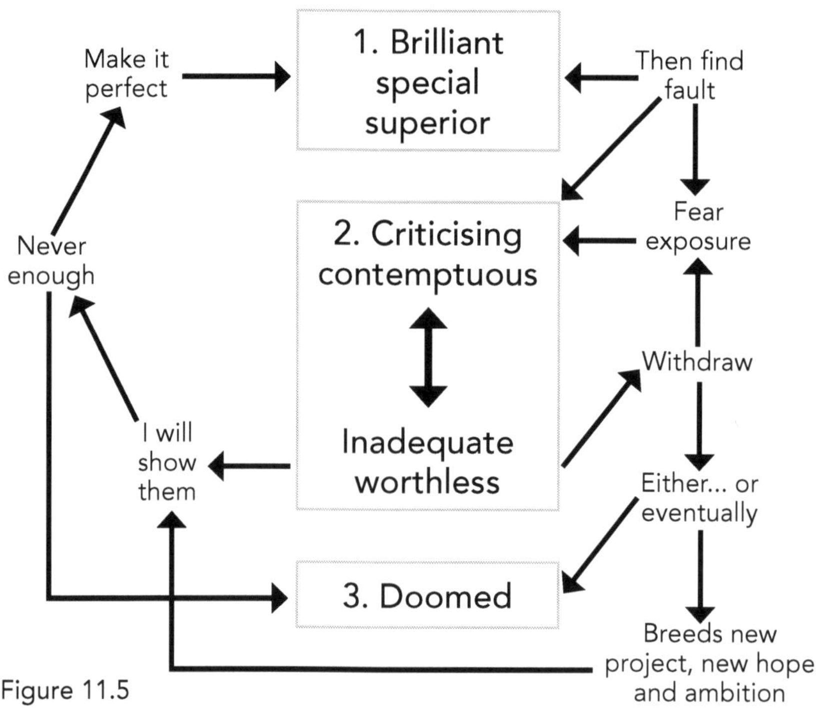

Figure 11.5

set off striving for perfection again. In part it may feel that it will never be enough, and we fear, or bring on, or let others bring on, a period of crashing down and feeling not brilliant but doomed as in box 3. The fear of this, or the reality of it, eventually breeds a new project and new hope and ambition and we set off striving again to make it perfect. Or we go round and round in box 2 criticising our efforts. Mostly perhaps it is quite normal to move around these boxes in the process of seeking to achieve something and the importance of conversational awareness is that we have the courage to talk about the highs and lows with someone who can listen and map with us helpfully.

In all these examples the thought comes to mind of the ever-growing number of life coaches, mentors, counsellors, psychotherapists to whom we all turn for inspiration, guidance and validation. In any, and all, of these roles we need to be mindful that when we join in an intimate conversation when are joining the person's inner talk and potential confusion of voices about their hopes and fears. Our challenge is to know our part in the dances we are joining.

Talking with our bodies

Conversational awareness applies to our bodies. How we talk about them with doctors and nurses, with fitness coaches and dietitians is a neglected subject. Most doctors and nurses aim to have a patient-centred bedside manner. They generally want to help the patient become knowledgeable about their condition. They have training in interpersonal skills, and role play training in interactions with patients. But do we know how to join them and play our part in a conversation through, with and about our bodies? In my lifetime, the conversation with medics has moved from excessively deferential or avoidant to more entitled on the one hand and more knowledgeable on the other. Creating conversations that lead to what is called the expert patient requires a conversational awareness not just interpersonally between doctor, nurse and patient or other health care profession. It needs the whole system of medicine to be conversationally aware. This applies to early intervention and treatment compliance. There is a rich literature on the talk that is needed to develop the expert patient.[68] If we are going to change the treatment, the diet or the exercise regime, do we also need to change the conversation?

Conversations with our bodies need to be compassionate and curious whilst also being general and specific. The template map in Figure 11.6 starts with wondering with my body, or part of my body or any attribute of my body (my sleep, exercise, eating patterns). The left side box points to what my body is doing and how I respond in what I feel and think. The up-arrow points to what we would like our body to be doing and what that would make us feel. Having that out on paper can help us think of other angles and the effort at this point is not to be judgemental or solution focused but to use the words on paper to help move a conversation out into the open. The down arrow points to what we don't want our body to do or don't want us to respond to the body by doing. The box at the bottom of the map can help fill in the thoughts and feelings about how my body would feel and I would feel if I was doing what I don't want to do with my body. At the heart of the template map are the yoyo moments, feelings or actions that might need kindness and attention as we shimmer or hover in reflection and response between hopes and fears.

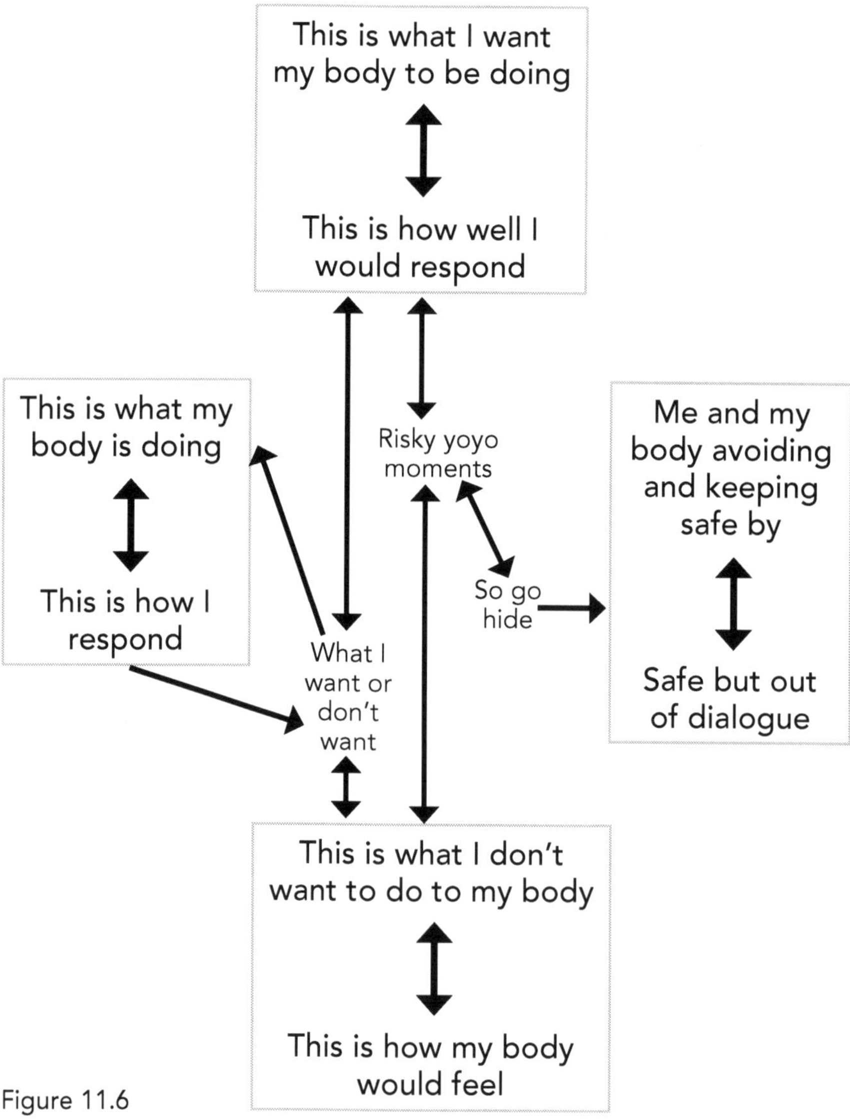

Figure 11.6

To name the feared place we (body and me) should say in our separate ways what we don't want to be doing because of what that would make us feel. Finally, we might look on the map and fill in where we go to make ourselves safe, and/or hide and avoid the yoyo up and down between what we want and don't want. The map can help us be more in conversation with our mixed feelings and small changes. Having made a map, it may be helpful to write a letter to me and my body. Dear my body and me.

Conversational intimacy love and care

A book that explores conversational awareness in search of better relationships would be a disappointment if it did not make a tentative map of how we do and don't talk in the context of love, intimacy and sexual relationships. There is indeed so much to say and many lessons to draw about power, tenderness and difference from the way a society talks about sex and love. We have come a long way in a few generations towards more open and equal public and private conversation. There is still so much to negotiate and navigate and each generation and each society is finding new freedoms, new injustices and new ways of talking. The legacy of a sexist and racist social system around the world will still need generations of active healing. We need to be answerable about the past and curious in conversation about the present for fear of otherwise being isolated within our like-minded silos. Perhaps there are as many variety of ways of doing the 'loving and hurting, helping and hindering' of appropriate intimacy within social types and identities as between groups. There are elements of the highs and lows of intimacy which is the same regardless of gendering and sexuality. A relationship is intimate in many ways, but it is conversational intimacy and trust which is key to all the others. From the perspective of conversational intimacy perhaps the voice can make a claim to be one of the most important organs.

Part of our conversational awareness is of the boundary between private and personal and public and personal conversation. How to be loving or how to be sexual does need a capacity to be intimately conversational. So much needs noticing, naming and negotiating. The ethics of conversation and the ethics of love and sex are similar. We first have a chance to learn this in teenage years.

Part one: first love is first conversations

When Lisa and Gary met in their mid-teens, they were immediately attracted but also surprised. It took them years to recognise what they had found with each other and what had been so missing from their lives before. They had found space to talk and had never talked so personally before. They were making a private realm of conversation. They talked about their families, their lives, politics and their dreams. They took turns to talk. They didn't tease each other or wind each other up. Although they were at similar schools and had similar backgrounds of class, it felt to them as if they were from two different worlds. For them their first love was their first conversation. Sexual attraction and negotiation needs a conversational ethics and intimacy. The differences in expectation, power and gender backgrounds need voicing and discovering and negotiating. The reason to take first love slowly is not just that desire and trust builds slowly but that understanding and dialogue need time to develop. We are literally learning to map each other's values, ideas and emotions about intimacy and relating.

It is not a time to be mapping the moment, but a thousand different maps might emerge as to how we co-create a relationship that is both personal and potentially sexual within and across the dynamics of gendering and being gendered. The conversational awareness grid might be a useful reference for thinking about the bigger picture of personal relationships.

	A conversational awareness grid pointing to some of the qualities (poetic or otherwise) that can arise with map and talk	Four directions of talk			
		Between us	**Within me**	**Around us**	**Beyond us**
Four lines of talk	**Hovering** Links and gaps, in or out, pro and con, picture and detail	*Ideas = unmapped*	*Thoughts = curiosity*	*Theories = gendered*	*Myths = unreliable*
	Shimmering Hot and cold, here and there, open or closed, sweet or sour	*Feelings = embodied*	*Emotions = passion*	*Drama = live*	*Presence = intense*
	Participating Doing and being, making and sharing, now and then, with or for	*Roles = unchartered*	*Creativity = wide open*	*Politics= sexual*	*Congregate = dance floor*
	Authoring Owning and disowning, acting and answering, for and against, self and others	*Authority = shared*	*Conscience = immediate*	*Values = mixed*	*Humanity = central*

Figure 11.61

In the grid (discussed in detail in Chapter 6) the version above has possible connotations for each of the sixteen items. In each of the boxes there is an = sign and a key word that highlights how that component might be tagged and experienced in an ethical and conversationally aware journey towards sexual and emotional intimacy. Each of us may live through or look back on this differently but the general point is a respect for the central role of conversational awareness as we learn to negotiate sexual awareness and intimacy. The sensuality and the romance and the pleasure may be in the dynamics of the conversation.

Part two: the honeymoon phase

When the honeymoon is over is a common phrase. It points to a time of being wrapped in a partnership which partly keeps the outside world away. It has extended meaning beyond the early months of a romance or married life to the point of reality check that any partnership whether work, friendship or sexual will face. It could be two lovers, a football manager and his or her team, a politician in relation to her or his supporters or partners in a business enterprise.

As in the map (figure 11.7) the story starts at box 1 with one or more people making a commitment to be together and share a part of themselves. The state is one of being 'wedded' and of being of one mind and blissfully merged (box 2) but there are connotations of getting entangled emotionally with each other as implied by the phrase 'tying the knot'. Conversations will take on the qualities of the emotional state. There is a degree of loss of autonomy and loss of self to the union. It will vary whether this is a cause of dividedness within the person or wholeheartedly mutual; or a performance for those around; or some defence against the uncertainty of the future beyond the immediate honeymoon.

The blissful state can be so over-inflated and so dominate dialogue that it is fragile and point 3 on the map of shimmering and hovering with mixed feeling and ideas leads to point 4 and conflicting needs and views. Which produces a fear of losing the honeymoon feelings by falling out. Indeed, falling out with each other is like falling down from a state of bliss. The challenge is to recover a sense of each other as separate selves and this may involve conflict and finding hiding places in busy and separate lives (point 6). There may also be nostalgia for golden times and moments of recommitment and having faith that love and bliss in partnership can be restored. The feared place is that of breaking up and feeling abandoned and unworthy or ashamed which in turn may generate an attempt to try again to recreate the state of mind and dialogue in box 1 on the map. The challenge posed by the process of talking with a map of this kind (it will be unique for each 'honeymoon grieving partnership') is to have a capacity to talk to each other from outside the dance of patterns and shifts in positions. At any point in this process there are risky moments of being hijacked by one position; or of yoyoing between two contrasting positions; or ending up in the most unwanted position at point 5 on the map.

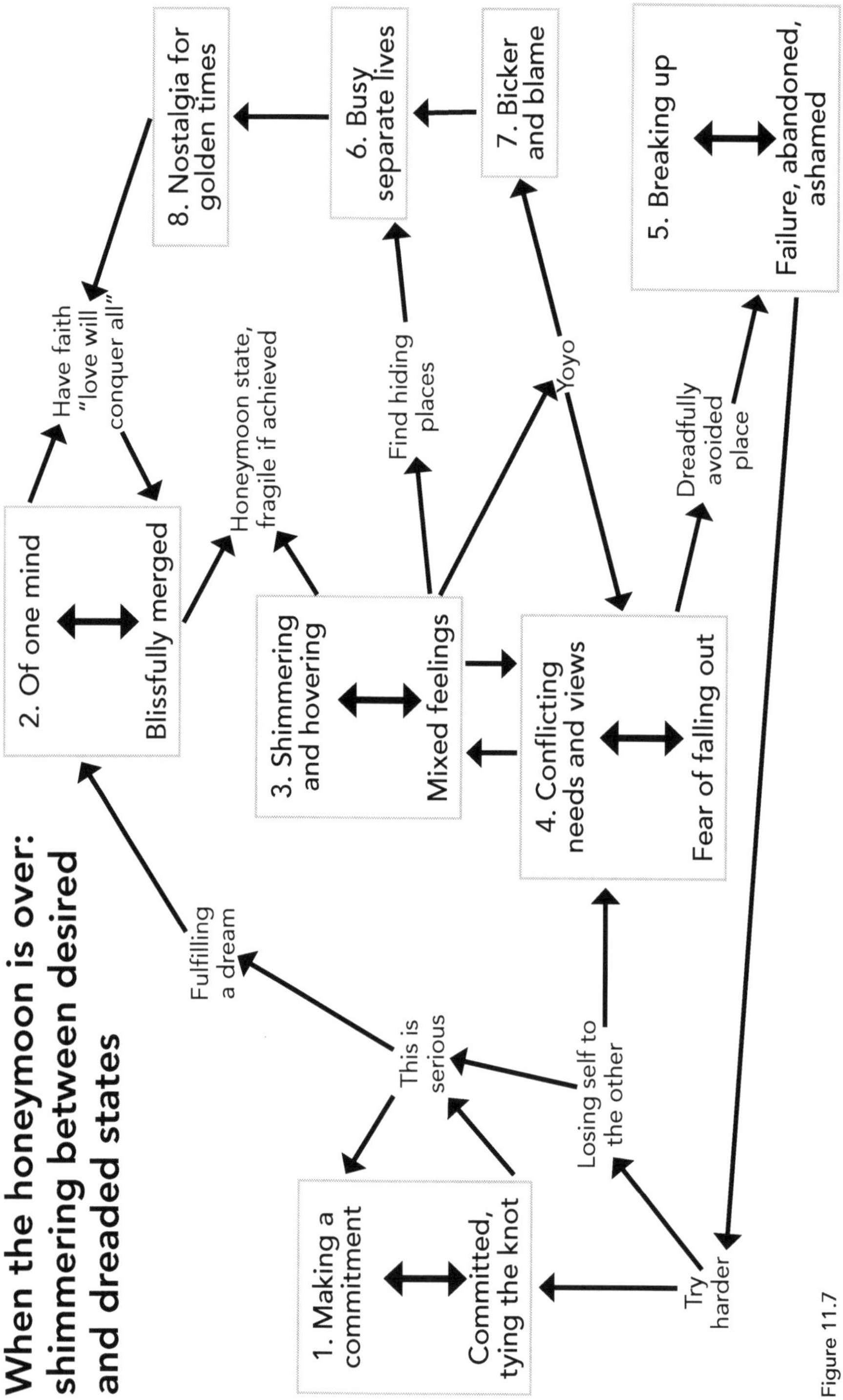
When the honeymoon is over: shimmering between desired and dreaded states
1. Making a commitment
Committed, tying the knot
This is serious
Fulfilling a dream
2. Of one mind
Blissfully merged
Have faith "love will conquer all"
Honeymoon state, fragile if achieved
3. Shimmering and hovering
Mixed feelings
Losing self to the other
4. Conflicting needs and views
Fear of falling out
Find hiding places
Yoyo
Dreadfully avoided place
5. Breaking up
Failure, abandoned, ashamed
6. Busy separate lives
7. Bicker and blame
8. Nostalgia for golden times
Try harder

Figure 11.7

There are parallels with the hopes and fears map in Chapter 4, the brilliant and doomed map in this chapter and the narcissism in ideas map in Chapter 12. This honeymoon phase map highlights the transferability of maps of one setting to another. It might be about a married couple, but it could equally be about a political movement, or business, or a partnership of any kind. You may find your way into the ideas of talking with a map by reflecting back on a particular honeymoon phase in your work or personal life and mapping in your own words.

Part three: bickering while driving

In this example the couple had one argument in front of the kids and the youngest was upset and the oldest went silent. Never again was their pledge, we don't argue in front of the children. For years they had driven into work together with one dropping the other off at their different offices. In the enclosed world of the car, they would bicker. They would use sour words and be unkind to each other; justifying the rudeness as home truths or tit-for-tat. This seemingly happy couple were like Jekyll and Hyde inside and outside the car. By the end of the journey, they hated each other and felt confused and disorganised. Their bickering was a kind of local war between them, and they were stuck in it. In the evening they were yearning for some familiar companionship and acted as if the bickering was something that happened only in the car. In mapping it out, once it came up when they went to couple counselling, it helped them change the conversation and had the following features. They could see the bickering only partly worked and was a form of emotional hide and seek giving them an illusion of control over their feelings. What the map helped them share and negotiate was that they were never satisfied by the bickering and were always left with what was named as a hidden vulnerability. The double elements of hiding their

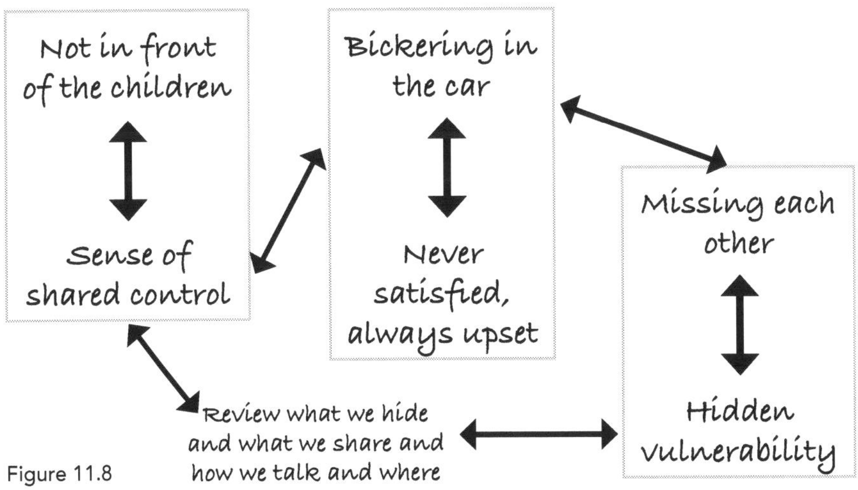

Figure 11.8

conversational bickering from the children and hiding their vulnerability from each other led to them reviewing what they hide more generally and when and where they talk. What helped them ultimately was a behaviour change when they went to work by bus.

Changing the conversation in arts and creativity

The conversational awareness invested in, stored by, and then drawn out through presenting or performing art is worth a book on its own. Artists work on their art through conversations with themselves with the work before them, with the world around them and with each other. These plural conversations go into the artwork: the painting, the novel, the play, the musical composition, the performance with the piano or guitar and many other forms and applications. The dialogues and conversations from all elements of the conversational awareness grid are held and contained in the artwork. It engages with how art is encouraged or allowed. How it perpetuates or subverts existing dominant perspectives or invents new ones. We should look to art for both reassuring and liberating conversations within ourselves and with others. We have to experience the art as audience and become conversational participants. We have to let it spill into our own artistic impulses and needs. We go to galleries, to concerts and festivals, or the theatre or cinema, or watch art programs at home and we hover and shimmer with our own efforts to recover or respond to the artist's conversation invested in their work. All the time we are asking questions of the artistic and creative and expressive side of ourselves. Here are some sample conversations.

Cubism and the art of fragmented perspectives

Bracques and Picasso, influenced by Cezanne and African art, changed the artistic conversation. You may say why pick them out, surely the impressionists changed the artistic conversation? Each new movement in painting changes the conversation by adding a different perspective but cubism seems highly relevant to how we talk to each other about how we see each other in the world. Like a conversation, the composition, the colouring, the form of a painting is so rich in possibilities. In the many conversations entangled in cubism we see within and beyond the fragments. We have to abandon the familiar forms of perspective taking and seek a variety of simultaneous points of view.

I am not a painter or an art critic but next time I go to an art gallery my aim as a visitor will be to feel the conversation that the artist has had with the work as they composed it.

I don't know why art galleries should feel like shuffling around a church or a museum. They should be conversational spaces. Each painting is the artful residue and expression of a unique kind of creative conversation. Each painting is waiting to be brought back into the dialogue from which it was made. The conversation between Bracques and Picasso was of breaking up the surface of a painting into multiple perspectives of seeing the person or object from all angles. Not impressionistic or expressionistic but fragmented in order to see the parts of the whole from all angles. For me it touches on our relationship with trauma buried by our capacity to keep up and manage by appearances. It is saying don't rush to clarity. Leave the conversation open. Cubism invites a conversation with all the other painting styles, opens the ground for choice, perspective and detail. Not just three-dimensional depth of perspective but realising the need for seeing the person or object or situation from multiple angles.

The conversational pianist

Alex Dariescu is a concert pianist. She has performed all over the world in many different venues to audiences of all kinds. Like any musician, Alex relates to her audience through her music and her instrument. The piano does the talking. But also, Alex does something extra whenever she can, by pausing at the end of her entry on stage, and before sitting down, she turns to the audience and introduces herself, and the piece of music, and her relationship with it. Her introduction is not telling the audience in the manner of a mini lecture but an invitation to join her in a conversation with the music and its performance, here and now, in all its vitality. It is almost as if she is saying: come on in, let's get side by side with this if we can.

Alex knows, like all artists, that we the audience make our own conversation privately within ourselves to the playing as it progresses. We go in and out of various emotional states and responses, some of which are tied to the movement of the music and some of which come from places within ourselves. Alex works with that and can also see how we draw upon a shared sensory response from the rows of people around us and the mass of people in the auditorium. It is a plural, orchestral conversation with more than one origin and it touches all sixteen of those elements in the conversational awareness grid in Chapter 6.

Artist must talk to themselves, but the rules of conversation vary with the medium and context of expression. Perhaps painters and others from the fine arts may hold on to their work because their conversation with it is hard to finish. The secret here is to adopt the stance that everything we do is unfinished or cannot be made final.[69] The performance is just another rehearsal.

When she is practising and rehearsing a new piece, Alex lets it talk to her, talks back to it and talks to herself about the playing, talks in her head to the composer. The conversation comes through her hands.

For Alex and all performers on stage there is a careful balance to be struck with awareness; not too much to trigger self-consciousness and anxiety but not too little to be unaware of the implicit conversation with the audience. There is a sweet spot (as introduced in Chapter 1) where the conversations within, between and around us go beyond somewhere to a higher level that is communal or transcendent and is hard to put into words without risking sounding overblown or cliched.

If you are an artist of any kind reading this book, look at the 'Too much-too little' awareness line, think of your (or your critic and mentors) conversation with the work and mark the sweet spot of awareness when it is not too over attentive, shaming or accusing and not too oblivious and unaware.

The painter or sculptor, the novelist, poet or playwright puts out a piece of work that creates a wall between the conversations put into the work and the conversation the onlookers draw from their participation in the finished piece. For musicians and actors there's no wall and the threat and the promise of the conversations is that they merge and blend and can become entangled. I see why performers both love and hate feedback at the end of a show. It is hard to know whose conversation with what and whom is being voiced in the feedback. I think musicians like Alex develop a special awareness of this and as long as they don't catch a glimpse of the man fast asleep on the third row they can simultaneously attend and orchestrate in the moment a conversation with their own talent, with the composer, with the audience.

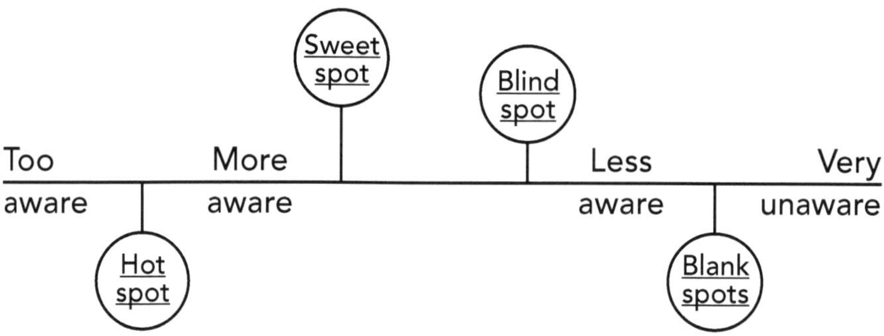

Figure 11.9

Alex like any performer goes through the sweet spots and hot spot and blank spots of performing. As in Figure 11.9 awareness needs working into the performance – shimmering between more or less awareness from moment to moment. Of course, Alex's lips are not moving when she is playing, her hands are doing the talking. How Alex conducts the conversation has lessons for all artists and indeed for all performers, including sports people.

Watching Alex Dariescu play on stage the movement between her hands and the piano seems seamless. Just as the final mix of lines and paints and brush strokes for the painter does. Everything moves so fluently and so fast and yet there are gaps. Alex can speak of these gaps. Each note is like a word in and of itself. It has its own musical story and part in the larger compositional conversation. It is the same for the playwright or novelist. Every word, every punctuation mark is a story in itself. Between each note is a link and a gap. The gaps are important. We mind them even if we don't notice them. To read Alex's story, listen to her play or see her perform go to https://www.alexandradariescu.com/my-story

Pride and Prejudice

One of the most acclaimed romantic novels in the English language is *Pride and Prejudice*. The author Jane Austen is an acute and compassionate, if also satirical, observer of the conversational highs and lows, the conversational riches and poverty of the small, enclosed world her characters are in. There is a lot of talking, and the conversations between Elizabeth Bennett and Mr Darcy shimmer and hover with attraction and antagonism. In a society where propriety was dominant, and the reputation of a woman was so controlled by a sexist discourse, a novel full of conversational awareness and a satirical tone invites the reader in as participant.

Throughout the book, the narrator is inviting the reader to reflect with her on the richness and poverty of the conversational world that swims in and around her characters.

The characters struggle to talk across differences in class, status and gender, but the reader is given a sense that some form of romantic common sense or authenticity can bring them together despite their petty narcissisms and conversational misunderstandings.

The novel ticks all the boxes in the conversational awareness grid. There is something very contemporary in this quote from the book (see also Chapter 12 on the narcissism in ideas) which might well stand as a definition of the distinction between healthy and harmful narcissism.

> *'Vanity and pride are different things, though the words are often used synonymously. A person may be proud without being vain. Pride relates more to our opinion of ourselves, vanity to what we would have others think of us.'*

The novel also invites curiosity through the grid of conversational awareness of what is excluded from discussion or attention for the reader. How did Darcy get his wealth? Was it through the slave trade and if not, why not speak of this? How scheming is Elizabeth Bennett? Does the narrator disguise her from a desperate need to be married and financially secure? Does her contempt for such needs get properly voiced? What sense do we have of the society and politics around them? As an example of the range of conversational awareness through the book here is Elizabeth Bennett naming the full extent of her shimmering and hovering between antagonism and attraction as we the reader are voicing the counter position, no this is not at all what you feel.

> *'From the very beginning – from the first moment, I may almost say – of my acquaintance with you, your manners, impressing me with the fullest belief of your arrogance, your conceit, and your selfish disdain of the feelings of others, were such as to form the groundwork of disapprobation on which succeeding events have built so immovable a dislike; and I had not known you a month before I felt that you were the last man in the world whom I could ever be prevailed on to marry.'*

You the reader might find it a useful exercise to go back to this popular book or film and see if you can make a map of the relationships linking Elizabeth and Mr Darcy and get a better sense of the quality of their awareness of the conversations which they are having.

Samuel Beckett's play Waiting for Godot

Similarly, in one of the world's most popular and acclaimed plays of the 20th century, the two characters are waiting for the proper conversation to begin only when Godot arrives. The two characters are tramps and are meeting in some nondescript intermediate space in transit, but not going anywhere. The play captures it as an absurd place to be waiting. But the situation is given humanity by how they are struggling in and out of making artful or humane conversation together. Their struggle distracts and entertains them and us, but they (and we) are not taken in by it. It is almost in the tradition of Laurel and Hardy (an apparent influence on Beckett) or Charlie Chaplin, but their struggle through conversation confronts us with the creative and complex range of language. The play seems to be asking if conversational language and all our efforts at communication are in the end not much more than slapstick? *Waiting for Godot* is a warning of the peril we face if conversation becomes the last buffer of humanity between us and the absurd. That is if language loses its good authority and its community roots. A dislocated conversation is in danger of becoming unreliable and without ethics. It is the conversational equivalent of whistling in the dark. As in the map, the conversation between the two characters seems to be trapped in a limbo of life with Godot and life without Godot. It is as if the waiting matters as a form of keeping busy inside ourselves and forever seeking another bit of banter to keep time going. The audience have a brilliant role in this play because we are there to make the link and fill the gap by mulling over and ruminating about it ourselves. The play might better be called 'chatting while waiting for the conversation to begin'. In one sequence Estragon says, 'Let's go', and Vladimir replies that they can't, to which Estragon asks, 'Why not?' Vladimir reminds him that why not is because they are waiting for Godot. To which Estragon despairingly replies, 'Ah!'

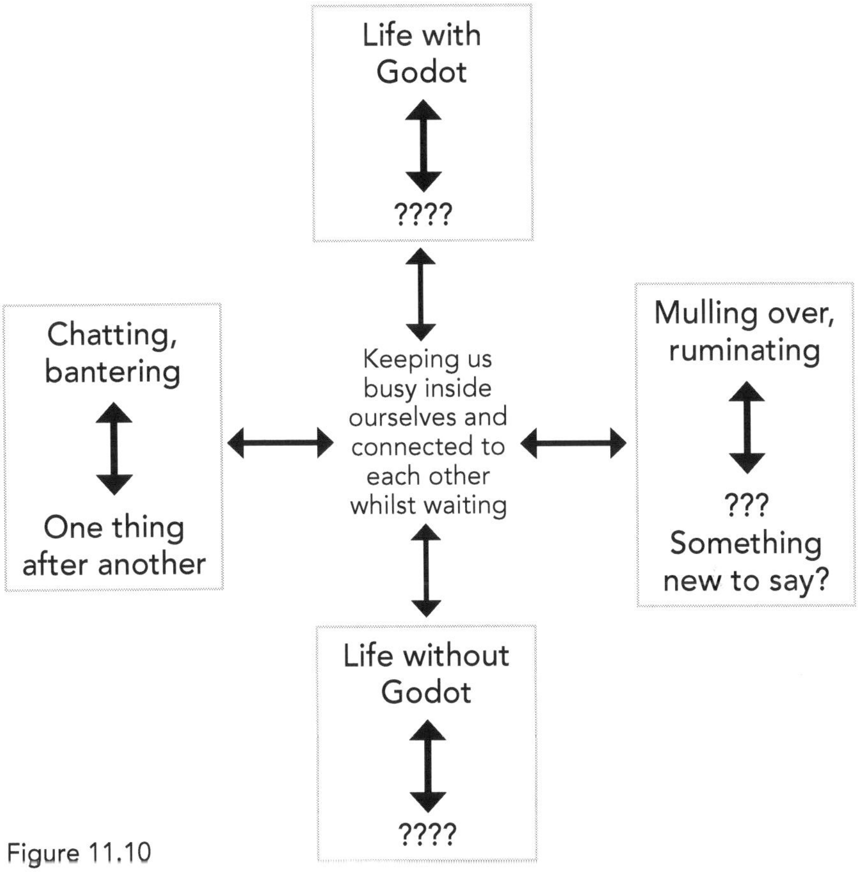

Figure 11.10

The play shows how at one level our efforts at conversation are time fillers, attempts to connect and find meaning. For Vladimir and Estragon there is hope and pleasure in conversational moments of awareness. Estragon in one scene says appreciatively of their recent conversation, 'That wasn't such a bad little canter'. In reply, Vladimir says plaintively, 'Yes, but now we'll have to find something else'.

Conclusion

This chapter has given a sample of the ways in which talking with a map can be applied at home, at work, in our personal and creative lives. It may indicate how a healthy and creative conversational awareness is central to teaching, parenting, managing, loving and creating and performing. We can take our learning from one context to another and find common conversational ethics. Movements and legislation that challenges sexism and racism and other forms of prejudice are seeking this common or universal ethics. How bullying or intimidation or disregard for turn taking gets established is for another book, but as said at the beginning of this book we can judge a society by how it talks. Parents, teachers, managers, artists and activists are the brokers of our conversational powers. It needs all of us to join in.

Chapter 12: Talking politics with a map

There is a final and important question to ask. How does conversational awareness show up in contemporary politics? How do we talk politically? Not just the policies, important as they are, but how do we talk about the polity of politics – the processes by which voices are heard and represented, decisions are made, values upheld, and societies governed? Conversational awareness is like the 'canary in the political coal mine'. To be afraid to negotiate how we give voice individually is to be in trouble collectively. The more freedom we have to orchestrate open discussion the richer our psychology and our society will be, both locally and globally. We have the time and the resources to nurture that freedom, but something holds us back.

The conversational awareness I have in mind is part of the governing and political process, but it has its roots in the voices of every man and woman. It is alarming to read that a large part of populations that can vote, don't, don't see the importance of political literacy and if views are held don't want to discuss them or don't feel safe in discussing them. The past centuries have seen an enormous human struggle and sacrifice of lives in support of freedom of speech, personal liberty, and more openly governed societies. In some parts of the world, we are freer than ever before to speak of our hopes and fears and find our voices and identities. Our culture and arts, our inter group relationships embody this freedom and hopefully our politics also. In other parts of the world there are brave and honest voices searching for and testing this freedom. Sadly, and painfully, there are forces that want to control what we say and restrict how we speak. We are struggling to find room for a conversation about what is honest and fair to say publicly and privately. The promotion of spectacle[70] and melodramatic outlets for mass expression of opinion creates an illusory sense of the will of the people and disorganisation of the spaces for thoughtful and compassionate discourse. Herein lies the conflict from right and left between pro-conversationalists and anti-conversationalists: a conflict which might well be as old as human society itself.

Overall, there is more space and time to talk about what matters. There is more education and astonishing means of distributing knowledge openly and freely, and yet we rarely have the deep talks, the long tutorials, or the conversational apprenticeships we need to share with and learn from each other. Where there is concern to talk politically it is scorned as part of the metropolitan elite or the chattering classes[71].

Politics in part is a battle for the control of the conversation in public, in the media, in our homes and our heads. It is a struggle to control what gets noticed, named and counted as political and what gets bypassed or supressed. It is about who is lauded and who is ignored.

How do we bring dignity, intelligence and limits to this struggle? What do we do about the powerful forces – now resurgent in many nations – seeking to undermine our political conversations and do away with democracy? What kind of conversation is possible with a mass of followers egged on by charismatic leaders who rally them to an extreme cause with lies and deceptions that cannot be sustained without violence and singular control of the machinery of government and the media?

I am not a political scientist nor a historian, but I am a democrat and want a fair and free society. It is one which can have an open conversation about its history and injustices, and which can face the facts of the climate emergency, and gross economic inequality around the world and the continuing force of patriarchy and sexism, colonialism and racism.

There are many powerful accounts of the dangers we face[72] and the hopes we can mobilise.[73] The balance of voices seeking open dialogue are matched by those set on undermining and destroying a culture of conversation in society. My point just now is not to argue for one view or another. I want to conclude this book by offering a map of one the most troublesome aspects of conversational ethics in contemporary politics. It is the psychology of a divisive and binary politics that leaves us so impoverished in our discussions and fixed and stuck in our ideas. It takes us out of dialogue with each other. How can we formulate why so many people are distrusting of political engagement, disenchanted with politicians and apathetic about the collective issues that threaten our global survival? Why does individual opinion take precedence over collective thought as if our vox pop choices of views are no different to choices of brands of cereal? It is as if the thoughtful processes and dignified exchange of ideas at the heart of democracy have been eviscerated. These are big questions that may either seem easy to answer or politically naïve to the reader, but I want to look at contemporary politics through the tools and methods of talking with a map and with conversational awareness in mind.

To make a small step in that direction I take the idea of narcissism and turn the spotlight off the politicians directly and wonder about the relationship between political ideas and people who rally to them and surrender their identities to them. My focus turns away from the palpable narcissism of some politicians and looks at the narcissism invested in the ideas which they promote and which we follow. It is a less confronting and a more relational and ultimately conversational approach. Instead of going head-to-head with leaders – which to some extent suits them and turns the exchange of ideas into a slanging match – the focus is on the psycho-social dynamics of the ideas and ideologies of supporters. Of specific concern is how a mass of people become so enthralled by an idea they not only lose themselves to the idea but lose their critical faculties and democratic capacity for open dialogue and truth testing. I will suggest that in defending the inflated position of a narcissistic idea there is a malicious phenomenon of disorganising our attachment to, and trust in, the political structures of society. It is not me versus you in the debating chamber but my identity versus the polity of the state. It creates an anti-conversational politics and a bewildering sense of anarchy which can only benefit the most extreme and dictatorial forces which may be its point.

The following pages define and then map out the 'anti-conversational' narcissism invested in an idea (Figure 12.1) and apply it to the political example of Brexit in the UK and similar patterns relating to Trump's campaign to be elected as president in the USA in 2016. These are just two examples of many that could be cited from around the world. The chapter concludes with another map (Figure 12.2) that tracks, in a positive and optimistic way, the qualities of discussion involved in a democratic relationship with political ideas. To get there we may, among other things, need to Map and Talk our way into more open and conversationally aware approach. We need to consider that movements such as Black Lives Matter and Me Too and the climate emergency awareness campaigns are not just addressing issues of racism and sexism and threats to the planet. They are not just seeking to change the conversation but are offering an opportunity to stop and think about how we talk to each other about our collective lives.

Throughout, narcissism is understood as a pattern of relating that operates within and between us individually, interpersonally and culturally. Exploring the narcissism of ideas in politics may help us see similar patterns in work and community organisations and in our social identities and cultural ties.

First, I am going back to the myth of Narcissus and Echo which gives us an instructive template for the micro-moments of narcissism in contemporary politics.

Narcissus and Echo

Wandering in the forest a young woman called Echo longs for a relationship with Narcissus, a handsome huntsman. He dismisses and ignores her and as punishment the Gods make him fall in love with nothing more than an idea of himself: an image of his own beauty in a still pool of water before him in the shade of the trees. He is innocently transfixed by love for this image and calls to it 'I love you.' He has no time or thought for anything else. Echo then mistakes his calling out to his image in the pool as a call to her and calls back in 'echo'. She pines away until only her echo of his love (of an idea) remains. Echo becomes an echo. Narcissus is completely hijacked by his idea and is incapable of dialogue or awareness outside of it. They both wither away for love of, or addiction to, an idea which is called for but points nowhere but to itself.

Imagine if Echo and Narcissus could step out of the confines of the myth and be in dialogue. Narcissus might acknowledge to Echo 'We were both losers in the end, me directly to the idea and you indirectly because of my neglect of you'. And Echo would reply, 'How humiliating is that? You chose a virtual relationship with an idea rather than a real conversation and relationship with me'. But Narcissus replies 'It felt perfectly real at the time. It was wonderful and complete. I never felt so intensely aware. I had no sense that there was nothing to it. I would have died without realising it was making me hollow inside'. Echo then echoes the words 'hollow inside' and wonders what it was about her position as a woman in search of love's dream that led her to be lost to an idea, just like Narcissus. Echo wondered about the difference between them and said, 'You know what, the Gods didn't bother to save me from the closed system they had set up to punish you.'

What if, as they talked, they discovered a truth that this Echo and Narcissus-like loss of self to a seductive and all-consuming idea, can only be countered by a capacity to talk about what is happening. Not just ordinary conversation but talking to each other with conversational awareness and all their faculties intact and all directions and qualities of talk in mind between them. The loss of themselves to an idea is the loss of conversational awareness. It is an abuse of conversational ethics. 'Look at us' they chorused. 'Out of dialogue with ourselves, with each other, with love and desire, with ideas and feelings and with words and conversation itself'.

Something similar happens in politics wherein we end up in the neat but deadly alliance of an Echo or a Narcissus trapped by our attachment to the image and sound of an idea.

Mapping the narcissistic use of an idea in politics

The following is a template for how an idea gets so over invested that first we lose our everyday political conversations to it and then we lose ourselves to it. Like Narcissus and Echo, we may be left with an identification with an image or an idea, but it is an empty connection. The places around the map are numbered to make it easier to navigate and discuss.

Starting in box 1, the world is complex and confusing, and we want it to make sense. Such a position is real and normal. We ask questions and share doubts with good will and an expectation of a democracy of ideas. But from box 2 someone with the power and pull to draw us in offers a neat, big and appealing idea that promises rescue by making sense of everything for once and for all. We join up – of course we do because it is the media and it has simplicity going for it. We become followers because it gives us something to attach to, some security and familiarity and above all it gives us that core childhood need for narrative coherence. It becomes a call to surrender ourselves to this way of thinking but also at the same time a call to join the 'supporters' club. It may be presented in a seductive, binary or prejudiced way. It may offer magic and ideal care and a freedom from having to think but in the process it offers an identity and a club to join.

Once we are at box 2 on the map the big appealing idea may meet a deep need for narrative coherence and a story which offers to sort things out for us as detailed in the map of open and closed stories on page 75.

Conversations like this happen all the time as we give ourselves to an idea – a football team, a faith, a view of the world that enhances us, a holiday destination. These temporary, weekend or part time attachment solutions, give us a hold on the world but don't take all of us. We can mock ourselves, stand back and cope with the hangover of disappointment when our team doesn't win or the holiday ends. Regardless of the content of the ideology involved, whether this is a healthy narcissistic attachment and identity solution or a harmful one, depends on how much we lose ourselves to it and in the process lose our ability to talk or think independently of the idea we are invested in and now attached to.

In the sequence of the map, our loss of self to the idea is at box 3. This is where our personal trouble and the bigger trouble for democracy and politics begins. You can ask yourself to what extent at some point in your life have you lost yourself to an idea to such an extent that the idea becomes defining and controlling of you? In mapping out a person's or a group's discussion of their investment in, and loyalty to, a specific way of thinking (as defined by point 3), can be judged by the question 'How much and for how long, and at what cost, do we become like Echo and Narcissus lost to and defined by the idea with nothing to say and no voice?' What can save us is a capacity to return to some form of conversational awareness and dialogue with our larger and wider view of self and others.

When we submit to an idea and gain identity and belonging it becomes our personal ideology. The price is twofold: it becomes a defining idea and other ideas are subordinated to it and the entire process of thinking and talking is narrowed by it taking us further into box 3. At the same time competing ideas, or groups who are rival idea makers, are attacked and dismissed as a threat (box 4). Or they are co-opted. Challenging questions, difficult conversations and the opposing ideas are satirising in a cruel and

The loss of self and dialogue to big appealing idea

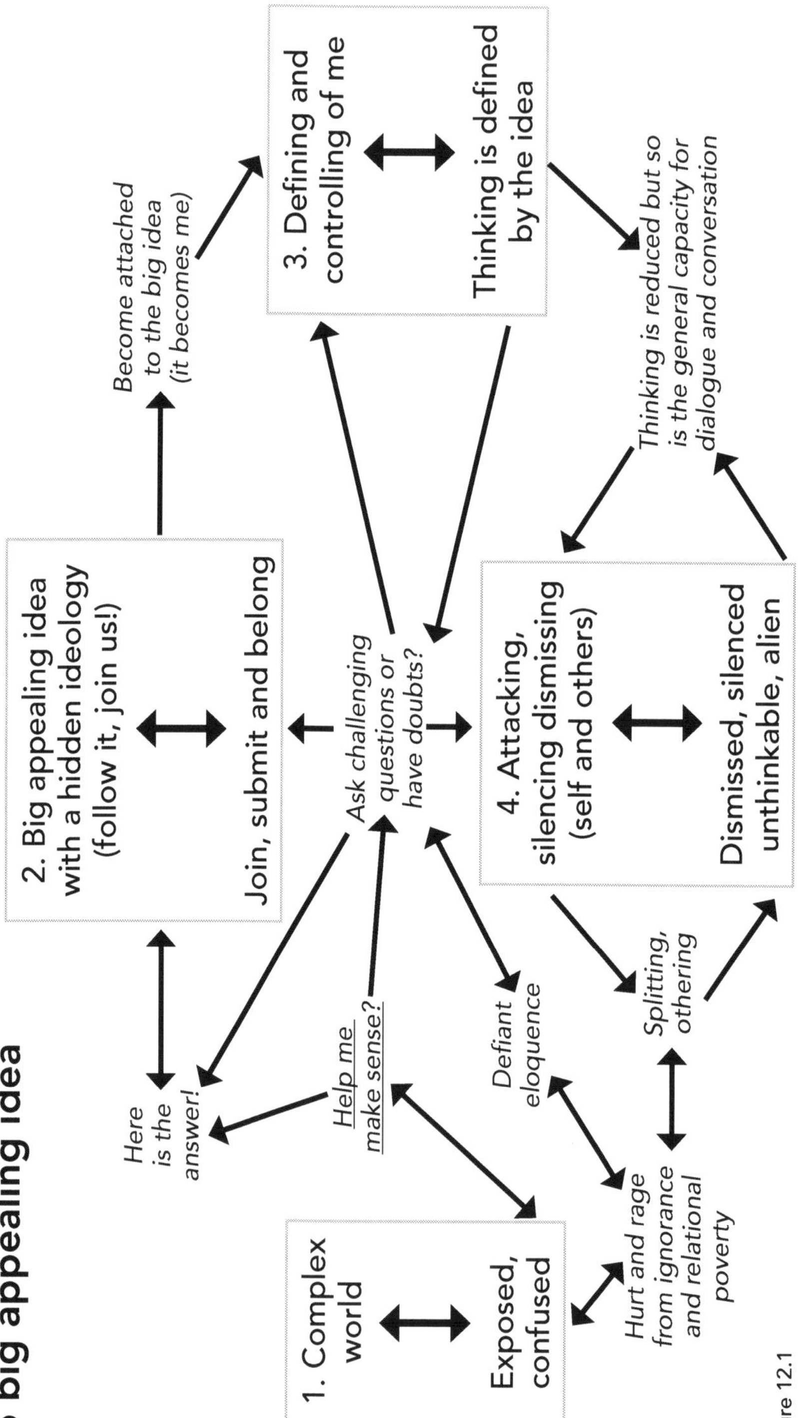

Figure 12.1

melodramatic style. This further locks in and narrows our thinking but also hurts us as we become aware of a stark reality: belong to the overvalued idea and feel included or be part of the devalued ideas and be excluded. The latter hurts the individual and the wider social and political culture. This is the dynamic that feeds binary thinking that features in racism and sexism and supports systems of patriarchy, colonialism and class divisions. Of course, there are economic and other forces involved but our world view and our internal identities become binary and divisive. We live with conflicting solutions to divided parts of ourselves.

This narcissistic surrender (as individuals or communities) to the force of the idea is compounded by an external loss of connection with the wider world of ideas and dialogue. In a process of selective attention and selective inattention, we cannot think freely outside the identity and social membership box in which the idea puts us. The process of association (these ideas are me/us) is tightly bound up with an equally powerful process of dissociation (those ideas are not me/us).[74] Those who attempt to think the unthinkable (dissociated ideas) are ridiculed or seen as stupid and alien (box 4). All ideas are tarred by the narcissistic brush and either overvalued or devalued. We become narcissistically defined by the ideas either in grandiose and entitled ways or martyred and antagonistic or vicarious ways. The public and private result is a greatly diminished capacity for debate and dialogue. Thinking is reduced but so is the general capacity for conversational awareness.

There is no difference between the collective macro-narcissism in the idea and the private micro-narcissism in the identity. This makes it a small step for the mass of people invested narcissistically in the idea to be easily encouraged to righteous, mob like behaviour. But most importantly, and in the context of mass media and social media, the whole fabric of political assembly, of debate and considerate political discourse can be cast as unreliable, disorganised and chaotic in nature.

This toxic splitting of identities and affiliations is fertile soil for those politicians who have an interest in binary politics and setting one group against another. Personalities and groups that are suited to such a climate tend to dominate. They thrive on going head-to-head. The more populist and crude elements of democracy (referenda, rallies, tweeting and campaign meetings) are overvalued and win out over the more nuanced, and challenging elements (parliaments, coalitions, committees and debate) which in turn are devalued. Events like a referendum (yes or no, in or out, for us or against us) feed and echo more polarised identity politics. They encourage an extreme narcissism of ideas in ways that narrow and limit our democratic resources and take us out of dialogue with ourselves and society. There is a 'twitter tunnel' effect as people who follow ideas by sound bites become more narrow, cynical or polarised and only follow their own trails. People become as thoughtful as the slogans on their T-shirts and lose themselves to a deadly politics of pantomime villains. A more personal pattern of voting according to the narcissism in the idea replaces citizenship and voting on balance of considerations.

Revisiting the conversational awareness grid with the narcissism of ideas in mind

It may be of interest to look at the impact of the narcissism of ideas map on the different elements of the conversational awareness grid considered in detail in Chapter 6. For each element the likely impact is indicated by an = sign. This is only a general guide and for any specific political conversation it needs colouring in for its unique context of time and place where it will evoke its own words, maps and conversations. The overall point is to open up spaces for, and steps towards, a more enlightened and democratic exploration of political ideas and processes. The reader could use the grid and the mapping template to assess the quality of a political or organisational conversation with which they are involved or familiar.

Just to go briefly down the four columns of the grid. The first column headed 'between us' might mean that ideas are fixed or fixated, feelings are merged within the group and no ambivalence or uncertainty is allowed or voiced. Roles in support of the ideas are superficial and authority is driven by a paranoia that the inflated bubble of ideas are under attack and need protection by making them sacred on the one hand and defining all opposing ideas as alien on the other hand. Going down the second column headed 'within me' might mean that thoughts are reduced to opinions and the emotions that go with them are heated and a genuine capacity for creativity is distorted and conscience is weak or absent. Down the third column headed 'around us' then theories are presented as ideology, the drama of emotions is pumped up, melodramatic and confrontational. Polity of politics and any pragmatic policies are bypassed and keeping power dictates public discourse and media. Finally, the fourth column instead of some transcendent or universal perspective myths cease to be a store of varied wisdom and are used divisively. In row two, the ineffable presence of being human together is idealised in heroic and epic terms and in row three congregation is a time for rallies and our core qualities of humanity end up feeling used.

For comparison, the opposite of a narcissistic inflation of ideas is mapped as below and the grid could be filled in with conversations along its lines.

A conversational awareness grid pointing to some of the qualities (poetic or otherwise) that can arise with map and talk		Four directions of talk			
		Between us	Within me	Around us	Beyond us
Four lines of talk	**Hovering** Links and gaps, in or out, pro and con, picture and detail	*Ideas = fixed*	*Thoughts = opinions*	*Theories = ideology*	*Myths = divisive*
	Shimmering Hot and cold, here and there, open or closed, sweet or sour	*Feelings = merged*	*Emotions = heated*	*Drama = melodrama*	*Presence = idealised*
	Participating Doing and being, making and sharing, now and then, with or for	*Roles = surface*	*Creativity = distorted*	*Politics= dictated*	*Congregate = rallies*
	Authoring Owning and disowning, acting and answering, for and against, self and others	*Authority = paranoid*	*Conscience = absent*	*Values = expedient*	*Humanity = used*

In dialogue with ideas

The opposite of losing self to the narcissism of ideas is a conversational awareness with our thoughts, feelings and ideas. It is that sense of being in society and among groups where all four conversations whether within ourselves, between us or around and beyond us have their metaphorical windows open and words can circulate. What would a conversational map of this look like? In Figure 12.2 the patterns of relating to ideas, loving them, investing in them in an open dialogue is mapped out using the same underlying template as Figure 12.1. We still want to make sense, ask challenging questions, and share our doubts in the face of a complex and confusing world. The response though, in leading to box 2 on the map, is to say, 'let us negotiate how we talk as much what we talk about'. Box 2 builds upon respectful, mutual, negotiation and shared curiosity. It leads to an openness of feelings and thinking wherein ideas resonate and connect and understanding grows. The interpersonal and group spaces for asking challenging questions and sharing vulnerability and doubts is valued and validated and the political conversation becomes open-minded showing that we can talk and think together despite our differences. Parliaments, debating chambers and committee structures have good authority and are protected against invasion. Differences of views are tolerated between us and recognised within ourselves. There is compassion not contempt for conflicting ideas and a process of loving ideas can be mixed with enthusiasm and scepticism.

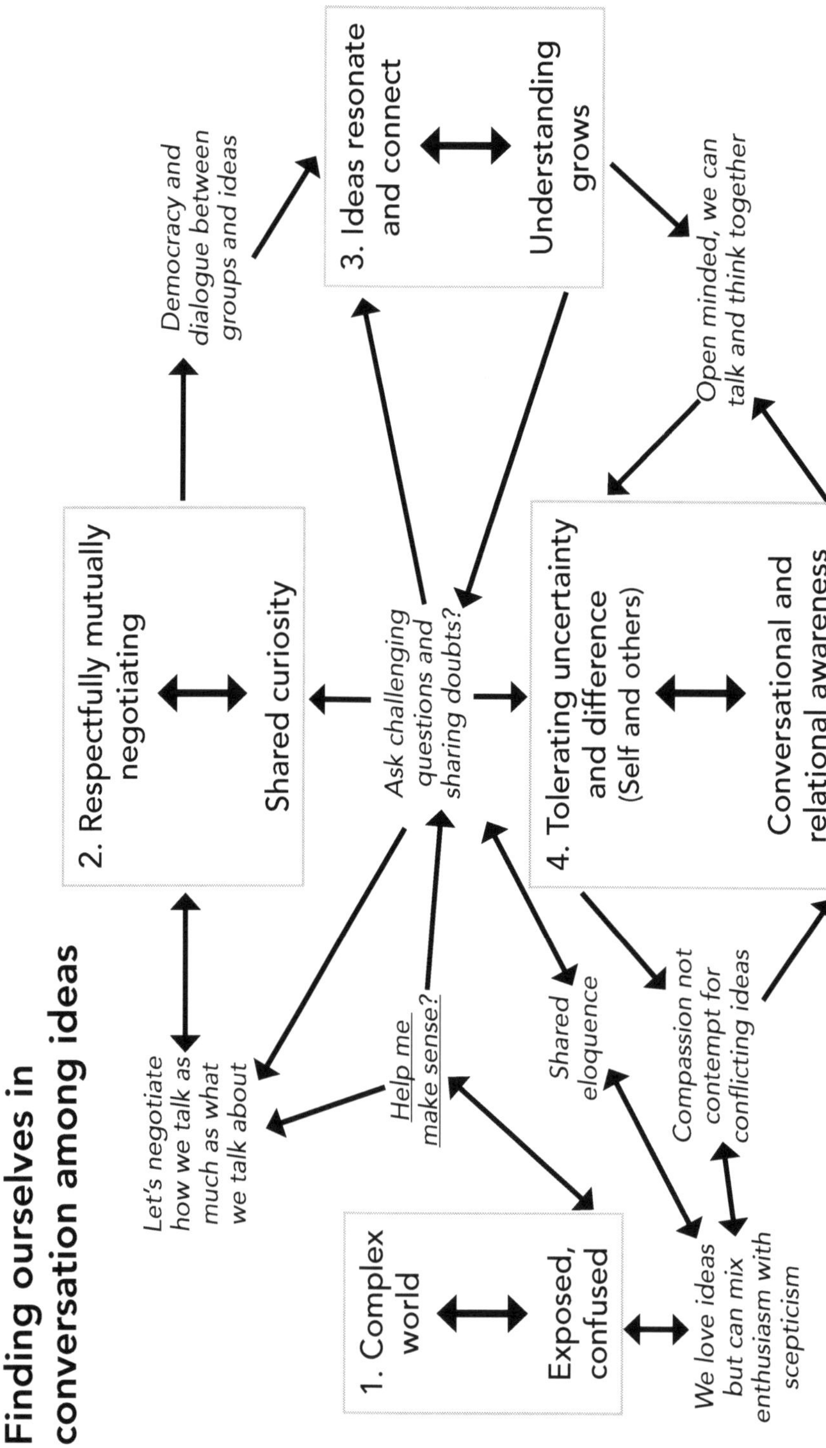
Finding ourselves in conversation among ideas
1. Complex world
Exposed, confused
We love ideas but can mix enthusiasm with scepticism
Let's negotiate how we talk as much as what we talk about
Help me make sense?
2. Respectfully mutually negotiating
Shared curiosity
Ask challenging questions and sharing doubts?
Democracy and dialogue between groups and ideas
3. Ideas resonate and connect
Understanding grows
Open minded, we can talk and think together
Shared eloquence
Compassion not contempt for conflicting ideas
4. Tolerating uncertainty and difference (Self and others)
Conversational and relational awareness

Figure 12.2

We are more likely to work side-by-side with competing ideas and not go head-to-head with the person who holds ideas divergent from ours. We still hover and shimmer between using ideas to share understanding and to affirm belonging. We still wobble between 'honest and transparent' thinking and 'group think.' But there is a conversational ethics in our everyday lives and thinking. The more open and aware our conversation the less the deathly folly of Echo and Narcissus can take root, either in petty or grandiose ways in our attachment to ideas. Of course, there are still conflicting ideas and still we are capable of inflating them with dreamlike qualities, but we don't solve the inner tension by attacking the person or group who is/are invested in opposing ideas. We reflect and take time to consider things. The increase in shared understanding and eloquence feeds conversational and relational awareness and this serves as a bulwark against narcissistic and fascistic threats to democracy. We value how we share our ideas as much as what they are about. We can put heart and soul into ideas but only if we can equally stand back from them and negotiate their worth. In summary, compassion and reflection replace contempt and ignorance.

Identity politics and identity awareness

What happens in informal, micro moments of dialogue can be scaled up to the macro politics of the day. At the heart of a narcissism in ideas and its threat to conversational awareness is the way we can over-identify with a world view and group outlook to the point it becomes group think.[75] Our narcissistic solution of losing ourselves to one ideologically driven identity is in the top right of the grid below (12.3). It is a fixed idea or identity solution that is very tightly held. From this corner of the grid there is no room for negotiation without moving across to the top left corner where sense of self can move its allegiances and be answerable to the challenges from others. 'I still care about my heritage and my life choices, but I can stand outside them as well as inside them.' In the top left there is a sense of self that can stand in among positions and identities. I can stand in between and apart from them as well as committing to one of them at certain points in time and place with certain groups of people and not lose myself to them unless temporarily for good cause (like in the final nervous hours of an election campaign when my party has a slim lead). The bottom right corner of the grid is ideas, roles and identities which I have been threatened with, or once had, or I saw powerful people in my life embody, and they are, 'definitely, fearfully and defiantly' not me. They might be seen as repressed or dissociated. They may have a subterranean part in our lives, or they may be part of the culture of our locality and threaten to colonise or hijack us.

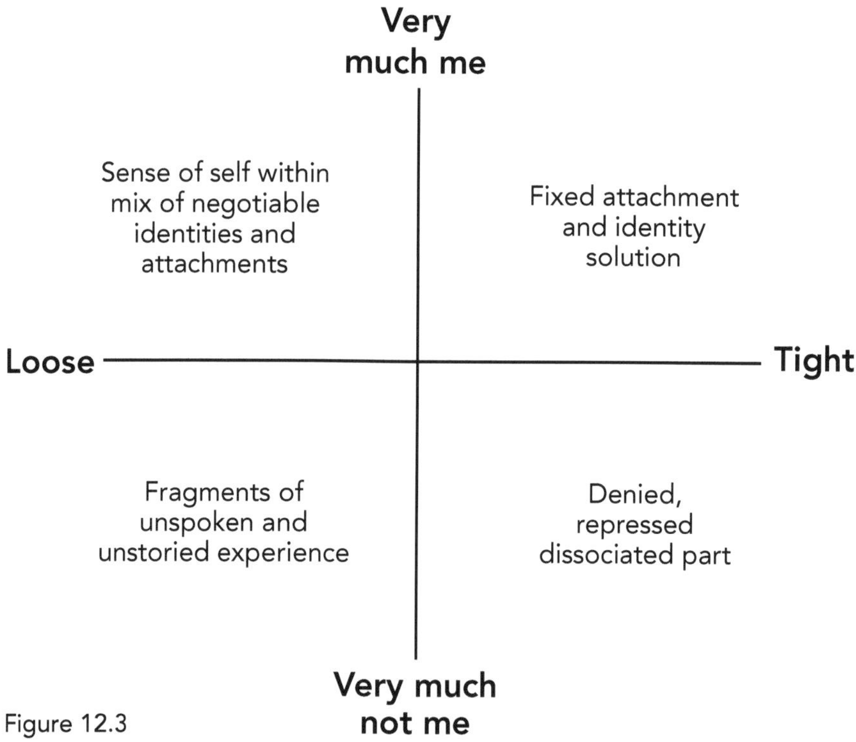

Figure 12.3

One way of understanding the narcissism in ideas is the appeal of over identifying with a branded, external ideology and identity around which we can congregate on mass (really or virtually) as a fixed defence against directly feeling the tightly buried parts that are bad and not me. Finally, in thinking about the bottom left corner of the grid there are, in all communities around the world, fragments of unstoried and unspoken experiences that drive our yearnings for a healing story or some force to bring clarity and make sense of things or bury fragments of feeling deeply away. Even a healthy democratic and conversationally aware process will push us around these quadrants. Hopefully we default to the top left-hand corner out of respect for the process of debate, regardless of our differences. What is alarming is the push to the extremes of fixed and tightly held views and identities leading to disorganisation and fragmentation of opposing views in the bottom left corner and the denial of any parts of our inner selves and life stories that does not fit with the tight and idealised narrative in the top right corner. Such divisive forces are elements in the social psychology that gives voice to the politics of fascism and dictatorship.

Epic, conversational or chaotic political discourse

Drawing upon the work of Mikael Bakhtin, the narcissistic investment in political ideas can be further explored in terms of three styles of conversational engagement. The three are listed as follows.

- Epic and heroic.
- Conversational and novelistic.
- Chaotic and disorganising.

Points 1 and 2 in Figure 12.2 come from Bakhtin and his distinction between epic (Superman) styles and novelistic (Dostoevsky) styles of literature. I have borrowed and applied his rich thinking, written in obscurity during the dark time of Stalinism in Soviet Russia and added the third style of speech which, in the context of different media and different global politics, seems to be key to the other two in our times. I have called this third column 'chaotic and disorganising' though it is not in the defiant spirit of riot and mayhem, but the deliberate stirring of chaos, disorganised attachment, uncertainty and mistrust in our social relations. Each of the three is considered in more detail. They are briefly described and their key points are tabled for easy comparison. Then the interaction between the three is highlighted.

The qualities listed as 'epic' are all linked to a narcissistic overvaluation and over identification with one set of closed ideas. The middle column of novelistic qualities are the product of open dialogue and rely on conversational awareness. They are seen as threat from the viewpoint of epic systems of political and cultural conversation. In response to the threat the third column of chaotic experience of conversation is deliberately promoted to undermine the conversational qualities of the novelistic column. Any political conversation will weave in and out between epic, novelistic and chaotic as any observer of British parliament at Question Time can testify. What matters is where we find the best of ourselves and how the institutions and arrangements of politics and society, especially the mass media and social media, can support and protect the qualities listed in the novelistic column. In summary the continuous threat to democracy and free speech is a mixture of the overblown, and hence fragile nature of the elements in column 1 leading to the actions in column 3 and undermining the validity and power of the qualities in column 2.

Epic and heroic

These are the kinds of narrative that are closed, the story is storied and finalised before they are shared. They are spoken of in authoritative and declamatory ways and are anti- conversational or resist dialogue by being grandiose or contemptuous. The stories are one dimensional and people are reduced to fixed roles and ideas. Time is linear with this happening and then that following. For example, the slogan linked to taking back control in the ideology of Brexit was 'Get Brexit Done' implying that once done the country would be forever in a new time. For Bakhtin, epic as a genre was represented by the classic Greek adventure stories as exemplified by Homer's Iliad and Odyssey. These are epic stories that define and unite a people. The epic narrative is simplified, heroic, out of time and non-negotiable. The form of congregation is a single-minded and devotional form of a mass movement in a binary world.

Epic styles of talking and story telling would rather turn to chaos than become novelistic		
Epic	**Novelistic**	**Chaotic**
■ Closed and finished ■ Certain, authoritative and given ■ Storied ■ One dimensional ■ Fixed roles and ideas ■ Then, and then ■ Declamatory ■ Resisting dialogue	■ Open and unfinished ■ Uncertain, to be discovered ■ Storying, inviting awareness ■ Multi-dimensional ■ Contextual and creative ■ Here and there ■ Conversational ■ Inviting dialogue	■ Teasing and deceiving ■ Borderline ■ Unreliable ■ Fragmenting ■ Disorganising ■ Everywhere is nowhere ■ Melodramatic ■ Faking dialogue

Conversational and novelistic

In contrast for Bakhitn was the novelistic genre. Like a good novel there is a sense of immersion in several threads, lines and directions of story and conversation. The outcome and the meaning are open for debate and discovery. Hovering and shimmering and the openness to find ways to participate, own and author our lives is novelistic. An open and pragmatic society is novelistic. Science is novelistic, and art can be. Uncertainty is tolerated and story telling is conversational, drawing on experience. The novelistic approach moves here and there in time and place and is always open and unfinished.

Chaotic, confusing and disorganising

One of the more challenging anarchist slogans of the Paris uprising, very representative of the 1960s, was 'Order is to be feared more than chaos'. The slogan worked because it pointed to two extremes. Too much order and there is no room for vitality and spontaneity or difference. Too much chaos or mess and there is too much anxiety for thoughts and feelings to be processed either internally or interpersonally. The anarchist end of the order and chaos equation seems to have been taken up by Machiavellian figures behind some of the leading political dictators around the world (or would be dictators). There are plenty of forces around who seek to provoke disorder and chaos so as to draw people to the other extreme and the protective hold of what then turns out to be an authoritarian extreme of order. It is relevant in the 21st century context to draw on the attachment thinking of Bowlby when studying infant development. One type of childhood attachment solution is described as disorganised attachment.[76] There is a teasing element to contemporary society with its mix of 'come-ons' and put downs, inclusion and exclusion that generates a painfully disorganised sense of self which we carry individually as our own burden. The politics of heroic or chaotic exploit this private sense of disorganised attachment which is then offered salvation by the addictive neat ideology.

Two political examples

There are multiple examples of the narcissistic investment in political ideas and the distorting effect on the political conversation. Two are highlighted here for the way they separate the narcissism in the politician from the narcissism in the idea. The first is a snapshot in the long saga of Brexit in the UK and the second is the rise to power of Donald Trump and the movement behind him. Both typify a closed anti-conversational triangle between people, ideas and politicians. The issue is not just the moral standing of the politician and the threat posed to democracy but the divisive nature of recruiting followers. From the perspective of a narcissism in ideas and conversational awareness the hope is to illuminate ways of restoring open dialogue within and between groups.

Brexit means Brexit

The narcissism in and of the idea of Brexit is that the political processes that sustain and govern a country can be reduced to a few slogans. Undoubtedly there are many valid arguments in terms of governance and economics for being in some form of federation of nations or not, but these weren't the material of a thoughtful and measured political debate. Brexit was promoted as the idea that brings with it all manner of benefits: national sovereignty, lower immigration, money back for the health services but the narcissism is invested in the idea of 'taking back control'. We, like Echo to Narcissus, hear the words 'take back control' and whisper in echo to ourselves 'With Brexit I will take back control of my life, of my identity, of me'. The slogan 'take back control' is a crude and distorted simplification of the complexities of governance and economics involved in international and domestic policy. The texture of what we will 'take back control of' is so idealised, it takes on dream-like quality and while being empty it can be the projective space for all kinds of needs. Its social, economic and political hollowness is precisely its psychological purpose. We fill the slogans with our own stories until we are stuffed so full of bite sized opinion, we are no longer able to think. This binary thinking is bad for the brain. It may be that the poet T.S. Eliot had the measure of it in his poem the Hollow Men when he speaks of headpieces 'filled with straw' and dried voices, 'when we whisper together are quiet and meaningless'[77].

Each politician responded to the narcissism of the idea of Brexit in a different way but the power of the idea was further inflated by the noise of their diverse support. All political policies are more complex than can be conveyed in a campaign, so they need simplifying. Ideas which have no specific policy are the easiest to simplify since there was nothing complex behind them in the first place. At a pre referendum evening rally and debate widely seen on TV in the UK, Boris Johnson stole the finale of the show with a rousing and Shakespearean 'Cry Harry for England' with his arms pumping the air with the call to take back control as if the people of the British Isles were back in the dark days of World War II.

The up and down, yoyo dynamic of a narcissism of ideas shows up in the sequence for Nigel Farage (BBC, 2016) of carrying a narcissistic wound from his early years promoting a British exit from the European Community and being met in the European parliament by laughter (as he recalls it). On attending the European parliament after his referendum triumph with the Brexit idea he was strident and contemptuous of his parliamentary colleagues, saying, 'You are not laughing now'. Shortly after he resigned as leader of UKIP saying, as if he was Narcissus waking from his loss of self to the idea of Brexit 'I want my life back'.[78] A politician risks losing themselves to an idea and thereby losing the capacity to be in dialogue with it. He may well get his life back but the people he egged on to invest narcissistically in his Brexit idea are left with their lives caught up in it for better or worse.

Boris Johnson (British Prime Minister at the time of writing) occupied a different position. He was suspected of aggrandising himself through betting his personal political fortunes on the Brexit idea. As if by pumping up the idea with Churchillian gestures he can pump up his own reputation.

Extremists can prevail from all sides in a climate saturated by a collective narcissism of ideas. The increase in hate crimes and the tragic murders of MP Jo Cox in 2016 and MP David Amess in 2021 show how extreme forms of narcissistic investment in ideas can lead people to lose themselves to an idea in ways that are a danger to others. The direct appeal to people, the provocative use of language to play on nationalism and racism; being contemptuous and loose with the truth; all undermine the political ethics of conversational awareness as detailed in the awareness grid earlier in this chapter.

Slogans about how ('take back control', 'make great again', 'will of the people') are mixed with slogans about what ('control immigration', 'have money back for the health service'). A good test of politics would be the extent to which the 'how' gets equal air and chamber time as the 'what' of debate and discussion.

Behind Brexit was another idea of the will of the people that has a democratic ring to it but does not pass any conversational awareness 'test'. Claiming she was acting out of a duty to the 'will of the people' was a key slogan for Theresa May as prime minister (2016-19) and one assumed by Boris Johnson once he was prime minister, more vehemently in the slogan 'Get Brexit Done'. In a blog post from the LSE in April 2019 titled 'Is Brexit the will of the people? the answer is shown to be not quite that simple'[79] Professor Christian List questions the assumption of Theresa May that 'the will of the people' is to be defined as 'the will of the majority'. He examines how the relatively slim majority in favour of leaving (in a referendum which was 'officially only advisory' can be taken as the binding will of the people. Professor List writes of several complicating factors.

> 'First of all, the majority was narrow. There were 17.4 million votes for Leave, 16.1 million votes for Remain, and 12.9 million abstentions. A further 18 million people living in the UK were not on the electoral register, including all young people below the age of 18 and many long-term residents who are not citizens, though they contribute to British society and have a stake in it. So, although 17.4 million is a large number, it is only a relative majority, not an absolute one.'

List goes on to write that another major complicating factor lies in what was meant by politicians and understood by voters as to the meaning of leaving Europe. In an understatement he notes:

> 'As we now know, there are several different versions of Brexit, and it is not clear which one voters had in mind. This problem was exacerbated by the fact that the pre-referendum campaigns were arguably not as deliberative, honest, and respectful as one might have hoped.'

He concludes that such important decisions about the future of a nation needs careful deliberation and full information. In the context of talking with a map it might be argued that what was missing was an ethics of conversational awareness and space on the political landscape for talking about all elements of the political process.

Without solid ground and if exposed to reasonable debate the various ways of leaving 'Europe' had to be reduced to narcissistically inflated slogans and the continuing political process had to be disorganised. The contrasting qualities of more or less presence of narcissism and 'showmanship' of Theresa May and Boris Johnson as political personalities is relevant. They both needed to promote the hollowed-out slogans of Brexit and put the narcissism into the ideas of the people, the nation and its heritage. In this context the politician takes something of the egging-on position or midwife to the political baby rather than its direct parent. It is voiced in the third person telling us about our relationship with a nation and its proposed destiny. It is very different to the I-thou address as most famously in the 'I have a dream speech' of Martin Luther King.[80] The comparable example of former president Trump in his campaign for election is instructive in this respect, as explored next.

People say means people say

A different relationship to the narcissism in and of ideas is a feature of Donald Trump's 2016 election campaign where inflated ideas are chanted back and forth between him and his followers: 'Crooked Hilary' 'Make them Pay' (Mexican people for a border wall), 'Make America Great Again' (New York Times, 2016). The audience are intoxicated by the ideas and bond with each other and Trump through them. Trump's skill is to be enchanted by the ideas he throws out but not the author of them. He talks of 'we' as if he is part of the crowd following a movement of ideas that is greater and truer than he and they can know. He is the mischief maker, egging on our inner Echo and Narcissus to be carried away by an image. The flag waver becomes the flag.

A striking example is his promotion of the idea that US President, Barack Obama was not born in America. With his arms outstretched and hands open as if confessing a truth which is not of his own making Trump declares it this way: 'People say, people say, Obama was not born in America. People say this. I don't know, but people say this'. What this leaves, is a sneaky truth claim built around the idea that 'people say' and that what people say is important. The politician who eggs people on plays as if follower to the voice of the people while taking the lead as their spokesperson and personification. Trump draws his own narcissistic fuel from the idea but at the same denies responsibility for it. The narcissistically inflated idea calls the tune and defines the relationship with his supporters who also draw strength by his apparent solidarity with them. There are many subsequent examples in his political reign and comparable examples from other politicians whether narcissists on a global scale or parish narcissists on a local stage.

Like Narcissus's love for his idea of himself these political ideas are hollow inside. Nothing can be asked of them because once inflated nothing is there to discover except a large and fragile bubble of an idea. The phrase 'people say' is the banal conduit for our prejudices and projections. People say can mean anything. People say means people say. Who can disagree with it?[81]

Conclusions

This chapter has invited the reader on the one hand to think differently about political talk and on the other to think differently about our relationship with ideas. Political history gives us plentiful accounts of the collective, narcissistic inflation of an idea that draws a mob or a dictatorship in its support. Equally there are plentiful examples where the narcissism in an idea becomes institutionalised and part of a national tradition covered by layers of ceremonial paint and theatrical pomp. 'God save the King', 'Rule Britannia', 'A nation once again.' We may also turn good politicians into narcissists, simply by the way we and the media wed them to their ideas indefinitely. Identity politics and confrontational movements are the drivers of this narcissism in ideas. 'By this belief we will be defined and live or die'. It is the opposite of a conversational and pragmatic politics. In the context of this book, it is at odds with the versatility and openness of which we are capable when we talk.

We need to talk to bring our thoughts and our powers of thinking back out of the conversational silos of personal ideologies. An ideology is a fixed set of views that is wired together and needs to be inflated to keep out of the rough and tumble of honest conversation. Ideologies are kept in the air by slogans, manifestos and pundits and the more they are inflated, the more all ideas – not just opposing ones – have to be either co-opted, deflated or slurred. This makes bad politics, bad government and is bad for our mental health, but even worse is when the ideology becomes personal and my whole capacity to share my thinking is hijacked. I talk at you and I talk at myself in binary ways.

It may seem odd to end here in a book about conversational awareness. However, if the conversation at the level of the politics is disorganised and undermined the loss of trust extends all the way through society to the classroom, the business meeting, the bar, the church, the therapy room and the extended family dinner.

Conclusion to the book

I am very grateful and appreciative if you have delved into this book or got to grips with parts of it and found something useful. *Talking with a Map* is to be judged by its capacity to help us share our personal and collective stories in conversational ways that enable us talk across our differences more openly and compassionately. Hopefully, in the process our conversational awareness is engaged and improved, and we talk better with each other.

Talking can be a beautiful and precious activity. Conversation is our uniquely human superpower. It can be jarring, clumsy, fluent and eloquent. It can be fun and serious and at times painful and difficult to find the words. In every way it is essential. Talking comes easily to us on the one hand and yet is difficult and complex at the same time. We shimmer between trusting and doubting each other and ourselves to be honest and open. I have tried to capture this by the idea of the conversational awareness grid and the interplay of different qualities of talking and relating as we carry our conversations in four directions of address at once. It is the orchestration or disorganisation of these four directions that is the focus of *Talking with a Map*. The challenge we face is to be mutually conversationally aware of moments when we are too focused on each other; or lost in a conversation with ourselves; or speaking in conformity to social expectations surrounding us. Or bypassing all of these by focusing our talk on connecting with a magical and rescuing dialogue with a world beyond our reach. We need to be versatile and answerable to each other to avoid losing ourselves to any one of these directions of speech.

Talking is how we care for each other, go against or away from each other, show tenderness and negotiate desires for support, for intimacy or understanding. It shows how we come to terms with pain and pleasure or hopes and fears. Learning to talk in our earliest months and years is how we learn to think and to relate to ourselves and others and manage our emotions. It is how we find the places we have been given in the world and how we negotiate new places and positions. If we want to review them and revise them, we need to talk them through.

At the heart of *Talking with a Map* is an ethical and democratic stance to conversational and relational awareness. In writing this book and teaching and applying the ideas and methods gathered within it, I cannot make up my mind whether what is offered here is conversational first aid or instructions for a conversational revolution. The latter would be a somewhat a grandiose idea, but it has felt, in my lifetime, that we so much need something like a renaissance in how we go about talking with each other.

Perhaps conversational first aid and conversational revolutions go arm-in-arm. You, the reader, must decide.

This book might be judged to have an optimistic and rosy view of the power of talking. For that I don't apologise. Observe and listen to a two-year-old searching for words in a safe and responsive environment and you will see optimism and hope. On the whole, the more we try to have honest conversations the better we manage our relationships with ourselves and others. Of course, we can talk in bad ways. We can talk to control or exploit, humiliate or shame. We can talk to deprive or undermine. We can talk to replay and inflict our own wounds on others. We can talk to excuse or justify our acts of harm or neglect. We can talk to defend or protect ourselves from risk or, in a form of inner speech, talk to dismiss one side of ourselves in relation to another.

I hope I have not ignored our powers to talk persuasively while lying, deceiving and exploiting. I have perhaps not looked enough at the forces that give rise to conversational poverty and the dictatorial and anti-conversational movements. But my search has been for ways of showing how conversational awareness, boosted by the methods of talking with a map, can be an antidote to these influences. It may be an innate quality of being human to have an eye, an ear or a nose for honesty. We need to be to be able to say, 'Are you kidding me?', 'Is that true?', 'Are we being straight with each other?' We judge the honesty of our talk by what is often called a feeling of authenticity. However, as the great sociologist of café society and community life Richard Sennett pointed out, we can also be caught up in a tyranny of authenticity.[82] The trap set by the narcissism invested in ideas is that each group of followers of an inflated idea believes in its truth with all their heart. Sennett prefers the idea of sincerity to authenticity, and I agree. Sincerity is more something jointly created in view of our differences. We should be able to play with words and play hide and seek with our hopes and fears as depicted in Chapter 3 of this book. We may need to have a conversation where one side of ourselves is authentically connecting with one side of another person, but another side of ourselves has its needs for authentic expression bypassed for the moment. We need to orchestrate moment by moment our relationship with our true and false or role-playing selves. For Sennett sincerity is a better star to follow than authenticity and this makes sense in our contemporary world with multiple identities.

Writing this book has kept reminding me why we talk. We talk to carry our stories and truths from generation to generation and to negotiate our bonds and differences from group to group. We talk to discover or affirm a transition in our social identity or to realise membership of a group. We talk to say hello and goodbye. Or not. We talk to bear our losses and things that went undone and unsaid. The writing of this book has changed me. It has made me more willing to talk and more open to a thousand ways to have a conversation. I am more sensitive to the delicate and co-creative nature of conversation. I see conversation as an activity we do just as much as painters paint or singers sing. I am more aware of the causes of conversational poverty. The uniquely human form of language and conversational awareness as described through the book and evoked in the chapter on Cora, the mother of tongues, is that conversation is one part of what we need to reclaim or protect in the face of the forthcoming divergence into non-biological forms of intelligence.[83] I hope the exuberance of conversation, the random twists and turns and then the endless processing and backtracking will always be beyond even the most advanced machines. Where we already have to be careful is to not reduce our verbal transactions to the automatic and machine like.

One goal of the work described in the preceding pages is to take simple lessons from psychotherapy and apply them in everyday life. A conversationally aware society needs a broad based and diverse public and private resource of talking therapies. We all need a sense that there is someone to turn to or talk to who will help us gain perspective and direction when in social difficulty or hurt psychologically. Psychotherapy and counselling and all the related approaches in public and voluntary settings don't just help solve problems or help us manage difficult emotions and relationships, they help heal or develop our capacity to talk about our lives. *Talking with a Map* and its encouragement of mutual aid in conversations is not to detract from the richness and value of a great deal of psychotherapy, counselling and related professional help. Long may it be available in affordable ways. However therapy has three problems regardless of its effectiveness and merits. First, it cannot last forever and the need for help may still be there after the allotted number of sessions. Second, it cannot meet the demand. The figures are astonishing for those seeking help and those who would seek help if they could afford it or had the time.[84] Third, therapists, in the context of their expertise, should be careful not to professionalise and mystify ordinary conversational curiosity and compassion. There is a risk of making a mystique of ordinarily helpful and caring conversations. By making therapists expert we risk making ourselves (including therapists when they are not being therapists) lacking in conversational competence. The goal of any therapeutic help should be empowerment and teaching us as clients (therapists are clients too) how to learn to be our own therapists.

If you want to take the ideas and methods in this book further in practical ways, I hope you can get together with a group of colleagues and or friends and set up a 'Talking with a Map' conversational awareness skills training group. The idea is to sustain a space and time for conversations of mutual aid and discovery. If needed or helpful, attend one of the introductory workshop on Talking with a Map, see www.mapandtalk.com/bookings.

Arrange to meet weekly, every two weeks or once a month and use the guidelines and ideas in this book and your own thinking and ideas to have a conversational awareness club.

So, keep talking. Seek out conversations of mutual aid and discovery. Talk on the bus or the train. Go for a walk and talk. Stop the world and talk. There is no limit on how much more effectively we could talk about the important aspects of our lives. Where our discussions are stuck or civic dialogue is under threat, we can seek to turn things around and change the conversation. If we can get the conversation flowing and notice, name and negotiate how it is going, then something good enough will come.

Endnotes

1 Jerome Bruner (1968) *Acts of Meaning*. Cambridge, MA: Harvard University Press.

2 Vygotsky, L.S (1978) Mind in society: In: The Development of Higher Psychological Processes. Edited by. Michael Cole. Vera John-Steiner. Sylvia Scribner. Cambridge, MA: Harvard University Press.

3 See www.mapandtalk.com/bookings for 'Talking with a Map' skills training workshops for individuals, teams and peer groups.

4 See Chapter 11 in this book and in Marshall J and Kirkland J (2021) *Reflective Practice in Forensic Settings: A cognitive analytic approach to developing shared thinking*. Brighton: Pavilion Publishing and Media Ltd.

5 Stephen Mitchell offers a rich understanding of what he call the relational turn in psychoanalysis (1988) *Relational Concepts in Psychoanalysis*. Cambridge, MA: Harvard University Press and also Karen Horney Our Inner Conflicts (1945) Norton. Karen Horney gave a pioneering and overlooked account of how in seeking to be whole heartedly ourselves in a divisive world we develop dynamic coping patterns of relating to self and others that whilst seeking to manage anxiety and conflict produce further conflict within ourselves and with others.

6 See Hobson. R.F, (1985) *Forms of Feeling*. London and New York: Tavistock.

7 Ryle A and Kerr I B (2020, 2003) *Introducing Cognitive Analytic Therapy* Wiley, Potter, S. (2020) *Therapy with a Map* Pav Pub; Corbridge. C, Brummer. L, Coid. P, (2018) *Cognitive Analytic Therapy-distinctive features* Routledge; McCormick. E, (2017) *Change for the Better* Sage 5th Edition.

8 Potter S (2020) *Therapy with a Map*. Brighton: Pavilion Publishing and Media Ltd.

9 Potter S (2020) *Therapy with a Map*. see end note 7

10 The mental health consequences of events linked to a changing global climate include mild stress and distress, high-risk coping behavior such as increased alcohol use and, occasionally, mental disorders such as depression, anxiety and post-traumatic stress. https://psychiatry.org/patients-families/climate-change-and-mental-health-connections#:~:text=The%20mental%20health%20consequences%20of,anxiety%20and%20post%2Dtraumatic%20stress.

11 The phrase was first used in 1955 in a quaker pamphlet campaigning for racial justice and against violence https://en.wikipedia.org/wiki/American_Friends_Service_Committee#History but has developed wide currency as a pointer to the process of saying what is going on at the grass roots that is not being acknowledged by those in power or with leadership roles. For a contemporary link of the idea to management and leadership see https://www.ideasforleaders.com/ideas/speaking-truth-to-power-is-more-complex-than-you-think

12 Jerome Bruner's influence on cognitive psychology and narrative ways of seeing and his introduction of Vygotsky to educational thinking has been extensive, influencing Trevarthen, Stern and others. Bruner J (1990) *Acts of Meaning*. Cambridge, MA: Harvard University Press.

13 Lane R (2018) From reconstruction to construction: the power of corrective emotional experiences in memory reconsolidation and enduring change. *Journal of the American Psychoanalytic Association* **66** (3) 507-516.

14 William Wordsworth (1802) Preface to the Lyrical Ballads. Available at: https://sites.udel.edu/britlitwiki/preface-to-lyrical-ballads-full-work/ (accessed April 2020).

15 Josselson R (1995) *The Space Between Us* (p9),London: SAGE Publications.

16 Johannson S (2021) *The Dawn of Language: The story of how we came to talk*. London: Maclehose Press.

17 Jerome Bruner brought the ideas of Vygotsky to the cognitive development of children and pioneering researchers. For example, Colwyn Trevarthen and Daniel Stern took an interpersonal and relational perspective to how infants developed from the earliest day and weeks of life to the beginnings of childhood. This convivial, relational and social view of child development has so many implications for parenting, for understanding trauma and for education and therapy.

For references see: Trevarthen C (2017) The affectionate intersubjective intelligence of the infant and its innate motivation for mental health. *International Journal of Cognitive Analytic Therapy and Relational Mental Health* 1 11-53. and Stern, Daniel. (2010) *Forms of Vitality* London: OUP

18 Ryle A (1975) Self-to-self, self-to-other: the world's shortest account of object relations theory. *New Psychiatry* **24** 12-13.

19 The interpersonal relational school of psychoanalysis in the US has been very influential. For reference see Sullivan HS (1955) *The Interpersonal Theory of Psychiatry*. Tavistock Press. For an overview of the relational turn in psychoanalysis see Mitchell S (1988) Relational Concepts in Psychoanalysis. Cambridge, MA: Harvard University Press.

20 Stern D (2013) *Unformulated Experience: From Dissociation to Imagination in Psychoanalysis* (Relational Perspectives Book Series). London: The Analytic Press

21 Emma Raducanu won the US master open in 2021 as a complete outsider in a remarkable (to her and everyone) series of compelling victories. Her inner self to self 'conversational' coach (she has changed actual coach several times in one year) and flexible relational intelligence seemed to be a key resources in adapting her game to changing circumstances.

22 As described by Kimberlé Crenshaw in *Intersectionality Essential Writings* (2020) New York: New Press.

23 Samuel Beckett's 1952 play *Waiting for Godot*, see also Chapter 11.

24 One of Bakhtin's contributions was to explore the spontaneous and novelistic features of dialogue. His work is well described by Holquist M (1990) *Dialogism*. London: Routledge.

25 https://www.ted.com/talks/chimamanda_ngozi_adichie_the_danger_of_a_single_story?language=en

26 A dog story is one that is told in a closed way with no room for metaphor, dialogue or transference. At times, we all tell dog stories about our lives to defend ourselves from deeper connection and shimmering and hovering with mixed ideas and feelings. Potter. S, (2020) *Therapy with a Map Chapter 3 p65* Brighton: Pavilion Publishing.

27 Smith E (2020) This is Shakespeare. London: Pelican.

28 Horowitz M (1998) *Cognitive Psychodynamics; From Conflict to Character*. Wiley: New York.

29 Conversational awareness and mapping evaluation measures can be found and downloaded from the research page of www.mapandtalk.com

30 Marshall J and Kirkland J (2021) *Reflective Practice in Forensic Settings: A cognitive analytic approach to developing shared thinking*. Brighton: Pavilion Publishing and Media Ltd.

31 *Interpreting Simone Weil: Presence and Absence in Attention* by Ann Pirruccello, Philosophy East and West Vol. 45, No. 1 (Jan. 1995), pp. 61-72. Published By: University of Hawai'i Press https://www.jstor.org/stable/13995095

32 They link to the www.mapandtalk.com website where there are links to the evaluation measures on the research page and further exercises and videos and a blog.

33 A key aspect of talking with a map is the freedom it gives us to travel in time by looking back, comparing one time in the past with another or looking forward and planning and anticipating what we can or should do in the future. In his book on the origins of language, Johannson cites the ability to time travel, as he puts it, as a key gift that language gives us as humans. Swerker Johannson (2021) *The Dawn of Language* London: Maclehose Press Quercus

34 Buber M (2002) *Between Man and Man*. London: Routledge Classics.

35 Hobson RF (1985) *Forms of Feeling*. London and New York: Tavistock.

36 Seamus Heaney collection *Human Chain* (thanks to Angela Mohan for the quote and the emotional connection with the idea).

37 https://www. theguardian. com/music/2021/oct/30/his-lyrics-defined-the-times-paul-muldoon-on-working-with-paul-mccartney

38 Horney K (1945/1992) *Our Inner Conflicts*. New York: Norton

39 Philip Bromberg (1998) *Standing in the Spaces*. Brighton: Psychology Press.

40 See for a rich and recent example Seth A (2020) *Being You – A new science of consciousness.* New York: Faber

41 Todorov T (1984) *Mikhail Bakhtin: The Dialogical Principle.* Trans. Wlad Godzich. Minneapolis: U of Minnesota. Waiting for Answerability: Bakhtin and Composition Studies by Helen Rothschild Ewald.

42 Chapter 6, in *Therapy with a Map* (2020) but see more generally: Writing Cures; Bolton G, Howlett S, Lago L et al (2004) London: Routledge. And also, Forrester J (2016) *Thinking in Cases*. London: Polity Press.

43 These ideas are also considered in the context of Cognitive Analytic Therapy in *Therapy with a Map* (Potter 2020, Pavilion Publishing & Media Ltd) and *Introducing Cognitive Analytic Therapy* (Ryle and Kerr 2020)

44 Bakhtin referred to this as the novelistic and openly dialogic contrast to epic, closed and heroic accounts of the stories of our lives. (*Dialogism: Michael Holquist* (1990) London: Routledge).

45 *The Dawn of Everything* is a scholarly and passionate journey of revision into how we see our earliest origins. It invites us to look backwards outside of the frame of western philosophy, racism and colonialism. Graeber D & Wengrow D (2021) *The Dawn of Everything: A new history of humanity.*

46 Johansson guides us through the challenges of what we know and don't know and the likelihood of a pluralistic approach to the contributions over time to human language ability.

47 It is hard to think of the development of the brain apart from the interplay between mind, culture and social context after grasping Merlin Donald's idea of the hybrid brain. Merlin D (2020) *A Mind so Rare.* London: Norton.

48 Meares. R, (2016) *The Poets Voice in the Making of Mind.* P4. London: Routledge.

49 For a rich exploration see Johannson as above in Endnote 43.

50 Bakhtin – for a good introduction to his work see Dialogism: Michael Holquist (1990) London: Routledge.

51 https://mindmatters.ai/2021/11/astronomer-et-is-more-likely-to-be-ai-than-a-to-be-a-life-form/

52 Aspects of theory of mind, attachment and the role mentalisation in the development of self are explored in Fonagy.P. Gergely. G. Jurist. E.J, and Target. M, (2004) *Affect Regulation, Mentalisatom, and the Development of the Self* London: Karnac

53 Fotopoulou A & Tsakiris M (2017) Mentalising homeostasis, the social origins of interoceptive inference. *Neuropsychoanalysis* **19** (1) 3-28.

54 Jean Knox (2011) in her book on the developmental and neuro-science components of developing self-agency quotes Gallese, the Italian neuroscientist who proposes a central role for mirror neurons. '*Being a self depends on the acquired capacity to 1) recognise the existence of multiple frames of reference and 2) to put them in dynamic relation to each other by a continuous process of analogy and differentiation. [T]he emergence of the self can be seen as the adaptive tool able to give coherence to these interacting levels of representation.*'
(Gallese & Umilta (2002) page 37 quoted in Knox J (2011) *Self-Agency in Psychotherapy.* London: Norton.)

55 As above in 50.

56 For Freud and in particular Sandor Ferenczi (one of Freud's most capable collaborators until he was cast out of the Freudian circle) in a brilliant and brief paper there is a kind of childhood sexual trauma which gives rise to a confusion of tongues. By this he meant that the mix of making special, admiring and cherishing a child can then serve as a cover or seductive entrapment for then exploiting and abusing the child. For Ferenczi, it showed up as a compulsion to repeat this confusion with the therapist in the hope to meet in conversation with someone who does not join the confusing dance and helps make sense of it and free the person from their childhood entrapment. For a rich account of his work see Gutierrez-Pelaez M (2018) *Confusion of Tongues*. London: Taylor and Francis.

57 See references to mapping and working with these varieties of narcissism in: www.mapandtalk.com

58 Sandor Ferenczi is a pivotal figure in the development of psychotherapy and psychoanalysis and his paper (freely available online) is well worth reading. For more on the debate around him and the legacy he generated go to Gutierrez-Pelaez M (2018) Confusion of Tongues. London: Taylor and Francis.

59 While there are many sources of reference two key texts are Herman J (1992) Trauma and Recovery. London: Basic Books and Van der Kolk, B. (2014) *The Body Keeps the Score.* London: Penguin

60 Ferenczi. S, *Confusion of Tongues* (endnote 56 above)

61 Whilst Talking with a Map draws principally on the work of Ryle there is so much that resonates also with the work of Karen Horney. See Karen Horney (1945) Our Inner Conflicts Norton.

62 Freud's earliest understanding of transference as the compulsion to repeat a pattern of relating that caused emotional pain in childhood and was never given meaning or authorship but is repeated now in the hope the meaning and the authorship will be revealed through its re-enactment.

63 These four authors seem to my mind to be covering processes in similar ways to the that described by Karen Horney as disentangling -Horney. K, (1945) Our Inner Conflicts, New York: Norton. For Ryle a major purpose of or re-formulation was to notice, name and compassionately not join the clients dance (Ryle & Kerr, (2020). In disembedding Jeremy Safran means something very similar. Safran, J. (2000) Negotiating The Therapeutic Alliance p156. The end product is a capacity evocatively captured by the relational psychoanalyst Philip Bromberg in his idea of standing in the spaces. (Bromberg, 1998)

64 Solms. M.L, (2018) The neurological underpinnings of psychoanalytic theory and therapy Front. Behav. Neurosci., 04 December 2018 https://doi.org/10.3389/fnbeh.2018.00294
Lane R (2018) From reconstruction to construction: the power of corrective emotional experiences in memory reconsolidation and enduring change. *Journal of the American Psychoanalytic Association* **66** (3) 507-516. The idea of memory reconsolidation occurs in several points in this book.

65 Marshall J and Kirkland J (2021) *Reflective Practice in Forensic Settings: A cognitive analytic approach to developing shared thinking.* Brighton: Pavilion Publishing and Media Ltd.

66 Octopus brain reference: https://www.scientificamerican.com/article/the-mind-of-an-octopus/

67 Page 74 Meares. R, (2016) *The Poets Voice in the Making of Mind.* P4. London: Routledge.

68 An Expert Patient is a person who has been empowered with the skills, confidence and knowledge needed to play an active role in making informed decisions about their own health care and management of their chronic condition. Claire. S. Lightfoot BMJ 2003;326:1279

69 Bakhtin unfinished. Holquist M (1990) *Dialogism.* London: Routledge.

70 See Walter Benjamin and the Aestheticisation of Politics https://www.google.co.uk/books/edition/Aesthetics_and_Politics/rov-DwAAQBAJ?hl=en&gbpv=1&dq=aestheticization+of+politics+walter+benjamin&pg=PA1&printsec=frontcover

71 The notion of the chattering classes comes from Auberon Waugh and refers to a metropolitan elite engaged in armchair politics.

72 For example, cogent accounts of the threat to democracy and the rise of fascism in a twenty-first century form (Robert Reich https://robertreich.org/post/140705539195). There are many voices speaking for a conversational enlightenment through movements such as the Me Too https://en.wikipedia.org/wiki/MeToo_movement and Black Lives Matter https://en.wikipedia.org/wiki/Black_Lives_Matter and campaigns to alert a popular understanding of the climate emergency.

73 See for example: Joanna Macy and Chris Johnstone (2012) *Active Hope.* California: New World Library

74 This binary process of dividing and splitting self from others and good from bad was well described and developed in the teaching of Harry Stack Sullivan (1953) and in Barton (1995)

75 The term 'groupthink' was originally coined by the sociologist of social spaces William H. Whyte. See his classic text *The Organisation Man* (1956).

76 Disorganised attachment is one of the traumatising experiences in contrast to secure attachment that has grown from the extensive work on attachment theory by Bowlby and Ainsworth. For an overview see Anna Jellema: Dismissing and preoccupied insecure attachment and procedures in CAT: Some implications for CAT practice (March 2002) https://doi.org/10.1002/cpp.310.

77 T.S.Eliot (1925) The Hollow Men https://allpoetry.com/the-hollow-men

78 BBC interview: https://www.youtube.com/watch?v=3KlWLTdjpuc

79 https://blogs.lse.ac.uk/brexit/2019/04/11/is-brexit-the-will-of-the-people-the-answer-is-not-quite-that-simple/

80 Footage of Dr Martin Luther King Jr's I Have a Dream speech: https://www.youtube.com/watch?v=vP4iY1TtS3s

81 Quoting from Simon Tisdall in the Guardian Newspaper 'A majority of Republicans believe Trump's 'big lie' – that Joe Biden stole the 2020 election' https://www.theguardian.com/commentisfree/2022/jan/09/the-epic-struggle-for-americas-soul-is-just-getting-started. For a compelling account of Trump's journey through the Presidency and its implications for the political conversation in the USA see the second book by his niece Mary Trump, a clinical psychologist specialised in trauma work. Trump M (2021) *The Reckoning*. New York: St Martin's Press.

82 Richard Sennett in *The Fall of Public Man* (1977) gives a powerful account of what he calls the 'tyranny of intimacy' and contrasts it with the convivial social discourse of the coffee house. Also see Sennett R (2012) *Together: The Rituals Pleasures and Politics of Co-operation*. Yale University Press.

83 https://mindmatters.ai/2021/11/astronomer-et-is-more-likely-to-be-ai-than-a-to-be-a-life-form/

84 It is estimated that 75% of people with mental health problems in England may not get access to the treatment they need. Department of Health (2014) *Annual Report of the Chief Medical Officer 2013, Public Mental Health Priorities: Investing in the Evidence*: www.gov.uk/government/publications/chief-medical-officer-cmoannual-report-public-mental-health. See also https://www.mentalhealth.org.uk/statistics/mental-health-statistics-people-seeking-help